WHAT OTHER FIRST RESPONDERS ARE SAYING ABOUT *THE FIRST RESPONDER HEALING MANUAL*...

I had been the direct supervisor of the Granite Mountain Hotshot crew which lost 19 members on the Yarnell Hill Fire on June 30, 2013. The traumatic effects of that incident were taking a very heavy toll on me physically, emotionally and spiritually. I was invited to participate in a small group going through *The Combat Trauma Healing Manual* with a group of local veterans. I questioned why God would put this opportunity before me since I had never been in the military. After the first couple of sessions I figured it out. I needed help, I had been hiding the trauma I was going through and I related to the veterans and their traumatic experiences. I needed the Biblical truth on PTSD, I needed the frank discussion from the group, and I needed the decision points the manual brought forth. Finally I needed to hear God's voice from people who had gone through tragic events, sought help from Him, and were getting better. I have witnessed firsthand what LODDs (Line of Duty Deaths) will do to firefighters, family members, spouses and children. I had lived this for 16 months. I also know what a blessing it was to my life to begin to get better by getting honest with God. *The First Responder Healing Manual* is a must read if you really want to get better after a tragic event.

—Darrell Willis, Wildland Division Chief, Prescott, AZ Fire Department
38 years as a firefighter, paramedic, captain, battalion chief, deputy chief and fire chief

✠   ✠   ✠   ✠   ✠

Dear fellow urban heroes,

Yes, you are a hero! You may not have had a roof cave in on you, or bullets whizzing by your head or some other spectacular story but you are a hero because you stand watch every day prepared for and even expecting that major life threatening event in the service of mankind. More likely you face numerous less spectacular, but highly traumatizing events almost every day and have been doing so for years. Even more likely, you are carrying around a load of stress that you put in a little compartment every day so that you can pull on your turnouts or armor and be the strong guy for someone less fortunate. Take it from one who has been there: at some point that stress is going to do bad things to you. It's not because you are weak, but because you are strong. The principals in this manual have helped me to deal with a stress level which had become nearly unbearable at one point. I challenge everyone to whom I give this manual to at least seriously read Step 1 and apply it to yourself before you dismiss your need for it. If you decide not to go any further don't get rid of it, because at some point in your career odds are that you will need what is covered in these pages. God bless you, and keep you, and heal you! Thank you for laying down your life every day for others.

—John Franklin, Chief Investigator, Lane County (Oregon) District Attorney's Office
21 years law enforcement – Corrections, Urban, Rural, Marine, Dunes and Helicopter Patrol, Detective;
8 years US Army Attack Helicopter pilot and instructor (CWO2)

✠   ✠   ✠   ✠   ✠

This manual is a critical spiritual resource for the hidden injuries suffered in the line of duty. It is literally "Kevlar" for the soul for our battle-hardened first responders – our "closer to home" warriors so often suffering from what they are called to do every day on the job.

—Dr. Robert Hicks, Law Enforcement Chaplain
32 years Air Force chaplain (retired); professor of History and Ethics, Belhaven University, Orlando
Associate Staff, Cru Military
Author of *Masculine Journey, Failure to Scream, Trauma: The Pain that Stays,* and others

Having worked with officers and deputies for a number of years, I have known too many outstanding men and women who have suffered in silence after having experienced a line of duty traumatic event. The outward wounds are easily visible and quickly treated. Yet it is the inner – typically untreated – wounds of the heart, mind, and soul that often have the most devastating impact on the individual and their loved ones. In this manual, Chris and Rahnella Adsit reveal that there is hope for the most battle-scarred of people, and that the wound you carry you do not have to carry alone. You've probably tried all kinds of other approaches to push through the hurt. You owe it to yourself and to those who care about you to try one more time. It will take work, but with God's help, this manual can facilitate your rediscovery of the hope, joy, and sense of purpose you thought had been lost forever!

—Bret Truax, Lead Pastor, Calvary Baptist Church, Salem, OR
9 years as the volunteer lead chaplain of law enforcement agencies in CO and MI
27 years pastoring churches in the Midwest and Oregon

You have this book in your hands because you are curious and looking for something that perhaps you cannot describe. Or maybe a loved one, a friend, or a Circuit Court judge has given you the last warning to get your act together. Perhaps something has occurred in your career that gave you that "WTF!" moment and now many unanswered questions are floating in your mind day and night. What you are holding is a means to let you know you are not alone in your search, nor without answers. Jesus Christ is the center of this book. He wants to be the center of all our lives and bring about the healing and strengthening that we long for. With this book and a group of like-minded responders like yourself, you can begin to head in a new direction. Begin that healing process – allow God to mend the rift between you and what truly matters to you.

—Michael Anderson, retired Fire Captain, Eugene, OR
35 years as a firefighter/paramedic in several municipalities in Oregon
4 years as a police officer; 6 years in the US Navy and Navy Reserves

WHEN DUTY WOUNDS YOU

The First Responder Healing Manual

Biblical Solutions for Line of Duty Stress & Trauma

Chris & Rahnella Adsit

Branches of Valor, International

The First Responder Healing Manual: Biblical Solutions for Line of Duty Stress & Trauma is part of the **Bridges to Healing Series,** which is published by Cru Military.

Also in the series:

The Combat Trauma Healing Manual: Christ-centered Solutions for Combat Trauma

When War Comes Home: Christ-centered Healing for Wives of Combat Veterans

Group Facilitator Guides are also available for both of these, and will soon be available for *The First Responder Healing Manual.*

Published by Branches of Valor, International, a ministry to veterans, first responders and their families: PO Box 2212, Eugene, OR 97402. For more information about Branches of Valor, please visit our web site at www.branchesofvalor.org.

DISCLAIMER:

This book is not a substitute for appropriate medical or psychological care for those experiencing significant emotional pain or whose ability to function at home, school or work is impaired. Chronic or extreme stress may cause a wide assortment of physical and psychological problems. Some may require evaluation and treatment by medical or mental health professionals. When in doubt, seek advice from a professional.

Cover and interior design: Katie Brady Design, Eugene, Oregon

Publisher: Chris Adsit, Branches of Valor International

Prepared for The PTSD Foundation of America, Houston, TX www.ptsdUSA.org

Original funding by: The 100 Club, Houston, TX www.the100club.org

ISBN 978-0-9671227-8-6

Printed in the United States of America

The First Responder Healing Manual is dedicated to the memory of the nineteen courageous men of the Granite Mountain Interagency Hotshot Crew who lost their lives June 30, 2013 on the Yarnell Hill Fire in Arizona. We honor them for their sacrificial service, realizing that all first responders must stand ready to make the same supreme sacrifice in the line of duty as they did – as many of our beloved brothers and sisters have.

The hearts and prayers of all first responders are with the families and friends of that outstanding Crew. We all look forward to a grand reunion in heaven in the not-too-distant future. God remembers those men, and carved His own memorial dedication in the rock of Yarnell decades before the event…

Photo by Jason Coil, taken on Yarnell Hill about 50 yards south of the deployment site.

The motto of the Granite Mountain Interagency Hotshot Crew is
"Esse Quam Videri" which means "To be, rather than to seem." How
fitting that God's name for Himself is: "I am." (Exodus 3:14)

God doesn't always take us around life's furnaces.
Sometimes He meets us right in the midst of the flames.

Table of Contents

PTSD Foundation of America
PROVIDING HOPE AND HEALING FOR THE UNSEEN WOUNDS OF WAR

Office: 9724 Derrington Rd. Houston, TX 77064 – Mailing: PO Box 690748 Houston, TX 77769
24-hour PTSD Veteran Line: 877-717-PTSD (7873) – Office: 832-912-4429 – Website: www.ptsdUSA.org

Three-Fold Mission:

1. To combat Post Traumatic Stress by:

- Bringing healing to our military community through pastoral counseling and peer mentoring, both on an individual basis and in group settings.
- Raising awareness of the increasing needs of the military community through public events, media outlets, social media, service organizations, and churches.
- Networking government agencies, service organizations, churches, and private sector businesses into a united "Corps of Compassion" to bring their combined resources together to meet the needs of the military community on a personal and individual/family level.

2. To give back to those who have given of themselves so selflessly by:

- Helping these warriors and their families adjust to non-deployed mode and find their "new normal."
- Combining with other existing community and faith-based organizations to offer a safe place where no one is judged, everyone is supported, and everything a warrior reveals remains confidential.
- Training others in the community to reach out to our warriors and their families, letting them know they are NOT alone.

3. To increase public awareness of Post Traumatic Stress by:

- Establishing relationships within the secular and faith-based communities to facilitate support systems for our military community.
- Locating and identifying churches currently (or interested in) ministering to the military community.
- Providing workshops and counseling manuals for the warrior and their families.
- Assisting the spouses and children of warriors struggling with Post Traumatic Stress.
- Keeping the issue before the media and general public through press releases, email newsletters, PSAs, websites, and Facebook.

Warrior Groups

The PTSD Foundation of America hosts fellowships for combat veterans and their families to share their experiences, testimonies of healing, compassion and hope in overcoming the invisible wounds of war. Not a treatment program, but rather a peer coaching and support program whose primary purpose is helping combat veterans find healing, balance and positive re-integration with their families and in society. Primarily in the Houston area.

Camp Hope, Houston

Camp Hope provides interim housing for our Wounded Warriors, veterans and their families suffering from combat related PTSD in a caring and positive environment.

The facility opened in 2012. It offers a 90+ day intensive peer-support and mentoring program that includes temporary housing, group lessons and support sessions with other combat veterans, individual mentoring sessions with certified combat trauma mentors, offsite activities (fishing, workouts, hiking, local events), and involvement with other local churches, businesses and volunteer organizations.

The Camp Hope staff is a unique team of combat veerans and civilian pastoral staff trained in working with victims of trauma and Post Tramatic Stress. The staff uses the necessary traditional counseling tools and incorporates a faith-based approch to help combat the effects of PTS. In addition, the staff assists veterans with a myriad of issues including job placement, coordination with the VA and reputable veeteran service organizations, and assists with claims and benefits, transportation to appointments, and peer support group integration.

Preface

FUNDING FOR THIS PUBLICATION WAS MADE POSSIBLE FROM THE 100 CLUB

5555 San Felipe Suite 1750, Houston, TX 77056

www.the100club.org

(713) 952-0100

The 100 club is a 61 year old (2014) non-profit organization composed of 31,000 citizen members who support both the law enforcement and firefighting community. In 1953, a handful of community leaders banded together to start the organization with a belief that they could provide financial support to the widows and children left behind from Houston Police Officers killed in the line of duty. From that early beginning, the Club grew to add all Municipal, County, State and Federal officers within Harris County to the coverage group.

Soon after the Club began to grow, the Board of Directors added a program whose goal was to prevent law enforcement officer line of duty deaths. The purchase of life protecting equipment for officers in the coverage area was put into place to provide funding when budgeted funds were not available for the needed equipment.

As the club, continued to grow, the Board added an undergraduate scholarship program for Law Enforcement Officers wanting to major in Criminal Justice. Today, the program is available at the University of Houston Downtown, Prairie View AandM University and Sam Houston State University. Additionally, a Master's degree in Criminal Justice is available for Law Enforcement supervisors at both Sam Houston State University and the University of Houston Downtown.

In the 90's, the Club's Board of Directors, knowing that crime doesn't stop at the City Limit Sign, approved expanding outside of Harris County to include some 18 counties where dependent families of both law enforcement officer and firefighters received financial support after a line of duty death. Law enforcement agencies may request life protecting equipment, and law enforcement officers may apply for 100 Club scholarships.

In 2001, the Club added both paid and volunteer firefighters to its line of duty death coverage. This was for all full time and volunteer firefighters in the 18 county 100 Club coverage area.

In 2006, the Club included any commissioned Texas Department of Public Safety Officers, Texas Parks and Wildlife Officers, and Texas Alcoholic Beverage Commission Agents killed in the line of duty anywhere in the State of Texas as part of the Club's dependent survivor financial assistance coverage.

In May of 2013, the Club added 13 counties, primarily in the Eastern part of Texas to its coverage area for financial support for dependent families of both law enforcement officers and firefighters killed in the line of duty.

This increases to 31 the number of Texas counties the Club provides dependent support for both law enforcement officer and firefighter line of duty deaths. Federal, State, County and Municipal officers are covered and both full time and volunteer firefighters are covered by The 100 club.

The 100 Club has provided over $41,000,000 of financial support since its beginning in 1953. Over $17,000,000 has been provided to the dependents of our Heroes killed in the line of duty with over $12,000,000 used in trying to prevent the loss of life with the purchase of life protecting equipment. The balance of the funding has been used for scholarships and to continue the Club's 60 year old annual tradition of honoring outstanding law enforcement officers and firefighters.

The 100 Club provides these resources to both our Law Enforcement Officers and Firefighters through our members. Your new membership helps us to continue an effective administration of our mission of helping those who put their lives on the line for each of us on a daily basis.

You can become a member of The 100 Club by joining on-line at: www.the100club.org or by calling the Club's office at (713) 952-0100.

The price of an annual membership is still the same as it was in 1953, only $100.

Acknowledgements

In the interest of full-disclosure, neither of the authors of this manual has ever served as first responders. Some might say this fact invalidates our platform as writers on the issues contained herein. However, we must point out that a heart surgeon doesn't have to experience a heart attack to be a good heart surgeon. He just needs to know a lot of stuff. God has given us the gifts required to comb through thousands of pages of first-hand accounts, research from stress and trauma specialists, instructive books and autobiographies by first responders, and various internet sites, and to dialog with numerous first responders struggling with line of duty stress and trauma in order to glean "the stuff" that will be useful to those reading this manual. In addition, as we completed each chapter we sent it to our "Review Team" made up of first responders and first responder chaplains. We asked them to give it the sniff test and let us know if we had written anything that was off-the-wall, incorrect, insensitive, unhelpful, heretical, culturally irrelevant or invalid. We incorporated their feedback. Moreover, we solicited specific clarification on many issues, and asked for personal accounts and stories from this group to use as illustrations of key points. Their stories appear scattered throughout the manual.

Every reader of this resource will greatly benefit from their insights and feedback, and all of us are extremely grateful for their help in this very important project.

The Review Team:

Mike Anderson – 35 years as a firefighter/paramedic in several Oregon municipalities in, including 5 years Lane County Paramedic and EMS Director; retired as a Fire Captain. 4 years as a police officer prior to firefighting career; 4 years in the US Navy during the Vietnam War, 2 years Navy Reserve.

Terry Bratton – 39 year senior police officer in Houston, TX. Instructor of law enforcement tactics across the nation, including the FBI, various state academies, and for the DOJ internationally. Recognized as a Use of Force expert in state and federal court, having reviewed thousands of incidents, including hundreds of officer involved shootings. Currently Executive Senior Pastor at a non-denominational church in Kingwood, TX.

Linn Burch – 28 years as a firefighter/paramedic in Eugene, Oregon. Currently serving as Aircraft Rescue and Firefighting (ARFF) instructor at the Eugene Airport.

Roanna Burch – 28 years as a firefighter's wife; Ministry Administrator for Branches of Valor, Int'l.

John Franklin – 21 years law enforcement in CA, HI, OR: Corrections, Urban, Rural, Marine, Dunes and Helicopter Patrol, Detective. Currently Chief Investigator for Lane County (Oregon) District Attorney's Office. 8 years US Army Attack Helicopter pilot and instructor (Chief Warrant Officer).

Brett Gilchrist – 34 years of pastoral ministry in Eugene, Oregon; currently Lead Pastor at University Fellowship Church; Chaplain, Eugene Police Department; bi-monthly chapel ministry at Oregon's maximum security penitentiary (OSP).

Chris Gillett – Began his career in the fire service in 1994. Pastored an inner city church for 5 years. Fire service Chaplain for 6 years. Currently a Captain, Fire Instructor, Training Officer and Chaplain in North Carolina. Former HUD Officer and a US Army veteran.

Rick Hartley – Began his career in Texas law enforcement starting in 1976, spanning a variety of responsibilities from television police reporter to Director of Media Relations for Houston PD, and Assistant Director of Texas Department of Corrections. Has served with The 100 Club of Houston since 1994, currently as Executive Director.

Ray Hunt – 25 year Houston police officer, 18 years night shift patrol, 10 years field trainer, currently President of the Houston Police Officers' Union.

Matthew Marin – Served four years in the US Navy and then went to work as a Police Officer for Houston PD. Matt was involved in two shootings where he had to take a life as a police officer – one as a DWI Unit officer and one as a patrol officer. He holds the Award of Valor from the State of Texas and the Hostile Engagement Award, two lifesaving awards, and an Officer of the Year award. Matthew suffers from PTSD, but is in the healing process after a few hard years.

Dr. Mike McCoy – 30+ years law enforcement in southern California and Oregon. Some of his assignments: field services, detention/jail, warrant and background investigator, police academy tactical officer, CIRT. Master Chaplain, CFMI. Department Chair for New Hope Christian College Crisis Response Degree Program. Air Force security police officer, Vietnam, 1968-70.

David McKernan –35 years with Fairfax County (VA) Fire and Rescue, the last 5 years as the Director of Emergency Management for Fairfax County. Some of his assignments during his career: medic, hazardous materials technician, fire investigator and operation chief.

Nancy Picha – 10 years Firefighter/EMT for the Auburn, Ohio Fire Department. Currently serving as a registered nurse in Dallas Texas.

Steve Ryan –25 years as a police officer in Idaho. 3 years police trainer in Iraq. Currently serving on the staff of the Law Enforcement Division of the National Rifle Association as a Law Enforcement Firearms Instructor Trainer. Prior to law enforcement career: 5 years a pastor in Burley, ID, one year as a firefighter.

Brett Truax – 27 years pastoring churches in the Midwest and Oregon; 9 years as the volunteer Lead Chaplain of law enforcement agencies in Colorado and Michigan. Currently Lead Pastor at Calvary Baptist Church, Salem, OR.

Rachel Turner-Benson – Wife of a 23-year law enforcement professional who is currently a lieutenant for a metro police force outside of Seattle and also a Desert Storm Marine veteran. Rachel is Director of Shields of Valor/Families and directs an internet talk radio program: Police Wives Talk Radio.

Chris Weinzapfel – 25 years of public service as a paramedic, 21 years of that time as a firefighter/paramedic, 19 years as a EMS educator and public speaker, 17 years as a tactical paramedic. Currently Director of Emergency Medical Services for Rowlett, Texas (Dallas suburb).

Darrell Willis – 38 years as a firefighter, paramedic, captain, battalion chief, deputy chief. Fire chief for 14 years. Currently serving as the Wildland Division Chief of the Prescott Fire Department. Instrumental in establishing the Granite Mountain Interagency Hot Shot crew in 2004 which lost 19 members on June 30, 2013 while he was their direct supervisor. Coordinated and participated in the removal of the deceased and assisting their immediate families in the incident aftermath.

Curtis Yamane – 33 years with the Seattle Fire Department, serving on ladder trucks, aid cars, and engines throughout the city. Currently serving as the Captain of Engine 35 in the Crown Hill neighborhood.

A special thanks to our team of intrepid and detail-oriented proof readers:

Roanna Burch, Susan Cumming, Ruth Linoz, Christopher Pace, and Debby Walker.

Finally, we want to express our gratitude to our long-time associate **Gene Birdwell**, Founder and President of the PTSD Foundation of America and Camp Hope in Houston, Texas. If it hadn't been for Gene's vision, facilitation and prodding, this manual would still be unwritten at this time. He has known all along that the stress and trauma that first responders deal with is very similar to what our veterans experience – perhaps different in source, but the same in crippling intensity. He also knew that the solution is the same for both populations: the healing power of Jesus Christ. Many first responders have taken advantage of the ministries and support coming from the PTSD Foundation of America, but Gene knew that there needed to be a manual that addressed the distinctives of the first responder culture more directly. With his facilitation, and with great encouragement from The 100 Club Executive Director **Rick Hartley**, and the Houston Police Officers' Union President **Ray Hunt**, and with the direction of the Healer Himself (Exodus 15:26), this manual has come into being. May God use it to accomplish His purposes in the lives of our heroic first responders – for whom we are the *most* grateful!

Introduction – Hide or Seek?

There are over three million first responders. They are involved in over 240 million incidents per year. Every day first responders immerse themselves in the chaos and confusion of other people's very bad days – up-close-and-personal – often risking their own lives to protect citizens from bad guys with guns, tripped out druggies, desperate criminals, deadly situations, medical emergencies, and natural disasters.

Impressive, but there are a few problems...

- The number one killer of law enforcement officers is suicide.[1]

- Firefighting is one of the most injury-producing, life-threatening and emotionally traumatizing occupations in America.[2]

- EMTs are paid less than garbage collectors and stick with their career an average of five years.[3]

- Nationwide, every cop can expect to be attacked with lethal intent every other year; with non-lethal intent many times per year.[4]

- First responders are the first on the scene of accidents, homicides, suicides and assorted acts of violence such as battery, rape, bombings, school shootings, etc.

- They extricate dead or dying children from mangled vehicles, and care for victims of domestic violence and child abuse.

- They respond to wildland fires, floods, tornadoes, hurricanes, earthquakes, and airplane crashes where there are often catastrophic sums of death and property damage.

- They provide medical assistance to homeless patients who are combative due to mind-altering drugs or alcohol.

- Despite their commitment and sacrifice, they are often derided, marginalized, insulted, spit upon, labeled as racists, second-guessed, overworked, underpaid, and underappreciated.

- They are fired, sued, prosecuted and sent to jail if they make the wrong split-second decision.

SOCIETY'S KEVLAR. Not everybody realizes who makes up the ranks of our first responders. Besides firefighters, paramedics, EMTs, police officers, sheriffs, state troopers, marshals, and their deputies, we can't leave out emergency room doctors, nurses and technicians, dispatchers, corrections officers, crime scene investigators, bomb squad, FBI, CIA, NSA, DEA, BATFE, TSA, Homeland Security, ICE, Secret Service, Border Patrol, court bailiffs, probation and parole officers, security guards, and others. All are part of the "Stress & Trauma Brotherhood and Sisterhood," and together make up the Kevlar of our society, protecting and defending us all against threats that come from people and circumstances who mean us harm.

> "With a broken arm I'd be a hero. With a broken brain I'd be fired."[5]
>
> —Police Chief William May, Townsend, MA

Does any of it ever affect you? Do you ever take a hit? How do you cope?

Suck it up and drive on, baby.

Right? That works – for a while.

HIDING. Most of you do your best to hide your invisible wounds and mask your symptoms. You are concerned that if you seek help for any indicators of stress or trauma, you'll be labeled as weak or deficient. You may be demoted. Assigned a desk job. Fired. These things *could* indeed happen in some towns. So you keep driving.

But eventually your cup of stress overflows, and driving on is no longer an option. There is no "Robo" in front of the word "cop." People get hurt. Marriages fail. Families disintegrate. Careers end.

Studies have shown that more than 125,000 active law enforcement officers on full duty are suffering with Post-traumatic Stress Disorder (PTSD). Other studies have shown that the rate of PTSD among firefighters is as high as 37% in some municipalities.[6] That's a huge number, and it's not even taking into account the even greater number who experience subsyndromal PTSD – stressed and traumatized but not quite meeting the criteria of full-blown PTSD. Yet.

What's In A Name?

Many first responders (and military) are put off by the term PTSD, mainly because of the "D." "I'm no fruit cake, no psyche job. I *don't* have a disorder!" Faulty self-image, peer pressure, concerns about getting canned, and the basic nature of PTSD symptomology all conspire to make them shy away from any association with that acronym. Understandable. But in doing so, many also shy away from *help*.

PTSI. Because of this, many professionals are arguing vigorously for changing the name of the diagnosis to PTSI – Posttraumatic Stress *Injury*.[7] This is a much more accurate description of your condition. You were injured. Wounded. Your body, mind and spirit are reacting to a three-pronged assault. Despite the "D" word, you need to keep in mind that this is the truth about your condition. The officer is down, but he can get back up again. He can recover from this wound.

So, though you understand that you are dealing with an *injury*, we will continue to use the appellation "PTSD" in this manual, only because it's the dominant term currently employed by the shrinks. Hopefully it will change soon.

⊕   ⊕   ⊕   ⊕   ⊕

The Healing Process

You have probably learned in the past that recovering from an injury is a *process*. It doesn't happen instantly by saying magic words or snapping your fingers. The same is true with PTSD.

You may not have recognized it, but your stress and trauma hit you at three levels: physically, mentally, and spiritually. Therefore, your bid for healing must encompass all three levels as well. Leave one out, and it's doubtful you will experience full healing. It's like a three-legged stool. You *can* balance on two legs, but it requires a great deal of energy and skill – and you will fall often. Adding the third leg brings efficiency and stability.

While your medical doctors and counselors can provide two legs, this manual seeks to point you directly to your Creator for the third leg. In fact, since He calls Himself "Your Healer" (Exodus 15:26) connecting with Him will greatly enhance the aid you receive at the other two levels. He wants to orchestrate your healing holistically. This manual will help you construct an environment in which God has optimal access to your body, soul and spirit for the purpose of healing.

WHAT'S "HEALING?" Most people who experience PTSD have one overwhelming desire: that things would go back to how they were before their trauma – back to "normal." We're not going to lie to you. You can't get back there. Your experience is a bell that can't get un-rung. The memories, the triggers, the sadness will always be there – at least to some degree. But with God's help, you *can* go forward to a new level of strength, stability and productivity that you never would have known had you not experienced what you did. The control and sting of your traumas can be greatly reduced. Rather than trying to suppress and deny the negative experiences of your past, God can help you integrate them into your present reality and help *you* control what happens in the future. You can get to a *new* normal that is superior to the old one.

Distress can become *eustress* – the kind of stress athletes need to excel, and the stress you engaged in as you trained to become the best first responder possible. God can transform disorder into order, weakness into strength, ashes into beauty, obscurity into prominence, darkness into light, mourning into dancing, loss into gain, death into life. He's real good at transformation – and resurrection.

COMBAT TRAUMA. In 2007, we produced *The Combat Trauma Healing Manual* which has provided a Christ-centered approach to dealing with war-related PTSD. Thousands of troops have been helped by it – or rather, by God. This manual employs many of the same principles, but is adapted to the unique components of the first responder experience and culture.

SEEKING. As you seek His help, may you experience what Jesus Christ promised:

> *"Come to Me, all who are weary and heavy-laden, and I will give you rest. Take My yoke upon you and learn from Me, for I am gentle and humble in heart, and you will find rest for your souls. For My yoke is easy, and My burden is light."*

> **– Matthew 11:28-30**

1. Mark Bond, Professor of Criminal Justice, American Military University. Article: Inpublicsafety.com, July 7, 2014: "How Do We Change Police Culture To Save Lives of Fellow Officers?"

2. Peggy Sweeney, President, The Sweeney Alliance. (Former volunteer firefighter, EMT-B, bereavement educator.) From Grievingbehindthebadgeblog.net, June 24, 2014: "Firefighters At Risk."

3. MedicCast. Article: mediccast.com/blog: "First Responder Pay Disparities."

4. Allen R. Kates, *Copshock: Surviving Posttraumatic Stress Disorder* (Tucson, AZ: Holbrook Street Press, 2010). p. 51, 406.

5. Police Chief William May, *Once Upon A Crisis.* p. 110.

6. Matthew Tull, PhD. Article: PTSD.about.com/od/prevalence/a/Firefighters, Jan. 29, 2012: "Rates of PTSD in Firefighters."

7. Dr. Frank Ochberg, founding board member of the International Society for Traumatic Stress Studies. Article: PolicePTSD.com, on Home Page: "PTSD or PTSI?"

Jeff[1] believed that if you sincerely try to do the right thing, you will be rewarded. A combat tour in Iraq had left him a little rattled, but he had worked through his issues well enough to join a major metropolitan police department. Whether as a soldier or in law enforcement, his passionate desire was to serve. To help. To make his world safer.

After two years on the force, Jeff had passed probation and was pushing a patrol car on the graveyard shift. A report comes in on a group of youths – probable gang members – possibly armed. Jeff responds quickly to the area and arrives well before his backup. Despite department policy requiring backup before attempting contact, Jeff parks his patrol car and walks toward the group. He doesn't want to appear afraid by waiting for backup to arrive.

The alley is dimly lit. He draws his Glock and commands them to show their hands. A few scatter. Others mutter obscenities but comply. One keeps his hands in his pockets and appears to be rummaging around for something. Jeff targets this individual and repeats his command, to no avail. Backup is taking forever. The other youths begin shouting at Jeff and demanding he leave their friend alone. He wonders if the ones who had scattered were now flanking him.

Suddenly the non-compliant youth brings something shiny out of his pocket and raises it up.

Instantly, Jeff's mind screams *"Gun!"* and his right index finger twitches three times. All three bullets find their marks, and the young man drops dead. The other youths sprint for cover, leaving Jeff alone with the dead youth.

The facts that emerge over the next few minutes would change Jeff's life forever. The youth had pulled out a cell phone, not a gun. He was only twelve years old, developmentally challenged and hard of hearing, unable to understand Jeff's commands. The "gang" consisted of the dead boy's big brother and friends, returning from a local youth dance.

Jeff is horrified and speechless. He is relieved of his gun and ammo by an investigating detective and transported to the office where he is interviewed like a common criminal. For the second time that night, he feels like his life is on the line. And it's not looking good for him. He simply can't remember certain details of the incident and he is afraid he won't be able to justify his actions.

Though he is cleared criminally by the shooting review team, Jeff is penalized for his violation of policy. Some fellow officers begin avoiding him, pegging him as unreliable and over-reactive. The public wants his head on a platter, and several civil lawsuits against him spin up. Because Jeff violated policy, the department won't represent him in court. His wife leaves him because of his depression, anger, flashbacks, nightmares and excessive drinking. It's only a matter of time before he loses his job.

Jeff is very angry at God, and will challenge you straight up: "God? Where was God when I was trying to do the right thing? Why didn't He stop me from shooting that boy? Why has He let me end up like this? If He even exists, God is irrelevant."[2]

⊕　⊕　⊕　⊕　⊕

? How about you? What are your thoughts at this moment about the existence of God?

_____

_____

_____

Natural Question

When a person experiences a horrific event, when evil triumphs, when the innocent are harmed, when a random, unexpected incident results in destruction and death, it's a natural human tendency to ask, "Where was God? Why didn't He prevent this?" It's natural and *normal.*

Since you're reading this manual we're going to assume that you have lived through one or more traumatic experiences. Maybe service-related, maybe not. Maybe it's the accumulation of months and years of stress. Did you wonder where God was when these things were happening? Did you question His existence, His ability, His goodness? Maybe you knew He was *somewhere*, doing *something*, but you shook your fist at heaven and cursed Him because He wasn't *there* doing what you needed when you needed it. It's okay. You're not alone. Some of the most godly, faith-filled men and women in history have done the same, more or less. Even Jesus Christ cried out from the murderous cross…

My God! My God! Why have You forsaken Me?

—Matthew 27:46

What do you know about God? Since He's infinite, it's hard to know a *lot* about God, but we're very sure about a few things. For instance, those who have walked with God very closely for a long time tell us that He is "supremely-good" and "supremely-powerful." But wait a minute. If God is supremely-good, He certainly wouldn't want bad things to happen. And if He's supremely-powerful, He certainly would be able to do what He wants and *keep* bad things from happening.

So… why do so many bad things happen in a world ruled by a God who is supposedly so good and so powerful?

Here's why…

"For God so loved the world…" You've heard that line before, right? God loves the world – and God loves *you* – at a depth and with an intensity that exceeds our understanding by infinity. His love isn't the sentimental, syrupy love that we see in the movies or daydream about. It's a love that is wise, selfless and freeing. It has eternity in mind, not just the here-and-now. However, this kind of authentic love is not something that God imposes on us…

Free Will

"Control freaks" are also characterized by depth and intensity. But they don't care about you – they have their own agenda. God is the opposite of a control freak. He is not going to force you to do anything. He will not impose His will on you. He's not interested in a group of puppets who will do what He says when He pulls the right strings. He *loves* you, and what He wants more than anything in all the universe is *your* love, sent back to Him of your own free will. If we are forced, it's not love at all. It's *physics*: simple action and reaction.

So God – from the very beginning – has deeply desired that we will decide on our own to respond positively to His loving overtures. Love cannot be coerced.

> Two things about free will:
>
> (1) It is a blessing from God because He loves us.
>
> (2) We often make it a curse because of our choices and decisions.
>
> —Terry Bratton,
> *39-year Houston PD veteran*

⊕ ⊕ ⊕ ⊕ ⊕

? Put an "X" on the line below that best describes how you feel toward God right now.

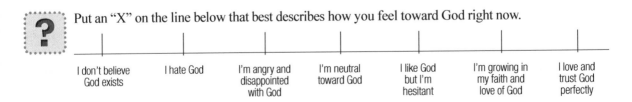

| I don't believe God exists | I hate God | I'm angry and disappointed with God | I'm neutral toward God | I like God but I'm hesitant | I'm growing in my faith and love of God | I love and trust God perfectly |

Love Rejected

"We do not want this man to reign over us!" That was Jesus telling a story in Luke 19 about how He was going to be rejected as King.

The story came true a few days later. *"Away with Him! Away with Him! Crucify Him! We have no king but Caesar!"* The people didn't want God – or His Son – as their ruler, so they killed Him. But this was nothing new. People have been rejecting God's rule in their affairs since the time of Adam and Eve. Mankind said "No" to God at the first opportunity and we've been saying "No" ever since – as a species, as nations, as individuals. God reaches out in love and says, "May I be your Shield, your Guide, your Guardrails, your Sustainer, your Companion, your Comforter?" And every one of us at one time or another has replied, "No, You may not. I would prefer to be the Captain of my own soul. Leave me alone. I'll do as I please."

God didn't change His mind about respecting our free will. He granted our wish. He backed off. But not very far. Always there, always ready to respond, always reaching out – but out of our way. "We don't need Him – we can handle things just fine by ourselves."

How are we doing?

Are we humans indeed handling things just fine, doing as we please? Consider just the last half of the 20th century. After six million Jews and six million Christians and gypsies were exterminated by the Nazis during World War II, the world vowed "We will *never* let that happen again." And yet between 1958 and 1961, Mao Zedong orchestrated the starvation deaths of at least twenty million Chinese as the world watched from the sidelines. In 1972, intake ducts in the dams of the Nile were plugged with the bodies of more than 300,000 Ugandans whom Idi Amin murdered with impunity. Between 1975 and 1978, Pol Pot executed two million of his own Cambodian people, and the rest of humanity remained disinterested. Did anyone try to stop Saddam Hussein from gassing thousands of Kurdish families in 1984? During three months of 1994 the world stood idle while a million Hutus and Tutsis hacked each other to death in Rwanda and Burundi. Today, armed militia in Sudan, Congo and Somalia rape and murder tens of thousands and have created more than two million refugees. We could go on. Suffice it to say that more innocent men, women and children have been murdered through genocide in the 20th century than have been killed in all previous wars in history.

But this is not a recent development. According to Pulitzer Prize winning historian Will Durant, there have only been 268 of the past 3,421 years when a major war wasn't raging somewhere on earth.[3] Man is at the helm and things are *not* getting better.

"If He even exists, He is irrelevant."

We can understand Jeff's deep frustration and despair. He was fed up with the injustice of it all, and the buck has *got* to stop somewhere! We can all identify with Jeff at some level. But isn't it ironic? We tell God to get lost and then blame *Him* for *our* unimaginable inhumanity toward each other. We have done this to ourselves. While we were supposedly captaining our souls and the souls of others with care and compassion – but without God – many used their power to enslave, torment and murder. They did as they pleased.

As one Jewish prisoner in Auschwitz remarked to his friend: "Where is God?" The other, pondering their sadistic guards and the unresponsive world, replied, "Where is man?"[4]

 Write down one incident that you observed while serving as a first responder that demonstrates man's inhumanity toward their fellow man (you might think of *many*, but just choose one).

_____

_____

_____

You've been on the street. You have experienced things that people were not originally designed to experience. You've seen people get maimed or die. You've held dead children in your arms. People have assaulted you and tried to kill you. You may have had to kill someone.

And now, even though it's all in the past, you can't shake it. The anxiety, the anger, the hypervigilance, the dreams, the hair-trigger rage, the depression – they're not getting better. Maybe they're getting worse.

Here's the most important thing you need to know about what you are currently experiencing:

Your condition is due to the evil actions of evil men – not God.

"Where *was* God, then? Where was He when I got shot? Where was He when that burning building collapsed on my best friend and killed him? Why didn't He stop that kid from running into the street? Did God sleep in that day? Was He busy with 'more important' things?" It might seem like that, but He was right there on the scene – ready to act in a way, and at a time, that is often elusive in the heat of the moment. He wept over the dead victims just as He wept at the tomb of His friend Lazarus (John 11:30-36). He is biding His time until the day He will judge and eliminate all evil and those who practice it. But in the meantime – right now – He is walking beside you and anguishing over the pain you are experiencing.

Harmonizing multiple free wills

And *protecting* you. Have you ever considered that? You may have been injured or wounded in the line of duty, and that experience is something you'll never forget. But do you know about all the accidents, assaults, blows and bullets He deflected to keep you alive? One thing's for sure: if you belong to Him, there were many. But you won't find out about them until heaven. He was there though, right with you, perfectly harmonizing your will, His will, the lawbreaker's will and your life-threatening circumstances to keep you alive, equip you better for eternity and bring glory to Himself. This is the supernatural juggling act of a sovereign God.

But why didn't He at least keep your partner alive? Save that child? Stop that madman? Sideline that drunk driver? We'll never know this side of heaven. There are too many variables for us to try to figure it out. It's like an ant trying to understand a computer. It – and we – simply don't have the equipment to sort those things out.

But we keep trying anyway. That's our nature. The Bible says that God put eternity in our hearts (Ecclesiastes 3:11). Because of this, we *know* there's something beyond this crazy life. We *long* for it. It makes us conclude that the present evil and suffering are *not right;* yet, we're utterly immersed in it. And not getting answers frustrates the heck out of us.

Here's a question that will help lead you to at least *some* answers:

Are you sure you know who your enemy is?

If you're a law enforcement officer, you have been trained to recognize when someone is a threat. However, this is not an exact science. Some of the worst criminals look and act like decent, law-abiding citizens, blending in and appearing harmless. You may have experienced the cruel consequences of *not* correctly identifying a threat.

Those assailants may have wanted to take your physical life, but you have other enemies who hold eternal objectives regarding you. Your thoughts, your spiritual and emotional health, your priorities, your plans, your allegiances, your productivity, your family, your heritage and your body are the disputed territories. Our *real* enemies aren't even human.

For our struggle is not against flesh and blood, but against the rulers, against the powers, against the world forces of this darkness, against the spiritual forces of wickedness in the heavenly places.

—Ephesians 6:12

Who, or what, do you think the preceding verse is talking about?

_____

⊕ ⊕ ⊕ ⊕ ⊕

Our Enemy's Bio

There is a real being known as Satan who has existed for thousands of years. He was once the Number One angel in God's kingdom, beautiful, intelligent and as powerful as they come. Back then his name was Lucifer – "Star of the Morning." Just like us humans, he had a free will. But he also had an audacious, prideful ambition: to take God's place. So before man had even been created, the Bible reports that he led a rebellion of one-third of the angels, attempting a cosmic coup – which he lost. As a result, he and all his cohorts were cast out of the Kingdom of Heaven onto the earth, and turned from angels into demons. (You can read about this in Ezekiel 28:12-19 and Isaiah 14:12-17.)

Satan *still* thinks he can overthrow God, and he and his network of spiritual combatants are continuing his assault even today. He hates God with a passion that surpasses anything a human has ever imagined. He hates God's creation, and most of all, he hates humans – because of how much God loves them. Satan and his demons deeply influenced the minds of people like Hitler, Stalin, Lenin, Pol Pot and others, who in turn unleash devilish oppression and wars on humanity. He seeks defectors from God's army that he can induct into his own. Human armies have their objectives, but many of them are subordinate to Satan's goals. He is just using them.

He has objectives involving presidents, dictators and nations. But he also has objectives for each and every one of us. If he can't use you, he'll seek to eliminate you. *"Be of sober spirit, be on the alert. Your adversary, the devil, prowls around like a roaring lion, seeking someone to devour."* (1 Peter 5:8) Don't miss this: he doesn't want to trip you up, make you feel bad, bum you out or hurt your feelings. He wants to *devour* you, and he won't quit trying until he's accomplished this ultimate objective.

He will use any weakness we have, any experience we've gone through, any vulnerability he can discover to fulfill his mission for us. You can be positive that he will use your traumatic service-related experiences to find the open gaps in your armor.

He is our enemy. Not God.

It's not the challenges you experience as a first responder that will do you in. It's the spiritual and psychological wounds that Satan can spin off those experiences that could. But there are counter-measures. You'll learn much more about this in Step 8: *How Do I Fight? – Rebuilding Your Defenses.*

⊕ ⊕ ⊕ ⊕ ⊕

Are you sure you know who your ally is?

Have you ever heard the term "the fog of war?" In the midst of combat when all hell's breaking loose, it's sometimes difficult to discern who's friend, who's foe, which way is safety and which way is death. A fireman in a smoke-filled building can get confused about which way leads out. An undercover cop might be mistaken about who he can trust, and who he can't.

In the Bible, Israel's greatest leader – King David – was a world-class warrior. He had personally led, fought in, survived and won dozens of campaigns during his forty years as king. But one thing he was never foggy about was who his #1 ally was. He *always* knew where to turn for aid: to God Himself.

Each of the Scripture passages below highlights a time when David was facing unbeatable foes, desperate situations and deadly consequences. But in each case, his foundational mindset and supreme confidence was that Almighty God, the Commander of the Hosts of Heaven, would rescue him, strengthen him and give him victory over his enemies.

Here he is as a mere teenager, addressing 9'8" Goliath of Gath, champion of the Philistines, while all the other soldiers of Israel stood back and wet their armor…

> *You come to me with a sword, a spear, and a javelin, but I come to you in the name of the Lord of hosts, the God of the armies of Israel, whom you have taunted. This day the Lord will deliver you up into my hands, and I will strike you down and remove your head from you. And I will give the dead bodies of the army of the Philistines this day to the birds of the sky and the wild beasts of the earth, that all the earth may know that there is a God in Israel, and that all this assembly may know that the Lord does not deliver by sword or by spear; for the battle is the Lord's and He will give you into our hands.*

> **—1 Samuel 17:45-47**

What character qualities were manifested in David because of his confidence in God?

_____

Now he's leading the armies of Israel in battle. He is the "theocratic warrior," an instrument of war in the hand of God. Not many can claim that position, but David could. God was not only his ally, but his comrade-in-arms *and* his commander-in-chief…

> *Arise, O Lord, in Your anger; lift up Yourself against the rage of my adversaries, and arouse Yourself for me; You have appointed judgment… O let the evil of the wicked come to an end, but establish the righteous; for the righteous God tries the hearts and mind. My shield is with God, who saves the upright in heart. God is a righteous judge, and a God who has indignation every day.*

> **—Psalm 7:6,9-11**

Check the statement that you think is correct:

❑ David was a blood-thirsty killer with an imperialist agenda and a lust for power.

❑ David saw himself as a servant of God – and he looked to Him to set the agenda, issue the orders and produce the outcome of the battle.

✠   ✠   ✠   ✠   ✠

Don't get the idea that David's life was all smooth sailing and victory parades. Many times, before the dawn of God's deliverance, he went through some very dark nights…

> *But You, O God, the Lord, deal kindly with me for Your name's sake; because Your lovingkind-ness is good, deliver me; for I am afflicted and needy, and my heart is wounded within me. I am passing like a shadow when it lengthens; I am shaken off like the locust… Help me, O Lord my*

God; save me according to Your lovingkindness. And let them know that this is Your hand; You, Lord, have done it.

—**Psalm 109:21-27**

How would you describe David's frame of mind as he wrote the above scripture?

_____

What was his attitude toward God?

_____

⊕　　⊕　　⊕　　⊕　　⊕

Chicks and Wolves

Have you ever watched a bunch of chicks with their mother hen? When danger comes, they instantly scurry toward their mother, who lifts her wings and gathers them underneath for protection. Could you imagine a wolf bounding into the chicken yard and one of the chicks running *away* from the hen and *toward* the wolf? That would be one very stupid – or confused – chick. And one very happy wolf.

And yet so many humans, when problems bound into their lives, decide to run *away* from the Supreme Problem Solver of the universe, rather than toward Him.

Why do you think that is?

_____

_____

In which direction are you running right now – toward God or away from Him? Why?

_____

_____

What's God got to do with anything?
He can't know what I'm experiencing. He's immune!

Are you sure? Here's something to chew on. Applied to any other so-called "god" on the planet, that statement could be true. Fake gods are always depicted as transcendent, all-powerful, above the wretched company of mere mortals, not limited by the things that limit us, pain-free, trauma-free, sorrow-free. Except for the God of the Bible.

He is the only "god" who has suffered.

The theology of the Trinity is difficult for *anybody* to grasp. God the Father, God the Son and God the Holy Spirit – one in essence but three in identity and function. Jesus Christ was the physical manifestation of God. When Jesus was born in Bethlehem, it was God Himself packed into that tiny little body lying in that dirty animal feeding trough. The baby grew into a boy and then into a man. Along the way, He suffered many things – everything that the rest of us humans do – and He learned from them. The only thing He didn't experience was guilt, because He never sinned.

But then He was rejected, scorned, falsely convicted, whipped, beaten beyond recognition, mocked, tortured and crucified. God was willing to endure this in order to pay the penalty that He Himself had set to atone for our sinful lives.

This is how our loving God defeats evil. He took it into Himself, experienced it at its worst, and then triumphed over it in the resurrection. He has earned the right to say, "I know *exactly* what you're going through. Whatever your ordeal, I've experienced worse."

> No one can ever go so low that God in Jesus has not gone lower. What other faith has at its heart a writhing body, torn flesh, shameful desertion and disgrace, anguished desolation, and a darkness that can be felt? God liberates not by removing suffering from us, but by sharing it with us. Jesus is 'God-who-suffers-with-us.'[5]
>
> —Os Guinness, philosopher, survivor of the Henan famine in China, 1943

> Jesus was not crucified in a cathedral between two candles, but on a cross between two thieves; on the town garbage heap; at a crossroad so cosmopolitan they had to write his title in Hebrew and in Greek and in Latin, at the kind of place where cynics talk smut, and soldiers gamble. Because that is where He died. And that is what He died about.[6]
>
> —George Macleod of Iona, clergyman and Scottish soldier in WWI

> The child was trapped in the car, and I *had* to get her out. With power that was not mine I moved mangled car parts to extricate her. But as I pulled her to safety, I saw what remained of her younger sister. Grief swept over me. That's when I felt the raindrops on my shoulder. As I moved away from the car, I realized it was a clear night. Not raining. Could it be that our Maker, the Creator of life and Victor over death knew my sorrow? Then the words of scripture rang in my head, "And Jesus wept."
>
> —T.B., Houston Police Department

Suffering happens. Can any good come out of it?

If you've ever been an athlete, if you've ever had a big dream, if you've ever pursued excellence in *anything*, then you know that not only *can* suffering produce good results, it's practically a requirement.

The same is true in the Kingdom of God. We're not saying that God has *caused* the trauma that you have encountered. It's been devastating, costly and very difficult – but it's not a total loss. In fact, over time God will *use* it to accomplish extraordinarily good things in your life – if you will let Him.

 What truth or principle about God and our adversity can you discover from each of the following passages? Write your observations down after each Scripture.

And we know that God causes all things to work together for good to those who love God, to those who are called according to His purpose.

—Romans 8:28

_____

_____

_____

Blessed be the God and Father of our Lord Jesus Christ, the Father of mercies and God of all comfort, who comforts us in all our affliction so that we will be able to comfort those who are in any affliction with the comfort with which we ourselves are comforted by God.

– 2 Corinthians 1:3,4

For God, who said, "Let light shine out of darkness," made His light shine in our hearts to give us the light of the knowledge of the glory of God in the face of Christ. But we have this treasure in jars of clay to show that this all-surpassing power is from God and not from us.

—2 Corinthians 4:6,7 (NIV)

[Joseph, great-grandson of Abraham, had two sons while he lived in exile in Egypt – where he eventually became the second most powerful man in the world.] Joseph named the firstborn Manasseh, "For," he said, "God has made me forget all my trouble and all my father's household." He named the second Ephraim, "For," he said, "God has made me fruitful in the land of my affliction."

—Genesis 41:51,52

✠　✠　✠　✠　✠

Be honest. Right now, today, do you think knowing and experiencing God at a much deeper level might eventually make your current level of anxiety and pain worth it?

✠　✠　✠　✠　✠

Conclusion

Does cold exist? Yes and no. We've all been cold. But cold is merely the absence of heat. We can measure heat with a thermometer, but cold is defined only by how hot it isn't.

Does darkness exist? Again, yes and no. We all *think* we've seen darkness, but actually we've not seen it at all. Darkness is only the absence of light. No one can measure darkness, but light is easily measured by various instruments.

Does evil exist? We've all seen evil. Many of us are marked by its scars. But just as cold is the absence of heat and darkness is the absence of light, evil exists only in the absence of God. As the Christian theologian C. S. Lewis once said, there are only two places in the universe where God does not exist: in some human governments and in some human hearts. He was speaking metaphorically, but the point is that wherever God is not vitally present, evil pours in propelled by dark forces of demons and men.

Just as heat overcomes cold and light dispels darkness, the presence of God drives out evil. The trauma you experienced was because of evil. Its continuing effect is because of evil. Only as you allow the light and heat of God to enter those wounded areas will you be able to experience His healing and His victory.

He loves you with an infinite love. He has loved you since before you were born, since the day He created the earth. He loved you when you were experiencing stress and trauma on duty, or emptiness and anxiety off duty. He knows everything about you. He knew ahead of time what you were going to experience and He knows how to heal you. He may not do it as fast as you'd like or in the manner that you'd prefer, but He'll do it perfectly – if you will let Him.

When "Shots fired – officer down" is transmitted over a police radio, there are instantly endless numbers of units racing to the scene to assist. The biggest danger is everyone crashing into each other as they converge to help their fellow officer. This level of response pales in comparison to what God is willing to do to come to your aid when you ask Him to. It may not be as openly dramatic, but it will be eternally consequential.

Prayer Seed

Father, You know how much I hurt. You know the depth of my anxiety, anger and confusion. You know how much I just want to be normal again. Please hear my prayer, asking for Your help. Forgive me for not giving You full access to my life up to this point. I know now that I can't fix this. But You made me. You know what to do. So I ask You to lead me out of my darkness into Your light. Help me to cooperate with You in this process. Give me patience and the ability to see Your hand at work in my life. Increase my faith. Thank You that You are my cover. Amen.

---

1. Name has been changed.
2. Story from John Franklin, Detective for Lane County Oregon District Attorney; also CWO2 Army Apache Helicopter pilot eight years.
3. Quote from Will Durant found at www.brainyquotes.com.
4. Os Guiness, *Unspeakable: Facing Up To The Challenge of Evil* (New York: HarperCollins, 2005). p. 46.
5. Ibid, pp. 147, 148.
6. Quote from George Macleod in Os Guiness, *Unspeakable*, p. 148.

Step ② What Happened To Me?
...Understanding the Physical/Psychological Context of Your Trauma

Your Trauma's Root of Honor

Edmund Burke wrote, "The only thing necessary for evil to triumph is for good men to do nothing." *You* – as opposed to so many on our planet today – *did something*. You decided to fight evil directly, along with all the damage and pain it inflicts, and became a first responder. Like young David in the Bible *running* to engage Goliath in a battle to the death, you gear up every day and look for opportunities to go where evil is breaking out. You run into buildings that everyone else is running out of.

When you joined, you may have been proudly carrying on the honorable tradition of several generations of first responders. Or you may have felt the mystical thrill of being the first one among your family and friends to launch into a first responder career.

Maybe you spent some time in the military. The discipline, esprit de corps, and the gravity of your responsibilities resonated with you, and you wanted to build on those sensations in the civilian arena. The combat-related adrenaline rush felt great. When downrange, you were engaged in some of the most significant activity in your life – life and death stuff. You wanted more.

As a first responder, you were driven by a desire to see justice served, pain alleviated, danger averted, crisis deflated, and the helpless defended.

But there were adversaries lying in wait who attacked you in ways you hadn't expected. The attacks weren't physical – although assaults may have been involved. The deepest and most debilitating wounds were the psychological and spiritual ones that spun off from the trauma. They hit you as you were putting your life on the line for others. Your physical wounds, the weariness from shifts that were too long and stressful, the injuries you suffered while doing your job – all those can heal. But the invisible wounds of trauma and stress don't seem to go away.

> "I continued to give myself to the job, and to lose pieces of myself along the way."[1]
>
> —Paramedic James Meuer

Nevertheless, you performed well in the face of your challenges. Some people may have thanked you for your sacrifices. You may have even gotten commendations, a mention in the paper, promotions. But while those pleasant moments fade, you're still making sacrifices. And you probably hold two thoughts concerning the unanticipated symptoms associated with your heroic acts of service:

1. I don't know how or why I have these feelings.

2. I want them gone.

This Step will try to address that first thought. The rest of the Manual will help you with the second one.

? Take a moment and consider ... A sacrifice generally means "something was given up." Because of your experiences as a first responder, what are some of the things you have given up (or that were taken from you)?

_____

_____

_____

First Responders and Operational Stress Reactions

"Operational Stress Reactions" describes a continuum of distressing responses that a person may have when they experience a horrific event, a series of events, or a long period of stress. Everyone involved in the emergency service occupations is regularly exposed to stressful and traumatic situations. Some will experience anxious reactions and improve quickly without any outside help, while others will get "stuck" at a certain reactive level and won't get better for a long time – or ever.

Our country is awash with stress. According to the American Psychological Association, up to 90% of all visits to medical doctors are stress-related complaints.[2] Obviously, unresolved stress in first responders can be extremely debilitating, career-threatening, and even life-threatening.

One cannot classify or assign absolute values to the severity of traumatic events, but we all have a general sense that incidents involving children, multiple fatalities or a personal near-death experience shake us up a lot more than transporting a drunk to jail or rescuing a cat from a tree. Nevertheless, it's not the incident itself that generates stressful reactions, but our perception of or reaction to the event. Everyone is wired differently and responds differently.

For public safety professionals, personal history, repeated trauma, and long-term stress can also wear down our psychological and spiritual defenses, making us more susceptible to stress reactions. But experiencing a traumatic incident does not automatically mean we will develop full-blown Posttraumatic Stress Disorder (PTSD). Our actual responses can fall anywhere along this spectrum, from "Mild" on the left to "Severe" on the right:

Operational Stress Reaction Spectrum

MILD					SEVERE
Duty/Home Transitional Stress	Occupational Stress Reactions	Adjustment Disorders	Acute Stress Disorder	Posttraumatic Stress Disorder	

- **Duty/Home Transitional Stress** – Tension resulting from on-duty stress or traumatic events which the first responder brings home; difficulty shifting from cop/paramedic/ firefighter mode to spouse/daddy/mommy mode. Symptoms include irritability, angry responses, impatience, self-isolationism, sleep difficulties, jumpiness, etc. These symptoms are relatively mild, and often dissipate within a few minutes or hours, or may trend up or down depending on conditions on the job.[3]

- **Occupational Stress Reactions** – Emotional or behavioral symptoms that develop due to exposure to the characteristically stressful elements of normal first responder employment; when environmental stressors exceed a person's capabilities and resources, leading to negative outcomes.[4] These reactions can develop from three categories of stressors:

  1. **Critical Incident Stress** – Negative psychological reaction to sudden, unexpected events that have an emotional impact sufficient to overwhelm an individual's usually effective coping skills.[5] Some of the most significant stressors are: line of duty death or injury, suicide of a working partner, injury or death of a child, prolonged exposure to a victim who dies, a multiple injury/fatality accident, and catastrophic events.[6]

  2. **Cumulative Stress** – Negative psychological reaction due to chronic and frequent exposure to stress-producing incidents over an extended period of time. In addition, long-term burdensome shift work, on-going conflicts with co-workers or command, exhausting work tempo, inadequate or interrupted sleep, rapid technological advances, increased specialty responsibilities, position insecurity, and reorganizations can break down a first responder's resiliency.[7]

3. **Derivative Stress** – A non-medical term describing strong, long-lasting emotional reactions which derive their impact from trauma that happened to another person.[8]

    a. **Secondary Tramatic Stress** – The natural consequence of caring between two people, one of whom has been initially traumatized and the other of whom is negatively affected by the first's traumatic experiences (even though they did not actually experience them) often mimicking their symptoms.[9]

    b. **Burnout** – A negative emotional reaction created through long attendance in high stress workplaces, characterized by physical, mental and emotional exhaustion, depersonalization, decreased motivation and apathy.[10] Often experienced by those in "helping" professions (besides first responders) such as counselors, dispatchers, emergency room personnel, doctors, nurses.

    c. **Compassion Fatigue** - The emotional residue or strain of exposure to working with those suffering from the consequences of traumatic events.[11] Often happens to those who are particularly empathetic, compassionate and self-sacrificing. Secondary Trauma + Burnout = Compassion Fatigue.

If not addressed, Occupational Stress Reactions can worsen and shift to the severe end of the spectrum. But with proper, intentional care and with God's help, these reactions will abate, and the first responder will return to a place of strength, stability and resiliency.

- **Adjustment Disorders** – Out of proportion emotional or behavioral symptoms developing as a response to a specific stressor or multiple, chronic stressors (such as financial trouble, divorce, disabling medical condition, etc.). Symptoms are more severe than Occupational Stress Reactions, and include depression, tearfulness, hopelessness, anxiety, anger, decreased performance at work or school, and "disturbance of conduct" (violation of another's rights such as fighting, vandalism, reckless driving, etc.). Once the stressor (or its consequences) has terminated the symptoms resolve within six months.[12]

- **Acute Stress Disorder** – PTSD-like symptoms experienced during or immediately after (within one month of) a traumatic event and lasting at least two days. Dissociative symptoms are common (numbing, detachment, dazed, amnesia), as are flashbacks, nightmares, avoidance of triggering stimuli, hypervigilance, paranoia, startle response, low energy, sleep impairment, etc. Impaired social and occupational function is prevalent. Usually requires intentional counseling to experience progress. If the symptoms don't resolve within four weeks, the diagnosis is changed to Posttraumatic Stress Disorder.[13]

- **Posttraumatic Stress Disorder** – The development of characteristic symptoms (lasting longer than one month) following exposure to a traumatic event or series of events in the following contexts:

1. **Direct exposure** to a traumatic event(s) such as war, threatened or actual assault or sexual violence, robbery, childhood physical abuse, kidnapping, torture, terrorism, natural disaster, severe vehicle accident, etc.

2. **Witnessing** a traumatic event(s) in person.

3. **Indirect exposure** by learning that a close relative or close friend experienced a violent or accidental traumatic event.

4. **Repeated or extreme indirect exposure to horrific details** of the traumatic event(s) in the course of professional duties (e.g. collecting body parts, repeatedly exposed to detailed reports of child abuse, etc.).[14]

The characteristic symptoms are categorized in four clusters:

1. **Intrusion** (or Re-experiencing) – Recurrent, involuntary memories, flashbacks, nightmares, sleep fighting, fixation on traumatic event(s), spontaneous dissociative episodes (one thinks they are actually back in the traumatic situation), panic attacks, phobias, intense or prolonged distress, etc.

2. **Avoidance** – Avoiding anyone or anything that reminds one of the traumatic event(s), self-isolating, anxiety in crowds or traffic, substance abuse to "numb," etc.

3. **Cognitions and mood alterations** – Forgetting key elements of the traumatic event(s), persistent and distorted self-image or world view, persistent and distorted blame of self or others for causing the event(s), strong negative emotions (fear, horror, anger, guilt, shame), diminished interest in previously enjoyed activities (sex, hobbies, exercise), feeling alienated from others, emotionally flat, etc.

4. **Arousal and reactivity alterations** – Irritable, aggressive, self-destructive or reckless behavior, hyper-vigilant, easily startled, reduced cognitive ability, sleep difficulties, substance abuse to "un-numb," suicidal and homicidal thoughts, etc.

The symptom profile for any individual will include a **unique mix** from the four clusters, not *all* of the symptoms by any means. Social and occupational functions will be impaired. These symptoms may surface immediately after the traumatic event(s), or they may not become apparent for weeks, months or even years.[15]

 Put an "X" on the **Operational Stress Reaction Spectrum** (page 20) which you feel represents where you are right now. You don't have to perfectly line up with the definitions of each designation on the line – just estimate where you fit on the "Mild" to "Severe" continuum.

What's the Target?

The medical and mental health communities are finally beginning to understand the immense impact that line of duty stress and trauma has on first responders and their families. Due to the high-profile traumas that our combat troops are experiencing in the Mideast, the topic of Posttraumatic Stress Disorder is becoming more common. It may be a condition that *you* are worried about. But remember: PTSD is a technical term that describes a set of symptoms at the severe end of the spectrum and this may not be your lot. However, in this manual we will often be focusing on PTSD. Even if you don't have this condition, you will be helped. It's a good principle: if you have to fight a whole gang, go for the biggest, baddest dude first. That's what PTSD is and, just like the gang leader, if we fight it correctly it will go *down!*

PTSD isn't new

In a military context, PTSD has been called by many names over the centuries. This makes it clear that it's a disorder not unique to modern wars, but common to all wars. During the latter half of the 1600s, the Swiss observed a consistent set of symptoms in some of their soldiers and called it "nostalgia." German doctors of the same period used the term *Heimweh* and the French called it *maladie du pays*. Both terms are roughly translated as "homesickness." The Spanish called it *estar roto,* "to be broken." During America's Civil War it was called "soldier's heart." They called it "shell shocked" in World War I, "combat fatigue" in WWII, and "war neurosis" during the Korean war. In the 1970s they coined the phrase "Vietnam Veterans Syndrome."

Each of these terms shows facets of the disorder. The soldier's heart *does* get profoundly altered by war. Nostalgia and homesickness describe the desperate longing of a PTSD sufferer to leave the chaos of the battle and return to the safety of home. Emotionally something is indeed broken inside these wounded warriors, resulting in various psychological neuroses – a familiar, persistent syndrome of symptoms. As a first responder, you may identify with many of these facets.

It wasn't until 1980 that the American Psychiatric Association formally identified, named and defined Posttraumatic Stress Disorder, and it's been in the official diagnostic manuals of the medical profession since that time. More research is constantly being done on this mystifying disorder. But here is the first thing that you need to know – upon which *all* the experts agree:

Posttraumatic Stress Disorder
is a *common* reaction to an *uncommon* event.

Common

If you have PTSD, it may be difficult for you to imagine that your anxiety-riddled behavior – which is so different from how you were before – could be "common," but that's exactly the case. Your symptoms are what we would *expect* from someone who experienced what you did. They are common to *millions* of other courageous men and women who have been first responders or fought in wars down through the centuries. For a person who saw, smelled, felt, heard and tasted the things you did, it's *common*.

And you are far from an isolated case. Some studies have shown that as many as 37% of first responders have experienced PTSD at some point in their careers.[16] You are most definitely *not* alone.

If this information is new to you, let us spell it out:

- PTSD is not rare or an aberration – it is a common response to an uncommon stressor.

- Millions of men and women are in the same boat you are.

- It is normal to be affected by pain, atrocity, horror and gore.

- Facing death changes a person.

- It would be abnormal if you weren't affected.

- It shows that you are human and that the horrific, stressful events that you saw or experienced matter.

Here is the next thing that you *must* know:

You are not weak, weird or cowardly.
You have been wounded.

What can cause a wound? We normally think of physical implements, like a knife or a bullet. But one can receive "soul wounds" that are as bad as or worse than physical wounds, affecting you more deeply and lasting longer than anything a gun could produce. And we're not talking sentimental psychobabble here – this is as real as it gets. You know. You're living it.

As we mentioned in the Introduction, PTSD could be more accurately termed PTSI: "Posttraumatic Stress Injury," highlighting that there is always an identifiable event or series of events that precipitate the condition. It doesn't manifest without some sort of specific cause, as many other neuroses and anxiety disorders do.

The word "trauma" is from a Greek word which means "a wounding." When applied to the physical realm, it refers to an event in which some external force has damaged a part of your body. The normal defense mechanisms (such as the skin, muscle, skull, internal bone framing, etc.) were unable to prevent the injury. For a while, you won't be able to function the way you used to because of the wounding. The punch that knocked the wind out of you will keep you doubled over for a few moments. The cast on your leg will temporarily prevent you from walking normally.

Time and Treatment

In a similar fashion, we can receive psychological wounds that incapacitate us. Events can get past our normal defenses and severely disrupt our emotions, our souls and spirits, our faith, our self-identity, our confidence, our trust in others, our sense of security and even our will to live. After this, we won't be able to cope, think, react, plan, or function in the ways we used to – at least not for a while. We will need time and treatment to bring about the healing. **To immediately try to resume life-as-usual – physically, emotionally, or spiritually – will only deepen our wound and prolong our healing process.**

If you were physically injured, it would be important for you to be able to tell certain people about it – such as a doctor, family member, good friend. Take a few minutes to think about how to describe your "soul wounds" and then write it out in the space below.

_____

_____

_____

⊕   ⊕   ⊕   ⊕   ⊕

What Causes PTSD?

Not just combat. A psychological shock or event that makes a person think they could be severely injured or killed, witnessing a traumatic event, or repeated exposure to horrific reports *can* trigger PTSD (remember: we're referring to the far left end of the spectrum). We emphasize *can* because it doesn't mean it necessarily *will*. One study determined that approximately 75 percent of Americans have had a traumatic experience significant enough to cause PTSD, but only about 10 to 25 percent of those actually develop the disorder.[17] Experts do not fully agree as to why some do and some don't, but it seems that the *intensity* of the experience or multiple experiences has a lot to do with it. In addition, if a person has been traumatized at a younger age (physical or sexual abuse, abandonment, kidnapping, assault, etc.) it increases their likelihood of developing PTSD as an adult.

Experiences that can produce PTSD are: combat, sexual and physical assault, being held hostage, terrorism, torture, natural and man-made disasters, accidents, receiving a diagnosis of a life-threatening illness, violating one's conscience by engaging in mutilation or other violations of the Law of Armed Conflict, or the killing of innocents (accidentally or on purpose). Witnessing or hearing about these incidents happening to a friend or close associate *can* cause PTSD. It can be especially severe or long-lasting when the trauma comes from an intentional human act, rather than from an accident or a natural disaster.

 Did you ever experience any of the events listed in the previous paragraph? If so, which?

_____

_____

⊕   ⊕   ⊕   ⊕   ⊕

The Physiology, Psychology and Theology of PTSD

One of God's top design priorities when He created us was that we be equipped to defend ourselves and survive in a wide variety of dangerous situations. To this end, He equipped us with an amazing set of response mechanisms.

Our brains are divided into two halves. The left side is our analytical side. It scrutinizes incoming information logically, thinks rationally, explicitly, in concrete terms. It is on this side that we store practical information, our ability to speak, read, write, spell and do math. This side remembers names and craves precision.

If our left side is like a "computer," our right side is more like a "photo album." This side remembers faces and craves rapport and relationship. It's our emotional side. It is intuitive, spontaneous, experience-oriented, artistic, and creative. It stores emotions. We dream on this side of our brain. And very importantly, this is the "alarm" side of our brain.

Beneath these two halves is our "lower brain" or brain stem. This part of our brain controls all automatic life functions, such as our breathing, digestion and heartbeat. The lower brain always trumps the two halves of our higher brain. It doesn't matter how logical it may seem or how passionately you might want to do it, you can't make your heart stop beating just by thinking about it. You can hold your breath for a little while, but before long your lower brain once again asserts its dominance.

The Science of Trauma Reactions

When we encounter something that we feel threatens our life, a cascade of hormonal reactions is triggered. A nerve shoots a message to our adrenal glands to dump adrenaline and noradrenaline into our bloodstream, causing our heart to beat faster, our lungs to pump harder and getting the rest of the body ready to either fight, fly or freeze. Our pupils dilate, giving us tunnel vision so we can focus on the threat and not be distracted by peripheral action. Thousands of small muscles in our arms and legs constrict, sending blood away from our skin and into our muscles for quick movement – and so that if our extremities are wounded, we won't bleed as badly. Our blood sugar and free fatty acids instantly ramp up, giving us more energy. At the same time, up to 70 percent of our brain-bound oxygen is quickly shunted into our muscles so we can run, kick or punch like we never had before. Additional hormones give us uncommon strength and quickness. Our perception of time is altered – ten minutes in a burning building may seem like only a minute… or an hour.

But something happens deep inside our brains, too. Our right-brain alarm goes off and drowns out the logical analysis of our left brain. It screams, "Less thinking, more action!!" It also starts taking pictures like mad – the noradrenaline heightens the emotional aspects of the situation making it more vivid and notable. Very strong and clear memories are being recorded, probably so that we will remember this event and avoid it in the future.[18]

Whatever It Takes

At this point, our lower brain takes over. It's live-or-die time. With this organ in control, nothing else matters. It automatically directs the rest of the body in very complex but focused ways to do whatever it takes to survive. Sometimes a person may involuntarily respond in a way they wouldn't normally respond – ways that some might later describe as self-serving or even cowardly. Trauma survivors may feel shock or shame about this.

Research has shown that your body will exhibit these built-in survival techniques no matter what your race or gender is, whether you come from a privileged background or the ghetto, whether you are mentally slow or highly intelligent, whether you come from a happy family or a broken one, whether you're a cheerful person or a total pessimist. But it's important to know two things:

1. God gave you this reactive pathway so that you would be able to do whatever was necessary to survive. It kept you alive. God knows that when our lives are threatened this behavior needs to come out or we could die. At that point, all the rationality, dignity, intelligence and decorum in the world is absolutely useless.

2. No matter how hard you might have tried, you couldn't have stopped this reaction. Can you stop your heartbeat? No. Neither are we able to control ourselves when our brains have clicked into this mode.

⊕　⊕　⊕　⊕　⊕

Can you remember having one (or more) of these "automatic" reactions while you were on duty? Place an "X" on the line below indicating how severe it was.

MILD——SEVERE

⊕　⊕　⊕　⊕　⊕

PTSD Persistence

"Ok," you say, "The crisis is over now. I survived. What happened wasn't pretty, but the score ended up Me – 1, The Grave – 0. So why can't I move on? Why do I keep reliving what happened?"

Often, a trauma survivor can go through a short period of decompression and processing and return pretty close to "normal." But if the traumatizing event was exceptionally violent and life-threatening or if there were multiple episodes, the brain stays "stuck" in this crisis-alert mode.

Think of it in terms of walking across a frozen lake. As you walk, you feel confident and enjoy sliding on the ice. You might even do a few aerial leaps and spins like the skaters on TV, just for fun. Suddenly you hear a loud pop and you notice the ice is cracking under your feet. You instantly freeze. Your arms reflexively shoot out from your sides for balance and your feet spread wide to distribute your weight. Your muscles are now tight, your shoulders bunched up, your eyes are the size of softballs and you begin to take very small, careful steps back the way you came. After about twenty yards, you're beyond where the cracks were. Do you think you'd go bounding merrily the rest of the way to shore? You'd probably remain on high alert the rest of the way, because you are now aware that the ice *could* give way beneath you at any time.

Getting Stuck

After a traumatic event, your brain knows that it just had an incredibly close call, and it is determined to be ready to react if the danger comes by again. Good idea – except if it gets stuck in that mode, which is essentially what PTSD is. It's like the ice-walker tiptoeing two miles of sidewalk to get home.

The shock physically alters parts of your brain. Your reactive pathways modify, your brain chemistry changes and becomes hypersensitive, overreacting to normal stimuli. Your hippocampus – the part of your brain that interprets and calms your emotional responses – shrinks and works less effectively. Your left and right brain hemispheres have trouble communicating and balancing each other – so you're either all emotion and unordered, or you are emotionless, cold, withdrawn and not much fun to be around. Sometimes each of them inside of five minutes.

And whenever your brain senses that it's getting near the "scene of the crime" via some sensory trigger (a smell, a sound, a sight, a memory), it quickly opens up the photo album it created during the earlier traumatic event and puts on an intense slide and video show to remind you that you don't want to go there again! "Are you *nuts!??* We almost *bought* it when we were there last time!! Get away!!" The technical term for this is "re-experiencing."

The opening of the photo album can also have another function. It's a flare being sent up by the trauma survivor's inner self alerting the outside world that he's been through more than he can handle and he needs help dealing with it. We humans aren't meant to suffer our traumas alone and not bother anybody else about them. We are an *interdependent* species, ordained so by our Creator. We need each other. And if our "outer self" won't take action, our "inner self" will keep up the pressure until we do. By the way, it seems to work. More PTSD sufferers finally decide to seek help due to their re-experiencing symptoms than any other reason.

⊕　　⊕　　⊕　　⊕　　⊕

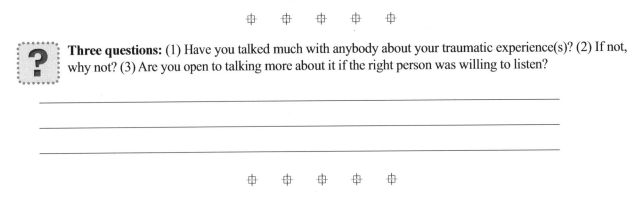

Three questions: (1) Have you talked much with anybody about your traumatic experience(s)? (2) If not, why not? (3) Are you open to talking more about it if the right person was willing to listen?

_____

_____

_____

⊕　　⊕　　⊕　　⊕　　⊕

PTSD Symptoms

Since the American Psychiatric Association first defined Posttraumatic Stress Disorder in 1980, and with additional research done since then, experts seem to agree that there are four categories of symptoms that characterize this disorder. Read through the list that follows and put an "X" in the box of any symptoms that you have experienced in the past or are currently experiencing. If your experience of a symptom is mild or very infrequent, give it a light, small "x." The more intense or more frequent the symptom, enlarge and darken the "**X.**"

Symptoms

1. **Intrusion Symptoms:** (Re-experiencing) Memories and images of the traumatic events may spontaneously intrude into the minds of those with PTSD, causing intense or prolonged distress or physiological reactions. Sometimes the images can be so vivid a person believes the trauma is actually reoccurring.[19]

In the past but not now / Experiencing currently

❑ ❑ Nightmares

❑ ❑ Sleepwalking, sleep fighting

❑ ❑ Unwanted daytime memories, images, thoughts, daydreams

❑ ❑ Flashbacks, feeling like you're reliving the traumatic event

❑ ❑ Somatic flashbacks (physical pain or a medical condition emerges, linked to the feelings or bodily states associated with the traumatic event)

❑ ❑ Fixated on the traumatic event, living in the past

❑ ❑ Spontaneous dissociative episodes (the world vanishes and you're suddenly somewhere else, experiencing some sort of trauma)

❑ ❑ Panic attacks, undefined distress, dread or fear

❑ ❑ Phobias (what kind?)

2. **Avoidance Symptoms** Traumatized individuals attempt to avoid situations, people or events that remind them of their trauma. They feel numb, emotionless, withdrawing into themselves trying to shut out the painful memories and feelings.

In the past but not now / Experiencing currently

❑ ❑ Intentionally avoiding anyone, any place, or anything that reminds you of the traumatic event

❑ ❑ Physical/emotional reaction to things that remind you of the traumatic event

❑ ❑ Self-isolating, dread of social interaction

❑ ❑ Anxiety in crowds, traffic

❑ ❑ Very reluctant to talk about your traumatic event

❑ ❑ Substance abuse to "numb" yourself (drugs, alcohol, food)

3. **Cognitions and Mood Alterations:** They may be unable to recall key features of the traumatic event, have a very negative self-image and/or world view, strong negative emotions, and disinterest in things that interested them deeply before. They are unable to show appropriate affection and emotion which causes friends and family to feel rejected by them.

In the past but not now / Experiencing currently

❑ ❑ Reduced cognitive ability (slow thinking, confusion, poor problem-solving, poor memory)

❑ ❑ Inability to recall key features of the traumatic event(s)

❑ ❑ Persistent, negative trauma-related emotions (fear, horror, anger, guilt, shame)

❑ ❑ Persistent, negative, distorted self-image ("I am bad.")

❑ ❑ Persistent, negative, distorted view of the world ("The world is always dangerous.")

❑ ❑ Persistent, distorted blame of self or others for causing the traumatic event(s)

❑ ❑ Lack of interest or motivation regarding employment, recreation, former hobbies, sex, exercise

❑ ❑ Relationships that were once close and even intimate are now strained, cold, distant, requiring too much energy to maintain, feeling detached or estranged

❑ ❑ Neglect/abandon personal care, hygiene, nutrition

❑ ❑ Emotional numbness, flat, can't get happy or sad, "dead" inside

❑ ❑ Inability to trust others

4. Arousal and Reactivity Alterations: Fearing further trauma, PTSD sufferers are always on the alert, on guard, jumpy, unable to sleep, angry, irritable. Many also have concentration and memory problems.

In the past but not now *Experiencing currently*

❑ ❑ Anger, irritability, "short fuse," fits of rage

❑ ❑ Hypervigilance (always on guard), always need to be armed with knife or gun; could also include "emotional" hypervigilance

❑ ❑ Easily startled, react to loud noises, jumpy

❑ ❑ Substance abuse to "un-numb" yourself (drugs, alcohol, food)

❑ ❑ Trouble falling asleep or staying asleep, insomnia, night sweats

❑ ❑ Accelerated heart rate, rapid breathing, heart palpitations for no good reason

❑ ❑ Physical fatigue

❑ ❑ Question/abandon faith, feeling of being betrayed or abandoned by God, mad at God

❑ ❑ Becoming violent, provoking fights

❑ ❑ Homicidal thoughts

❑ ❑ Suicidal thoughts, attempts

❑ ❑ Anniversary reaction (become anxious nearing the monthly or yearly anniversary of the traumatic event)

❑ ❑ Adrenaline junkie (taking risks, getting hyped-up)

❑ ❑ Self-mutilation, cutting, excessive tattooing

What do you miss most about how your life was before you experienced your trauma?

_____

_____

Traumatic Brain Injury (TBI)

Medical professionals treating those who have been wounded in the recent conflicts in the Mideast tell us that many troops diagnosed with PTSD actually have *Traumatic Brain Injury*. These two conditions exhibit many of the same symptoms, hence the confusion.

Traumatic Brain Injury (TBI) is usually the result of a sudden, violent blow to the head, or being in close proximity to an explosion. The skull can often withstand a forceful, external impact without fracturing – but a powerful blow or the percussive force of an explosion can launch the brain on an internal collision with the skull. The result: an injured brain inside an intact skull.

A brain injury may also occur when a projectile, such as a bullet, rock or fragment of a fractured skull, penetrates the brain. The severity of brain injuries can vary greatly, depending on the part of the brain affected and the extent of the damage. A mild brain injury may cause only temporary confusion and headache, but a serious one can be fatal. Read over the list of TBI symptoms below, and you will see how troops and first responders could be misdiagnosed with PTSD. The symptoms in **bold print** are the same ones you'll find on lists of PTSD symptoms.[20]

Read over the list of TBI symptoms below, and you will see how troops and first responders could be misdiagnosed with PTSD. The symptoms in bold print are the same ones you'll find on lists of PTSD symptoms.

TBI Signs & Symptoms[21]

1. headaches
2. dizziness or vertigo
3. **memory problems**
4. balance problems
5. ringing in ears
6. **sleep problems**
7. **poor word recall**
8. difficulty reading
9. **difficulty concentrating**
10. visual disturbances
11. **irritability or anger outbursts**
12. **impulsivity**
13. lack of forethought
14. obsessive/compulsive behavior
15. inflexible in thought

16. **anxiety**
17. sensitivity to light, touch, sound
18. gets lost or becomes misdirected
19. **depression**
20. **negative attitude**
21. **antisocial or isolated**
22. slowed or impaired motor skills
23. **poor judgment**
24. speech problems
25. balance problems
26. seizures
27. loss of sense of taste or smell
28. **change in sexual drive or ability**
29. **avoidance behavior**
30. **restricted range of affect (e.g., unable to have loving feelings)**

Though we don't have the space to go into the subject of TBI in this manual, it's important for you to be aware of this alternative diagnosis. Only a healthcare professional can properly determine if you have TBI or PTSD, but if you have experienced a head trauma, and your symptoms seem to match the above list more closely than the previous list of symptoms for PTSD, you may want to investigate it. The treatment for the two disorders is *different!*

The Way Out

According to memory expert Dr. Daniel Schacter, there are three basic types of memory:[22]

- **Procedural memory** – learned activities that we do automatically, like walking, bike riding, tying your shoe or spelling the word "cat."

- **Semantic memory** – involves remembering concepts, words, facts, data and other bits of knowledge, trivia, etc., like quoting the Lord's Prayer or the Pledge of Allegiance.

- **Episodic memory** – memory of an event that occurred in our lives, usually engaging the senses, including images, feelings, behaviors and meaning, like, "Remember the time we went body-surfing in Hawaii?"

Traumatic soul wounds are episodic memories – very negative ones, in dire need of processing and integration into our lives, values, beliefs and sense of well-being. One very effective way to release the unprocessed emotions of the past, heal traumatic memories and counteract some of the physiological consequences of your trauma is to experience a *more powerful* episode, which involves Jesus Christ entering your episodic memories of your trauma experience. When this happens, images, senses, feelings, actions and meanings of the past are confronted, re-experienced, processed, released and overpowered by this new episode with Jesus.

Later in this manual (page 61), we'll be helping you set up and experience those "episodic encounters with Christ." A lot of the groundwork and preparation will involve faith, discipline, work, and some pain. It will involve time, commitment, and patience – with God, with yourself and with the process.

But you *will* experience healing. The trauma you experienced has changed you. You're not worse, just different. And as you cooperate with Christ as He works in you, you will absolutely end up better than ever! There is *much* to be hopeful about!

> For over three decades, I have studied victims of overwhelming stress – concentration camp survivors, POWs liberated from years of captivity, terrorized hostages. Repeatedly, I have been inspired by the countless cases that run counter to "expert" predictions. Instead of a pattern of deficit and defeat, there is one of coping and conquest. Indeed, rather than being devastated by their suffering, many survivors have actually used the experience to enrich their lives … Human beings have a magnificent ability to rebuild shattered lives, careers, and families, even as they wrestle with the bitterest of memories.
>
> —Dr. Julius Segal[23]

 If there's one thing you would like to include in your personal definition of how life will be when you are "healed," what would it be?

_____

_____

PTSD expert Dr. Aphrodite Matsakis divides the process of healing from severe trauma into three stages: Cognitive, Emotional and Empowerment.[24] Our intention is to cover these three stages in a non-linear fashion as best we can in this small manual:

Cognitive Stage – Remembering the trauma and constructing it mentally

- Gaining a broad understanding of how things work in the Kingdom of God
- Identifying the facts about your trauma
- Deepening your faith and relationship with God
- Helping you reconstruct your identity based on God's truth
- Helping you construct an environment that will give God maximum access to your wounded soul

Emotional Stage – Feeling the feelings associated with the trauma

- Facing the episodic memories of your trauma and reintegrating it into your present reality with Christ's help
- Dealing with issues of forgiveness (needing to receive or needing to give)
- Identifying and eliminating bitterness
- Recognizing and dealing with repressed feelings caused by the trauma
- Understanding and entering into the grieving process

Empowerment Stage – Finding meaning in the trauma, redeeming it, mastering it and becoming a victor rather than a victim

- Healthy re-connection with your family, community
- Reaching out to others who are hurting
- Vital relationship with an "encourager" friend(s)
- Victory over triggers and fears
- Setting healthy, achievable goals

We're not saying this process is going to be a smooth, uninterrupted flight path to the moon. There will be setbacks, slow times and detours. But stick with it! It will be worth it in the end. As Ralph Waldo Emerson once said:

Our greatest glory is not in never failing, but in rising up every time we fail.

And as God said in Proverbs 24:16 (NLT):

The godly may trip seven times, but they will get up again.
But one disaster is enough to overthrow the wicked.

Trauma is a thief. The self-defense mechanisms that God built into you were vital at the time your body and mind were attacked, but now – not so much. As a first responder, you sacrificed. But more has been taken from you than you bargained for. God wants to reimburse you for what has been taken, if you'll let Him:

Then I will make up to you for the years that the swarming locust has eaten... You will have plenty to eat and be satisfied, and praise the name of the Lord your God, who has dealt wondrously with you; then My people will never be put to shame

—Joel 2:25,26

⊕　⊕　⊕　⊕　⊕

Prayer Seed

Heavenly Father, You know that my intentions were honorable when I became a first responder. I trained hard. I worked hard. I was willing to sacrifice for the sake of others. I did the best I could trying to serve and protect my community. But I have been seriously wounded. I didn't know how seriously at the time. Now I do. I need Your care and healing. This disorder is bigger than I am – but I know that You are bigger than it. Please come to my aid, show me the way out of this and bring health and restoration back into my life – body, mind and spirit. Amen.

1. Quote from James Meuer from *Damaged: A First Responder's Experiences Handling Posttraumatic Stress Disorder* (Bloomington, IL: WestBow Press, 2013). p. 36.

2. Article by American Psychological Association: Expert commentary: "Stress, Part Two – Getting a Grip," Nov. 10, 1997. Retrieved from www.discoveryhealth.com/DH.

3. Various sources: "Spouse Battlemind Training," brochure produced by Walter Reed Army Institute of Research, January 2007; "Courage To Care: Becoming A Couple Again" handout by the Uniformed Services University of the Health Sciences (www.usuhs.mil), Summer, 2004; "Roadmap To Reintegration" by U.S. Army Europe found at www.per.hqusareur.army.mil.reintegration, June, 2008.

4. Article by A. Shirom: "What is organizational stress?: a facet analytic conceptualization." Journal of Occupational Behaviour, 1982. vol. 3, pp. 21-37.

5. Article by Jacoba De Boer: "Work-related critical incidents in hospital-based health care providers and the risk of Posttraumatic stress symptoms, anxiety, and depression: A meta-analysis." Social Science & Medicine, 2011. (pp. 316-326).

6. Jeff. Mitchell, Ph.D. & Grady. Bray, Ph.D, "Emergency Services Stress: Guidelines for Preserving the Health and Careers of Emergency Services Personnel" (Englewood Cliffs, NJ: Prentice Hall, 1990).

7. Applied research project paper by Suzanne Todd (CA Dept. of Forestry and Fire Protection/Placer County Fire Dept): "Managing Cumulative Stress In Fire Service Personnel: Strategic Management of Change." (National Fire Academy Executive Fire Officer Program, February, 2001).

8. Non-medical, general term coined by the authors, intended to encompass the three familiar and medically well-defined conditions that are listed.

9. Dr. Charles Figley, *Compassion Fatigue – Coping With Secondary Traumatic Stress Disorder in Those Who Treat the Traumatized* (NY: Brunner-Routledge, 1995). p. 11.

10. C. Maslach & M. P. Leiter: "Stress and burnout: the critical research," in C. L. Cooper (Ed.), *Handbook of Stress Medicine and Health* (Lancaster:CRC Press, 2005). pp. 155-172.

11. Dr. Charles Figley (Ed.), pp. xv, 2,3,14,15.

12. American Psychiatric Association: *Diagnostic and Statistical Manual of Mental Disorders, Fifth Edition* (DSM-5). (Washington, D.C.: American Psychiatric Publishing, 2013). pp. 286-289.

13. Ibid., pp. 280-286.

14. Note: this does not include exposure through electronic media, television, movies, or pictures, unless this exposure is work-related. (DSM-V Criterion A: Stressor)

15. American Psychiatric Association: DSM-5, pp. 271-280.

16. Article by Matthew Tull, Ph.D.: "Rates of PTSD in Firefighters" (About.com; January 29, 2012): "Studies have found that anywhere between approximately 7% and 37% of firefighters meet criteria for a current diagnosis of PTSD." Also, article by Mark Bond (prof. of Criminal Justice at American Military University): "How Do We Change Police Culture To Save the Lives of Fellow Officers?" (inpublicsafety.com; July 7, 2014): "Many police researchers estimate there are 125,000 active law enforcement officers on full duty who are suffering with Post Traumatic Stress Disorder at any given time." Also, applied research project paper by Lieutenant Lori Beth Sanford (Allen Park Police Department): "Critical Incident Stress and the Police Officer: A Pro-Active Approach" (School of Police Staff and Command Program, Sept 19, 2003): A Michigan study of police officers revealed that "Thirty-one percent (31%) reported they had experienced PTSD." Also, article by Sheila Myers: "PTSD and Suicide Among Law Enforcement Officers" (sheilamyers.hubpages.com: January, 2014): "Going with what has been reported, the best estimate is that 30% of all police officers suffer from PTSD at some point in their career."

17. Donald Meichenbaum, *A Clinical Handbook/Practiced: Therapist Manual for Assessing and Treating Adults with Posttraumatic Stress Disorder* (Institute Press, 1994), p. 23.

18. Observations from Dr. H. Norman Wright, *Crisis & Trauma Counseling* (Ventura, CA: Regal Books, 2003). p.198-205, and Patience H.G. Mason, www.patiencepress.com Post Traumatic Gazette, Issue 1, May/June 1995.

19. Portions of the descriptions of symptom categories are from The Australian Centre for Posttraumatic Mental Health: Australian Guidelines for the Treatment of ASD and PTSD (www.acpmh.unimelb.edu.au).

20. Definition from Mayo Clinic: www.mayoclinic.com/health/traumatic-brain-injury/DS00.

21. TBI symptoms from Brain Injury Association (www.biausa.org), Centers for Disease Control and Prevention (www.cdc.gov/ncipc/tbi), and Dr. Daniel Amen, M.D. (www.amenclinics.com).

22. Dr. Daniel Schacter, *Searching For Memory* (New York: Basic Books, 1996). p. 18.

23. Dr. Julius Segal, *Winning Life's Toughest Battles*, p. xii; quoted in Robert Hicks *Failure To Scream*, p. 79.

24. Dr. Aphrodite Matsakis, *I Can't Get Over It* (Oakland, CA: New Harbinger Publications, 1996). p. 143.

Step 3A Where's the Hospital?
...Constructing Your Healing Environment – Part A
[This Step is covered in two parts.]

"For I, the Lord, am your Healer."

—**Exodus 15:26**

> "Some people say that God is a crutch. God is not a crutch. He's a whole dadgum hospital!"
>
> —Dr. J. Vernon McGee

Robert Hicks is an Air Force Reserve specialist, counselor and expert on PTSD. In his book *Failure To Scream*, Hicks shares an experience he had as a young man assisting a famous neurosurgeon.

> At the end of the operation he asked if he could teach me anything about the brain. I asked, "What causes the brain to develop tumors?" He answered, "I don't know." Then I asked, "How does healing take place after we put the piece of skull back in place?" He laughed. "Listen," he said, "all I do here is take out the pieces of the brain that have died, and then God does the healing. *I just cooperate with the laws God has built into the human system.*" What a lesson from a humble yet brilliant man! I believe it is the same for psychological healing... We must cooperate with the laws that God has already ordained for proper human functioning. We are not the healers, but we can cooperate with the healing process.[1]

God has indeed ordained certain laws that will optimize your healing process. Two things are needed: you need to *know* the laws, and you need to *obey* the laws. Now, these laws are not things like, "Go to church three times a week, carry a Bible with you at all times, shower in holy water and live a perfect life." The laws you'll be reading about here have to do with your relationship with God, and how you can cooperate with His healing process by giving Him optimal access to your wounded soul.

When it comes to seeking God's help, many people envision God like a probie looks at a super-strict Recruit Training Officer during training academy. Does God have a clipboard and a check list, barking out orders and waiting to see if you'll respond correctly and measure up before you are considered worthy to advance to "Healed, First Class?" In reality, it's more like you're an injured sapling and God is the weather surrounding you: raining down life-giving water and energizing sunlight; bathing you with carbon dioxide for respiration; cool evenings and warm days for an invigorating rhythm; winds to strengthen your trunk. If the sapling wants to heal, it just needs to make sure it remains in the "weather." If it decides it doesn't like getting rained on or sun baked, pulls up its roots and takes up residence in a basement, it will never heal.

In the same way, God has set up a healing environment for you. The more you stay in contact with the elements of His "weather," the more healing you will experience.

The Essence of Healing

What are we looking for? When the subject of "healing" comes up, we usually think about doctors. A doctor will *do* something for you that will fix you up: set a bone, give you some antibiotic, remove your appendix. But they're not really *healing* you. They're just adjusting various factors in your environment so that the normal healing processes that God has built into every person can proceed unhindered.

That's what we're attempting to do in this Step. Building on the foundation of Jesus Christ being your Lord and Savior (if you're still confused about this, see Appendix A which will describe how to begin a personal relationship with Christ), we want to share **five vital elements** that are crucial to your healing environment:

1. The Holy Spirit – your divine power source

2. The Word of God – your divine food and weapon

3. Prayer – vital communication with your divine command structure

4. The Christian Community – your divine station house

5. Your Mindset – spiritual themes for divine healing

As you include these five elements in your life, they will facilitate the deepening of your connection to the Healer, so that He can accomplish His healing work in you.

Element #1: The Holy Spirit – Your Divine Power Source

Who is the Holy Spirit?

The Bible presents God as a "Trinity" – three-in-one. That is, God is frequently affirmed to be the one-and-only God (Deuteronomy 6:4; Isaiah 43:10; John 17:3; 1 Corinthians 8:4), and yet there are three distinct "persons" who are referred to as God:

- God the Father – John 6:27
- God the Son – John 20:26-28
- God the Holy Spirit – 1 Corinthians 3:16

One God presented in three different manifestations, each one with its separate and distinct function. All three have existed as a unit since before time began – never beginning, never ending. But each has had a different job.

In a way, God's different manifestations are like the work done by a fire engine and its crew, named and described based on the different ways they help people. When asked who they are, one observer might say, "They're **firefighters**, putting out fires that break out in the community." Another might say, "They're **EMTs**, helping people who are sick or injured." Another might say, "They're **fire protection experts**, educating people about how to avoid dangerous situations." A single unit with different manifestations.

In a nutshell, the Holy Spirit's job is to live inside of us, empower us, comfort us, heal us, enable us to live a righteous and satisfying life, and to help us communicate with God. The Old Testament Hebrew word for Spirit is *ruach*, which means "air in motion," "breath" and "life." The New Testament word for Spirit is *pneuma*, and means virtually the same thing. The Holy Spirit is the wind, breath and life of God entering our lives the moment we ask Him to.

 Study the following verses from the Bible and write down what you think it's saying about what the Holy Spirit does:

Jesus speaking: "When He, the Spirit of truth, comes, He will guide you into all truth." – **John 16:13**

_____

_____

_____

Jesus speaking: "I will talk to the Father, and He'll provide you another Friend so that you will always have someone with you. This Friend is the Spirit of Truth. The godless world can't take Him in because it doesn't have eyes to see Him, doesn't know what to look for. But you know Him already because He has been staying with you, and will even be in you!" – **John 14:16,17** (MSG)

_____

_____

_____

Jesus speaking: "You will receive power when the Holy Spirit comes on you; and you will be My witnesses in Jerusalem, and in all Judea and Samaria, and to the ends of the earth." – **Acts 1:8** (NIV)

_____

_____

Paul writing: "The Holy Spirit helps us in our weakness. For example, we don't know what God wants us to pray for. But the Holy Spirit prays for us with groanings that cannot be expressed in words." – **Romans 8:26** (NLT)

_____

_____

The Indwelling of the Holy Spirit

When you invited Jesus Christ into your life, He entered you in the form of His Holy Spirit. Once there, He's there permanently. This is called the "indwelling" of the Spirit. But what we shared with you in Step 1 about God not violating your free will still holds true. He's not going to _force_ you to go His way on any subject. You can decide to disregard His fellowship, His counsel and His offers of help. The Bible says we can "quench" the Holy Spirit by our disinterest (1 Thessalonians 5:19). We can also "grieve" Him through our disobedience (Ephesians 4:30). We can make it so it's _just as if_ He wasn't in our life. But He's always there – waiting for you to respond positively to Him.

The Filling of the Holy Spirit

In Ephesians 5:18, God gives us two commands, one negative, one positive. What are they?

1. _____

2. _____

To "be filled" with the Holy Spirit means to be controlled, empowered and guided by Him. The point of the verse is that, just as alcohol can control us in destructive ways, the Holy Spirit can control us in positive, constructive ways – if we allow Him to.

> _Don't be drunk with wine, because that will ruin your life. Instead, be filled with the Holy Spirit._
> —**Ephesians 5:18** (NLT)

⊕   ⊕   ⊕   ⊕   ⊕

Three Kinds of People...[2]

The Natural Man – "Captain of my own soul!"

S = Self, sitting on the throne or control center of his or her life.

✝ = Christ, outside the life.

Circles = Activities, interests, priorities and plans in discord with God's.

This represents the **non-Christian** who doesn't have a relationship with God. As he tries to direct his own life in his finite and usually self-interested way, it often results in frustration, despair and discord with God's perfect plans for him.

The Spiritual Man – "Walking in faith and obedience."

S = Self dethroned, yielding to Christ's Lordship in his or her life.

✝ = Christ on the throne, guiding and empowering the Christian.

Circles = Activities, interests, priorities and plans in harmony with God's.

This represents a **Spirit-filled Christian** walking closely with God. Since Christ is all-powerful and all-knowing, He can ensure the Christian's life will harmonize with God's plans for him, resulting in love, joy, peace patience, kindness, goodness, faithfulness, gentleness, and self-control (Galatians 5:22,23) – among other things! No guarantee of a problem-free life, only one that is in harmony with God's plans for him or her.

The Carnal Man – "I'll take it from here, thanks."

S = Self back on the throne, once again trying to direct his or her life independent of God.

✝ = Christ still in the life, but dethroned and not allowed to be Lord.

Circles = Activities, interests, priorities and plans in discord with God's.

This represents a **Carnal** or **Worldly Christian** who isn't walking with God. As he ignores or disobeys God's directions, his life falls into disarray. Comparing frustration levels, dead-ends and despair, it's difficult to tell the difference between the Carnal Christian's life and the non-Christian's life.

 Study the three diagrams and descriptions above. Which one would you say currently represents your life?

_____

Which one would you like to have represent your life?

_____

Five Steps To Filling…

1. Desire

Blessed are those who hunger and thirst for righteousness, for they shall be filled.

—**Matthew 5:6** (NKJV)

 What does Jesus say is required in order to be "filled"? What would this look or feel like in your life?

_____

_____

Search your heart. Do you "hunger and thirst for righteousness"? Do you actually *want* Jesus Christ as your Lord, and the Holy Spirit as your Guide? Are you willing to obey what God tells you to do? Don't expect His power to flow unhindered if you are simply "going through the motions." God looks at the heart, and He knows your heart completely.

2. Confess

If we confess our sins, He is faithful and righteous to forgive us our sins and to cleanse us from all unrighteousness.

—**1 John 1:9**

The reason the Holy Spirit may be "quenched" in your life is because of sin – saying "No" to God and "Yes" to your unrighteous desires. Ask God to reveal the sins that have been separating you from His plan and power. As He brings them to mind, agree with Him that those choices were wrong (that's the essence of confession). Ask Him to forgive you for each one.

3. Present

And do not present your members [body parts] as instruments of unrighteousness to sin, but present yourselves to God as being alive from the dead, and your members as instruments of righteousness to God… For just as you presented your members as slaves of uncleanness, and of lawlessness leading to more lawlessness, so now present your members as slaves of righteousness for holiness.

—**Romans 6:13,19** (NKJV)

 Do you think "presenting" ourselves as spoken of in the above verses involves a passive attitude or something different? What attitude is described?

_____

Most people associate slavery with demeaning oppression – and in every human case it is. In the spiritual realm, Satan desires to enslave you to his will, which will lead to destruction. As first responders, you have seen the devastating consequences of his enslavement in those you deal with and treat all the time. But God wants you to be "enslaved" in a different way: to *His* will for your *benefit*, leading to freedom from the things that tear you down, and a strong connection to the things that will build you up and bring you satisfaction, fulfillment and joy.

A crucial insight is found in **Romans 6:16-18** (MSG):

*You know well enough from your own experience that there are some **acts of so-called freedom** that destroy freedom. Offer yourselves to sin, for instance, and it's your last free act. But offer yourselves to the ways of God and the freedom never quits. All your lives you've let sin tell you what to do. But thank God you've started listening to a new master, one whose commands set you free to live openly in His freedom!"*

List some "acts of so-called freedom that destroy freedom?" How do they enslave us?

_____

_____

4. Ask

So I say to you, ask, and it will be given to you; seek, and you will find; knock, and it will be opened to you. For everyone who asks, receives; and he who seeks, finds; and to him who knocks, it will be opened. Now suppose one of your fathers is asked by his son for a fish; he will not give him a snake instead of a fish, will he? Or if he is asked for an egg, he will not give him a scorpion, will he? If you then, being evil, know how to give good gifts to your children, how much more will your heavenly Father give the Holy Spirit to those who ask Him?

—Luke 11:9-13

What astounding, superhuman exploits does this passage say you need to perform in order to "persuade" God to give you what you need? (Careful… trick question!)

_____

Remember what was said earlier about our free will? God won't compromise your privilege of choosing. Since you made a willful choice to depart from His will, you need to make a willful choice to get "reconnected."

5. Thank Him in Faith

This is the confidence which we have before Him, that, if we ask anything according to His will, He hears us. And if we know that He hears us in whatever we ask, we know that we have the requests which we have asked from Him.

—1 John 5:14,15

We can know that being filled with the Holy Spirit lines up with God's will because He commanded it in Ephesians 6:18 (see page 35). So, according to the above passage, what can we be sure will happen if we ask God to fill us with His Holy Spirit?

_____

If you ask for something from God and have confidence you have received it, the normal thing to do next would be to say thank you! As Bible teacher Tommy Adkins once said, "Saying thanks is always a sign that you have 'faithed' God."

Asking To Be Filled

When you pray to God, He isn't as concerned with your exact words as He is with the attitude of your heart. But sometimes it helps to express what is in your heart if someone else supplies the words for you. Here is a suggested prayer:

Dear Father, I need You. I hunger and thirst for Your righteousness, rather than for the garbage of the world. I want You to be my King and my Guide. But I confess that I have taken the throne of my life from Your control and have sinned against You. I've made many wrong choices. Please forgive me for this. I yield myself to You in obedience, desiring to serve You rather than myself or my enemy, the devil. Please fill me with Your Holy Spirit. I step down from the throne of my life and give it back to You. Based on Your promise, I have faith that You have heard my prayer and have filled me with Your Holy Spirit. Thank you! Amen.

Does this prayer express the desire of your heart? If so, are you ready to pray it (or something similar) right now?

If you prayed the above prayer or something similar today, write the date in here:

So, Am I Done With This Now?

Well… no. It's an unfortunate but natural part of the human condition for us to periodically re-take the throne of our lives by asserting our will and ignoring God's will. As we grow spiritually, our objective is for this to happen less and less. In the meantime, we must be prepared to recognize when we have slipped into the "carnal" category, and take measures to once again be Spirit-filled. Remember: this doesn't mean we are no longer saved or that the Holy Spirit has left us, it simply means we've temporarily pushed Jesus Christ off the throne of our life and are trying to run things ourselves.

"Spiritual Breathing"

Here is an illustration that will help you understand what to do when you need to be "refilled." Think of it in terms of breathing. When you exhale, you rid your body of harmful carbon dioxide. When you inhale, you draw life-giving oxygen back into your body. Out with the bad, in with the good. A similar thing happens in the realm of the Spirit.

Exhale

When you become aware of sin in your life, it's time to take a spiritual breath. First, you must exhale by **confessing** your sin. The Greek word for "confession" is *homologeo,* which means "to say the same thing as." God's Spirit tells you your action was wrong, and you agree with Him – that's confession. And if you truly agree with Him about it, you will not only say so, you'll also look for ways to stop doing the thing that was grieving Him. That's what **"repentance"** is: "to stop, turn around and go back the other way."

Inhale

Now breathe in the life of the Holy Spirit by asking Jesus to once again take the throne of your life. By faith, ask Him to control, empower and guide you. When you make this request, you can *know* that He will immediately grant it, based on His command in Ephesians 5:18 and His promise in 1 John 5:14-15. Hopefully, this exercise will also remind you that the Holy Spirit is God's breath and life, as mentioned earlier.

How Often Do I Do This?

As often as you need to. It may be once a week, once a day, once an hour or even once every few minutes! The important thing is to not lose heart and give up in defeat. As a drowning man will struggle frantically to clear his lungs of water and breathe in oxygen, so we need to recognize the critical need to keep Jesus Christ on the throne of our lives – confessing our sins and seeking His filling.

Spiritual breathing should become as natural and automatic as our physical breathing is. Each time you sense the conviction of the Holy Spirit, stop right then and take a spiritual breath. Some Christians have adopted the habit of starting out each day – even before getting out of bed – asking God if there is anything in them that is displeasing to Him, confessing it if there is, and then asking Him to fill them with His Holy Spirit.

Element #2: The Word of God – Your Divine Food and Weapon

When you received Jesus Christ into your life, you became a three-dimensional being, composed of a body, a soul and a spirit. We know that our physical bodies need to be fed. Most people are regularly reminded of it by hunger pangs. But our souls and our spirits also need nourishment. Our soul – our will, intellect, emotions, etc. – is nourished by things like truth, beauty, knowledge and friendships. Our spirit – the part of us that relates to God – is fed by the words of God: the Bible. As Jesus said in Matthew 4:4 (NIV), *"Man does not live on bread alone, but on every word that comes from the mouth of God."* And as Peter wrote in 1 Peter 2:2 (NKJV), *"As newborn babes, desire the pure milk of the word, that you may grow thereby."*

A Christian who doesn't get a regular diet of God's Word will end up with an emaciated, weak and sickly spirit. Perhaps you've seen photos of people being liberated from Nazi concentration camps at the end of World War II. If we could take photos of the *spirits* of some Christians today, they would probably look very similar to the physical bodies of those poor men and women who had been deprived of proper nourishment for so long. Don't let this happen to you! Be sure that you're getting a steady diet of God's meat and potatoes!

Based on the two preceding paragraphs, how would you complete this sentence? "The Bible is…"

?

_____

_____

Benefits of Reading the Bible

The following passages describe the benefits of studying and applying God's Word to your life. Write at least one benefit you observe in each passage.

God speaking to Joshua: *"Study this Book of Instruction continually. Meditate on it day and night so you will be sure to obey everything written in it. Only then will you prosper and succeed in all you do."*

—Joshua 1:8 (NLT)

_____

King David writing: *"The law of his God is in his heart; his feet do not slip."*

—Psalm 37:31 (NIV)

_____

King David writing: *"How can a young man keep his way pure? By living according to Your word… I have hidden Your word in my heart that I might not sin against You."*

—Psalm 119:9,11 (NIV)

_____

Jesus speaking: *"If you remain in Me and My words remain in you, ask whatever you wish, and it will be given you."*

—John 15:7 (NIV)

_____

Jesus speaking: *"If you hold to My teaching, you are really My disciples. Then you will know the truth, and the truth will set you free."*

— John 8:31,32 (NIV)

_____

_____

Your Personal Plan

The following illustration shows that there are five ways a person can get a firm "grasp" on the Word of God. Called the "Word of God Hand Illustration"[3] and created by The Navigators, it demonstrates the importance of getting a balanced input of the different methods of taking the Bible into your life. If you try to grasp it with only one or two fingers, you won't hold it very well. But if you use all five fingers, your grasp of it will be strong.

1. Hearing – Listening to a sermon at church, on the radio, or on a podcast or CD; listening to audio recordings of the Bible being read; discussing the Bible with your friends; etc.

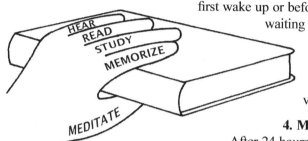

2. Reading – Sitting down alone and reading a chapter or two of the Bible, perhaps when you first wake up or before you go to bed; reading when you're on a bus or train; in a waiting room; during lunch; between emergency calls; etc.

3. Studying – More intense and focused activity than just reading; consulting commentaries; verse cross-referencing; outlining; answering questions; going slow and deep. Observation, Interpretation, Integration, Application.

4. Memorizing – Committing key verses of the Bible to memory. After 24 hours, you will remember: 5% of what you hear, 15% of what you read, 35% of what you study, but 100% of what you memorize. Running God's Word through your mind can affect your actions and *reactions*.

5. Meditating – Deliberately reflecting on God's Word, praying about it and considering how to apply it to your life. Just as your thumb can touch each of your four fingers, meditate on what you hear, read, study and memorize.

Personal Application

I will commit to a period of personal Bible intake (hear/read/study/memorize/meditate) lasting no less than _____ minutes, _____ day(s) a week, for the next _____ weeks, to start on _____ (date). I will ask _____ to check up on me, give me encouragement, and help me find answers to questions I come up with.

✛   ✛   ✛   ✛   ✛

Bible Study Plan

Here's a good format to follow as you study the Bible. Read through a chapter (the book of John is a good place to start, if you need a suggestion) and write down your thoughts and observations according to the **SPACE-Q** format:

S: Sins to confess

P: Promises to claim

A: Actions to avoid

C: Commands to obey

E: Examples to follow

Q: Questions I need answered

✛   ✛   ✛   ✛   ✛

Taking the Sword

God's Word has another function: it's a **weapon**. In Ephesians 6:14-17, the Bible talks about the spiritual armor that is available to every believer: belt of truth, breastplate of righteousness, sandals of the preparation of the gospel, shield of faith, helmet of salvation… these are all defensive implements of war. But the final item mentioned is *"the sword of the Spirit, which is the Word of God."* This is *both* a defensive *and* an offensive weapon.

You can read a great account of how Jesus used God's Word in a battle with Satan in Matthew 4:1-11. Twice Satan launched an attacking temptation at Jesus. Twice He countered with a verse of Scripture – defensive moves. With the third attack, Jesus not only repelled the devil's assault, but sent him into hasty retreat with a counterattack using the sword of the Word. Hebrews 4:12 (NKJV) tells us that "The Word of God is living and powerful, and sharper than any two-edged sword…"

Learn how to use it.

Your Weapon

A police officer is intimately acquainted with every square millimeter of his weapon. A firefighter's "weapon" is his hose, tools and his assigned apparatus – and he knows them inside and out. An EMT has drilled for hundreds of hours to be completely familiar with the human body and various emergency medical procedures. Now it's time to get cracking on a training program to become as familiar with your new weapon – God's Word – as you are with your service-related ones. It will keep you alive.

In *Step 8: How Do I Fight?* you'll be learning much more about spiritual warfare and how to defend yourself against the forces of darkness using God's Word.

Prayer Seed

Father, I know that You love me – and I am thankful that You do. But I am wounded and I need Your healing. You are the Great Healer and so I'm coming to You. Help me to follow the laws of healing that You have established. I desire with all my heart to cooperate with You in this. Thank you for the gift of your Holy Spirit. May He control and empower me every day. May I never quench or grieve Him. Help me to give Him full access to every area of my life. Convict me whenever I sneak back onto the throne of my life. I know I can count on your forgiveness and correction when that happens. May I frequently and regularly come to your Word for nourishment, guidance and encouragement. Let me see my growth and strengthening as a result of its intake. Please motivate me to become intimately familiar with this new weapon of spiritual warfare. May I use it with skill and discernment. And may You be glorified in my life. Amen.

1. Robert Hicks, *Failure To Scream* (Nashville: Thomas Nelson Publishers, 1993). p. 164.
2. William R. Bright, *Have You Made The Wonderful Discovery of the Spirit-Filled Life?* (Orlando, FL: Campus Crusade for Christ, 1966, 1995). Illustration used by permission.
3. Word Hand Illustration, Copyright 1976, The Navigators. Used by permission of NavPress, Colorado Springs, CO. All rights reserved.

Step **3B** **Where's the Hospital?**
...Constructing Your Healing Environment – Part B
[This Step is the second of two parts.]

There are three more crucial elements to your healing environment that still need to be considered ...

Element #3: Prayer – Vital Communication With Your Divine Command Structure

Trapped!

Engine Company 12 is a moderate-sized city firehouse with a crew of four. I'm the Captain. We had just micro-waved our perfectly-cooked station dinner for the second time that night when the tap out came for a structure fire. A third microwaving was in the cards for us later.

As we rolled up first in, we observed fire blowing out a corner window of the three-story house. We also noticed smaller windows at ground level indicating a basement. No smoke was emitting from those windows, and they appeared clear. Good news – we hoped.

Incident Command arrived and orders were issued to proceed with a direct attack of the fire. Engine 12 was to lead the attack as first in. We cracked the front door and air was immediately sucked in low while smoke billowed out high. This was not going to be a quick knock down.

I yanked the door shut, and we waited for the truck company to arrive and vent the structure. Shortly thereafter, the IC orders us to advance, and we're inside. Sounding proceeds using the head of an axe as we crawl along on our knees. Floor's solid. We're making good progress.

Within a few minutes, I realize it's excessively hot. I look down at my knees and notice that the carpet is melting. Everything just changed from controlled to uncontrolled. As I'm forming the words to abort and back out, we hear a sickening crack from below.

We are tossed into the basement along with a ton of flaming debris. My mind is racing. I look for my guys and pull them to me. Everything is dark. Very hot. I run through my options.

"I really ought to hit my emergency beacon – let them know we're in trouble. Maybe get on the radio and call in the Rapid Intervention Crew. Those dudes will rip this building *down* to get to us! Maybe we should..." Then I shake my head.

"Naaah. We'll be fine. Besides, I don't like the Incident Commander much. He's probably still sore about the disagreement we had about that call in the Cowboys/Broncos game. He might think I'm a big wuss – can't handle things by myself. Besides, this radio might not even work. Maybe it's melted. Maybe the RIC is on a dinner break. Waste of time to call."

I yell to my crew, "Looks like we're on our own here! Grab that hose and let's fight some fire!"[1]

Officer Needs Assistance

That was obviously a fictitious scenario. *Every* first responder on duty knows with 100% certainty he or she can rely on their command structure to respond instantly to a call for help or backup. And they wouldn't hesitate to ask for it, unlike the dufus in the above story. Why would *anybody* – especially someone who is in some big-time trouble – not take advantage of any and all avenues of help and support available?

The ironic thing is that Christians do it all the time. We have been given this incredible communication system – instant contact with our Creator and Savior by simply talking or thinking – and we don't use it nearly enough. In fact, you can ask just about any Christian if they think they should be spending more or less time in prayer, and they will *always* answer "More!" Prayer is the Christian's 9-1-1 call, yet we seldom use it.

⊕   ⊕   ⊕   ⊕   ⊕

 Why do you think so many people are reluctant to spend much time in prayer?

_____

_____

⊕   ⊕   ⊕   ⊕   ⊕

It could be that people don't have a clear idea of the purpose of prayer. Though God loves to answer the requests we make of Him in prayer, this isn't its only purpose. God is not a cosmic Santa Claus, existing only to grant us all of our desires and make us happy. We must never forget that Christianity is not supposed to be merely a religion or a philosophy of life. It is a *relationship* with our heavenly Father. And in any relationship, there must be communication. We don't always benefit directly from the communication itself, but the communication produces a deeper relationship, which opens the door to *all kinds* of benefits.

I talk to my wife on a very regular basis – because she's my best friend and I love her. We talk about *everything*. There's lots of give-and-take. Sometimes I talk and she listens, sometimes it's the other way around. Sometimes we don't even need words to communicate. Because of this, our relationship is very deep and satisfying for both of us.

But how would it be if the only time I ever spoke to her was to let her know that I wanted something? She *does* want to know what I want – because she loves me – but she wants to know a lot more than that! Our relationship would be pretty shallow if all I ever did was issue my demands to her.

 On a scale of one to ten, how much do you think God wants to hear from you?

| Not in the least | 1 | 2 | 3 | 4 | 5 | 6 | 7 | 8 | 9 | 10 | Very, very very much |

On a scale of one to ten, how much do you want to talk with God?

| Not in the least | 1 | 2 | 3 | 4 | 5 | 6 | 7 | 8 | 9 | 10 | Very, very very much |

⊕   ⊕   ⊕   ⊕   ⊕

What Does God Want You To Pray About?

God loves you with a love that is as eternal, intense and pure as anything we can imagine, and more. Proverbs 15:8 says, "The prayer of the upright is His delight." And guess what? Because of what Christ did on the cross for you, you are one of the "upright"! Imagine Jesus Christ, sitting by your bed when you wake up, saying, "Good morning! I love you! I can't wait to hear your delightful voice. Talk to Me, please!"

Here are a few verses in the Bible that will give you some insight about the things God invites us to talk with Him about. After each verse write what is being prayed *for* or *about*.

Give us this day our daily bread.

—Matthew 6:11

_____

_____

I love You, O LORD², my strength. The LORD is my rock and my fortress and my deliverer, My God, my rock, in whom I take refuge; My shield and the horn of my salvation, my stronghold.

—Psalm 18:1-3

_____

_____

In everything give thanks; for this is God's will for you in Christ Jesus.

—1 Thessalonians 5:18

_____

_____

My God, my God, why have you abandoned me? Why are you so far away when I groan for help?

—Psalm 22:1,2 (NLT)

_____

_____

If we confess our sins, He is faithful and righteous to forgive us our sins and to cleanse us from all unrighteousness.

—1 John 1:9

_____

_____

Lead us not into temptation, but deliver us from the evil one.

—Matthew 6:13

_____

_____

I Want Answers!!

God will answer *every* prayer that you pray in faith. Every one. But the thing to keep in mind is that, **if we have submitted ourselves to Him as our King and Guide**, He gets to decide *how* to answer our prayers. His answers will always be what's best for us and for His Kingdom. And since He's all-knowing, all-powerful and timeless, He ought to know! He'll answer our prayers in one of three ways:

1. Sometimes He might answer our prayer "**No**. It wouldn't be good for you." Like the good father saying no to the toddler who wants to play with the nice, shiny butcher knife.

>   For deeper study: Examples of God saying "No" (even to His Son!): 2 Samuel 12:15-18; Mathew 26:37-42; 2 Corinthians 12:7-10.

2. Sometimes He might answer our prayer "**Wait.** This would be a good thing for you, but not right now. Be patient. It's on the way." Like what I said to my fourteen-year old son when he wanted to borrow the car.

>   **For deeper study:** Examples of God saying "Wait": Genesis 15:2-5; Genesis 50:24,25; Exodus 5:22,23; 6:6-8. In each case, the fulfillment of the promise happened many years later.

3. Sometimes God might answer our prayer "**Yes!** This will be a *good* thing for you!" Like what my wife said to me when I asked her to marry me.

>   **For deeper study:** Examples of God saying "Yes": Psalm 32:5; 1 Samuel 1:11,19,20; 1 Chronicles 4:9,10; 2 Kings 6:15-18. In each case, God said "Yes" to their request.

Obviously, we would like to increase the percentage of "Yes" answers we get. Psalm 37:4 gives us some great insight on how to do this:

> Prayer is weakness plugged into strength. Prayer is saying, "I can't, but You can," and plugging into God's "I will."[3]
>
> —Dr. Jack Taylor

>   *Delight yourself in the LORD, and He will give you the desires of your heart.*

When the Lord is our delight – when our attitude toward Him is one of love, acceptance, submission and a quiet confidence that He always knows what's best for us, when we're willing to allow His will to be done rather than what we might prefer – this gives Him unhindered access to our souls and spirits so that our desires *will* line up with His before we even begin to pray. Then we'll be able to pray boldly the way Jesus prayed:

>   *Nevertheless, not as I will, but as You will.*

—Matthew 26:39b (NKJV)

Personal Application

Building muscle

OK. You've got the theory, but why make prayer a regular, disciplined part of your daily life? It would be foolish to assume that you would have the strength to subdue a suspect or carry out a victim from a fire if you never hit the gym. Simply *hoping* that the strength would be there at just the right time is not a risk you should take – for the sake of your partner, yourself or the public. So you regularly work those muscles (hopefully!) in order to ensure that they will respond effectively in all situations. Regularly talking with God about your concerns, hopes, dreams and questions is like working out your "prayer muscle" so that when the stress of your calling suddenly ramps up, you are primed to respond with God's help to any and all challenges.

My Plan:

I will commit to a period of personal prayer – either by myself or with others – lasting no less

than _____ minutes, _____ day(s) a week, for the next _____ weeks,

to start on _____ (date). I will ask _____ to check up on me,

give me encouragement, and help me find answers to questions I come up with.

Prayer Assignment

In Step 2, on page 30 you were asked this question: *If there's one thing you would like to include in your personal definition of how life will be when you are "healed," what would it be?* Assuming that you wrote something down (or at least, something came to your mind), begin today asking God if He would fulfill that desire for you. Ask Him *every day.*

As Jesus advised us in Matthew 7:7 (NLT):

> *Keep on asking, and you will receive what you ask for. Keep on seeking, and you will find. Keep on knocking, and the door will be opened to you.*

Element #4: The Christian Community – Your Divine Station House

You need a safe haven away from threats, danger, stress and demands – away from the streets and the fireground. You need a place where you can rest, recuperate, retrain, socialize, get updates, get resupplied, and get ready to go out again. Sounds like your local station house. These are also attributes of a church that is functioning as God intended it.

But PTSD sufferers tend to self-isolate, avoiding crowds *and* the church. Why is that?

Growing up, we all had our "crowd" – a group of people we preferred hanging out with. We were comfortable with their likes and dislikes, how they would react in certain situations, what would make them laugh or get mad. We all had similar goals and priorities, and we're OK with each other's hang-ups. We cut each other some slack for the sake of the friendship.

When a person becomes committed to a first responder career, we inherit a new crowd. Goals and priorities shift. Our life focus narrows. Training imposes a new and deeply engrained set of actions and reactions. Positive and negative events occur that affect us deeply in ways that we can't easily shake. We find more and more similarities with our new first responder crowd than we had with our old crowd. The new crowd has been through what we've been through – they understand us. The old crowd drifts, and we have less and less in common.

But along the way, more negative events may pile up. Stress, trauma, injuries, betrayal, loss, grief, compromise… Moods shift. People seem more annoying. Anger flames quickly into rage. Gatherings create anxiety. Loud noises produce exaggerated responses. The list of hang-ups lengthens. We don't want to go places that stress us out – that list also continues to lengthen.

Self-Isolation

So, with all this going on, we begin to assume we must appear very weird to our old crowd. We figure they could *never* understand our world, or who we are now. Or perhaps we don't want to burden them with the horrific things we see on an all-too-regular basis. So we avoid them – and their churches. But we also don't want our *new* crowd to spot any idiosyncrasies. Show no weakness! And in order to cloak anything that could be construed as weakness, we even begin avoiding *them*. And despite all the positive assets waiting at our "divine station house," going there becomes less and less attractive. So too often, when we are given the opportunity to socialize – with either our old or new crowd – we decline.

 On a scale of one to ten, how closely does the above scenario describe your experience?

Not in the least	1	2	3	4	5	6	7	8	9	10	Very, very very much

What has made you the most discouraged about trying to maintain relationships with your old, pre-first responder friends?

_____

_____

When you're struggling with the symptoms of stress and trauma, social isolation may seem like your best option. It feels more comfortable at first, and it's easier than trying to deal with people who don't understand. But it's one of the worst moves you can make.

Isolating yourself...

- severely diminishes your support network, which are often human conduits to God
- robs you of emotional closeness to people you like and who care about you
- gives you more time to worry and feel lonely, helpless and depressed
- causes you to play into Satan's key tactic – isolate the prey, eliminate all avenues of support, turn up the heat, then offer destructive ways to "fix" the problems
- keeps you from experiencing the *good* relationships that are energizing and healing
- makes your environment "encouragement neutral" – no minuses but no plusses either

In addition, this action goes against the basic design objective of our Creator. He made us to be a communal species. Companions were designed specifically for this kind of situation.

> *Two people are better off than one, for they can help each other succeed. If one person falls, the other can reach out and help. But someone who falls alone is in real trouble. Likewise, two people lying close together can keep each other warm. But how can one be warm alone? A person standing alone can be attacked and defeated, but two can stand back-to-back and conquer. Three are even better, for a triple-braided cord is not easily broken.*
>
> **—Ecclesiastes 4:9-12** (NLT)

God invented the Church to be like an incubator – a place where His children can grow, get strong, get healed and become stable and independent. And who is supposed to supply all this beneficial stuff? The Spirit-filled Christians who occupy the Church.

We're not necessarily talking about a building here – though that is often where "the Church" gathers. The Church is a living organism composed of Christians all over the world. The Bible refers to it as "The Body of Christ" as in, Christ is the head, and we are like His hands and feet, accomplishing His work on the planet. His intention is that we cooperate with each other – and in so doing it's much more likely we'll accomplish His purposes. The Apostle Paul shows us how it all works in 1 Corinthians 12. Let's look at a few key verses to gain some insight:

> *God's various gifts are handed out everywhere; but they all originate in God's Spirit. God's various ministries are carried out everywhere; but they all originate in God's Spirit. God's various expressions of power are in action everywhere; but God himself is behind it all. Each person is given something to do that shows who God is: Everyone gets in on it, everyone benefits. All kinds of things are handed out by the Spirit, and to all kinds of people! The variety is wonderful:*

> - wise counsel
> - clear understanding
> - simple trust
> - healing the sick
> - miraculous acts

> - proclamation
> - distinguishing between spirits
> - tongues
> - interpretation of tongues

> *All these gifts have a common origin, but are handed out one by one by the one Spirit of God. He decides who gets what, and when.*
>
> **—1 Corinthians 12:4-11** (MSG)

The Main Point

The Holy Spirit gives every person – including *you* – some kind of a gift (or gifts) that he or she can use to help others with. He knows exactly which gifts each of us would be best suited for, and He expects us to use them for the good of His body. He distributes them, but He also continually energizes them. Although the Spirit will accomplish a lot in your life by direct contact with you, He will also work on you through other gifted people.

I want you to think about how all this makes you more significant, not less. A body isn't just a single part blown up into something huge. It's all the different-but-similar parts arranged and functioning together. If Foot said, "I'm not elegant like Hand, embellished with rings; I guess I don't belong to this body," would that make it so? If Ear said, "I'm not beautiful like Eye, limpid and expressive; I don't deserve a place on the head," would you want to remove it from the body? If the body was all eye, how could it hear? If all ear, how could it smell? As it is, we see that God has carefully placed each part of the body right where he wanted it.

—1 Corinthians 12:14-18 (MSG)

 What do you think the main point of the previous passage is?

_____

_____

The way God designed our bodies is a model for understanding our lives together as a church: every part dependent on every other part, the parts we mention and the parts we don't, the parts we see and the parts we don't. If one part hurts, every other part is involved in the hurt, and in the healing. If one part flourishes, every other part enters into the exuberance.

—1 Corinthians 12:25,26 (MSG)

 What do you think the main point of the previous passage is?

_____

_____

⊞　⊞　⊞　⊞　⊞

So "Church" is simply a community of Christians. It could be a formal congregation based in a building, or it could simply be a collection of your Christian friends who are looking after each other in love, motivated and directed by the Holy Spirit. Whatever its configuration, it is crucial that you be vitally connected with a group of believers who know and love you.

 Below are a few verses that describe what is supposed to happen when Christians form a community that is intentional about making a place where God can help and heal. Write down what you observe in each verse:

Iron sharpens iron, so one man sharpens another.

—Proverbs 27:17

_____

_____

Laugh with your happy friends when they're happy; share tears when they're down. Get along with each other; don't be stuck-up. Make friends with nobodies; don't be the great somebody.

—Romans 12:15,16 (MSG)

_____

_____

Those of us who are strong and able in the faith need to step in and lend a hand to those who falter, and not just do what is most convenient for us. Strength is for service, not status. Each one of us needs to look after the good of the people around us, asking ourselves, "How can I help?"

—Romans 15:1,2 (MSG)

But encourage one another day after day, as long as it is still called "Today," so that none of you will be hardened by the deceitfulness of sin.

—Hebrews 3:13

Let's not merely say that we love each other; let us show the truth by our actions.

—1 John 3:18 (NLT)

What Happens Underground?

Have you ever spent time in northern California and walked among the majestic redwood trees in the various parks there? These are the tallest and most massive trees on the planet, many of them ascending over 350 feet. Some are as old as 4,000 years. You can't help but to be awestruck by their strength, endurance and tenacity.

But think for a minute. Have you ever seen a redwood tree growing all by itself in the middle of a field? Probably not – unless the area around it was recently cleared by man. And if so, it won't stand there for long. God has ordained that redwood trees must always live in groves, because He is aware of their secret: *shallow root systems.*

Unlike many trees that have deep taproots, redwood root systems grow laterally, and cover a huge area to efficiently absorb the small amount of rain that falls on their often rocky habitat. So, in order to keep from being blown over, redwoods *interlace* their roots below the surface, forming a solid platform that stretches for acres – even miles. When the storms blow through their valleys, they remain standing because they hold each other up.

This is an excellent picture of how the Christian community should function. The world can be a stormy place from time to time. As a first responder, you have been in some pretty bad storms. Any Christian – first responder or not – who tries to go it alone is vulnerable. It won't be long before he or she encounters difficulties that are more than they were designed to handle solo. This is why it is necessary for Christians to get involved in each other's lives, interlace their "roots" and hold each other up during the storms that come along.

Element #5: Your Mindset – Spiritual Themes for Divine Healing

To conclude this Step, we would like to give you one more prayer assignment. There are certain mindsets that are vital to creating a healing environment. If they are present, you will heal faster; if they're absent, it gets a bit iffy. No one can give them to you – no one but God, that is. If they aren't already a part of your personality, or if they got burned out of you along the way, start asking God to supply them for you. It's as simple as asking, "Lord, give me courage." He'll give you what you need for today. But follow Jesus' advice to "Keep on asking." (Matthew 7:7). Three very crucial mindsets for healing from stress and trauma are **courage**, **intentionality** and **optimism**…

Courage

Courage is not the absence of fear; it is the making of action in spite of fear.

—Dr. M. Scott Peck, *The Road Less Traveled*

If you are suffering from service-related stress or trauma, every day can provide a new surge of fearful thoughts that threaten to shut you down and turn you into stone. This condition exists *not* because you are weak or cowardly, but because you are wounded, and your brain is not processing incoming stimuli properly. But with God's help, as He instills you with His courage to act in spite of your fears, you *can* conquer them (more on this in *Step 12* in the section entitled *Facing Your Fears*, page 161).

You have problems. We all do. But why should *you* feel any reason to be courageous? Because you are vitally connected to the Supreme Problem-Solver of the Universe! And He says to you the same thing He said to Joshua, as he took over leadership of Israel after Moses died:

> *Have I not commanded you? Be strong and courageous! Do not tremble or be dismayed, for the Lord your God is with you wherever you go.*

—Joshua 1:9

God *wants* to give you the courage to take action and become the man or woman that He desires you to become. He intends for your life to *matter*, despite – and possibly because of – the traumatic experiences you suffered. He has a legacy in mind for you, but you need to have the courage to reach for it. If you reach, He will be sure you grasp it.

> Do not let your fire go out, spark by irreplaceable spark, in the hopeless swamps of the approximate, the not-quite, the not-yet, the not-at-all. Do not let the hero in your soul perish, in lonely frustration for the life you deserved but have never been able to reach. Check your road and the nature of your battle. The world you desired can be won. It exists, it is real, it is possible, it is yours.

—Ayn Rand, Russian-born American novelist and philosopher

Success is never final. Failure is never fatal. It's the courage to continue that counts.

—Winston Churchill

Intentionality

As we mentioned earlier, your service-related trauma is a wound. It's causing you pain and crippling you in some ways. Like any wound, you cannot deal with it by ignoring it. If you do, it will only fester and get worse. As a first responder, you are a man or woman of *action*. You know that in emergency situations, taking action is often the only way to stay alive. To be passive could mean death – yours, your partner's, or whoever you're trying to help. It's still true today.

Make at least one goal for each day. Combine your courage with your intentionality, and – as that great twentieth century marketing philosopher (Nike) once said – "Just Do It!"

You will miss 100% of the shots you never take.

—Wayne Gretzky, professional hockey legend

Never grow a wishbone where your backbone ought to be.

—Clementine Paddleford, pilot and writer

When a man does not know what harbor he is heading for, no wind is the right wind.

—Seneca, ancient philosopher

Optimism

Focus on your improvements rather than on your setbacks or stuck-points. You may lie awake at night and accusing thoughts begin to haunt you. "If only I'd done *that!* If only I hadn't done *that!*" With God's help, you can shift gears and begin thinking about the *good* things you did, the *right* decisions, the *positive* accomplishments. Your life might be characterized by "three steps forward, two steps back." So, focus on the cumulative total. It doesn't matter how many times a football team is behind during the game – it's the final score that counts. And as the great sports philosopher Yogi Berra once said, "It ain't over till it's over." And it ain't over for you. Your story is still being written. God has promised to bring you through this ordeal as a *victor:*

> *And we know that God causes everything to work together for the good of those who love God and are called according to His purpose for them. For God knew His people in advance, and He chose them to become like His Son, so that His Son would be the firstborn among many brothers and sisters. And having chosen them, He called them to come to Him. And having called them, He gave them right standing with Himself. And having given them right standing, He gave them His glory.*
>
> **—Romans 8:28-30** (NLT)

"I am not a failure. I've just found 10,000 ways that won't work."

> —Thomas Edison, who estimates he tried 10,000 different substances before he discovered the lighting element for the incandescent bulb.

"Optimist: A man who gets treed by a lion but enjoys the scenery."

> – Walter Winchell, newspaper and radio commentator

"Optimism is a force multiplier."

> —General Colin Powell

⊕　⊕　⊕　⊕　⊕

Prayer Seed

Thank You for Your provisions for my healing, Father. Thank You for your Holy Spirit and for Your Word. Thank You too for the opportunity to communicate with You any time, any place, through prayer. With the help of Your Holy Spirit, I'll do my best to delight in You, so that my desires will line up with Yours. I have confidence in the wisdom of Your answers to my requests. Thank You that You will say "Yes" to all of my requests that are in line with Your will and in my best interests. Thank You for the gifts You have given to Your body, the Church. Sometimes I'm reluctant to break out of my isolation and make contact with them. I've seen that none of them is perfect, by any means. But I know I need their encouragement and support. Lead me to friends who will truly be Your conduits – those I can laugh with, mourn with, and count on through thick and thin. And please build into me those three crucial mindsets: courage, intentionality and optimism. May they reside in me and help me to be receptive to everything You want to send my way. Amen.

⊕　⊕　⊕　⊕　⊕

---

1. Story from Michael Anderson, 35-year firefighter and paramedic in Eugene, Coos Bay, Florence and Albany, Oregon. Also served four years as a police officer and four years with the Navy. Michael was *not* the Captain in this story!

2. Whenever you see the word "LORD" in all capitals in the Old Testament, this means that the four-letter personal name of God was used in the original Hebrew – the name He called Himself (Exodus 3:15,16). The name of God was so holy to the Jews that they wouldn't even pronounce or write it. When they did write it, they removed the vowels from the name and just wrote "YHWH." Modern interpreters are of the opinion that the name was probably "Yahweh," pronounced "*Yah*-way."

3. From *Evangelism Explosion* by Dr. James Kennedy (Tyndale, 1977), appendix A.

Step 4 How Did I Change?

...Remembering What Happened

These things I remember, and I pour out my soul within me.

—Psalm 42:4

Numbness.
Not thinking about what happened.
Putting it out of your mind.
Suppressing it.
Turning it off with alcohol or drugs.

These actions are more comfortable than remembering. Easier. Recalling traumatizing events is painful, harder, stress-producing, and absolutely no fun at all. So why do it?

Because it's pro-active. It's intentional. It's courageous. It will aid your healing.

Stuffing It

When your line of work took you on the call that shook you to your core, or when you thought you were about to be terribly harmed or killed, your brain slipped into defensive mode in order to keep you alive and responsive to the threat (see Step 2). Many elements of that traumatic event were put on the back burner of your mind for the time being – things that should have been thought about, judged, responded to, emoted over, mourned, accepted or rejected, filed away properly. Your right brain took those videos of what was happening, and they're on your hard drive, along with all the soul-ripping emotions that went along with them. But they weren't meant to stay there. They're like computer viruses, disrupting your system at the most inconvenient times, leaking into other compartments of your hard drive and corrupting them. If they aren't discovered, brought out and dealt with, they'll get worse and the whole system will suffer. But if they *are* exposed to the light of God, their power over you can be weakened and removed.

Robert Hicks wrote *Failure To Scream* about the debilitating effect bottled up pain has on PTSD sufferers. What they went through *should* make a person scream in protest, pain, frustration and rage, but instead they stuff it in and don't deal with it. He wrote:

> What we have learned from the Vietnam experience is that denial and silence are not beneficial ways of coping. But talking about it, in some strange way, seems to be therapeutic. Naming and talking about our experiences, no matter how tragic, takes much of their control and power away…Silence and denial, no matter how subtle, only further break the heart and bring no healing to the scream.[1]

Ever had a splinter in your finger? It's not exactly life-threatening. But unless you're willing to do the work and dig it out, exposing it and the infection to the open air, that little thing will become a very *big* thing in your life, requiring all of your attention.

> *When I kept it all inside,*
> *my bones turned to powder,*
> *my words became daylong groans.*

—Psalm 32:3 (MSG)

We have no secrets from the all-knowing God. But sometimes, it's like part of our mind is trying to keep a secret from another part. We know what happened. And yet, in some kind of deep, self-defensive, self-anesthetizing maneuver, we try to keep the painful truth from our conscious self – and thereby from the rest of the world. But this maneuver has long outlived its usefulness. As Lt. Col. Dave Grossman, author of *On Killing*, wrote, **"You're only as sick as your secrets."**[2]

Getting the Secrets Out

God has written your story – you *are* His story. The Bible says, *"For we are God's workmanship, created in Christ Jesus to do good works, which God prepared in advance for us to do."* (Ephesians 2:10 (NIV)). In Greek (the original language of the New Testament) the word for "workmanship" is *poiema*, from which we get our English word "poem." You are a piece of God's creative writing.

"What?!" someone might exclaim. "If that's the case, He's a horror-story writer! How could anyone say that God was the author of *my* difficult, confusing, pain-filled life?" God wasn't the author of the evil, as we examined in Step One. But as He wrote your life and saw the waves of evil that would hit you, He factored it all in ahead of time. He knew how He was going to keep you alive, He's planned how He's going restore you, and He's eager to see you walking in strength and confidence once again. He won't erase the pain, but He'll incorporate it into your body, soul and spirit and make you more like Jesus Christ than ever before.

In this Step we are proposing that you undertake a journaling project about your traumatic experience(s) to help with your healing. If you're a writer-type, you are probably already looking forward to this exercise. If you're not, you're probably dreading it. In either case, you need to see it for what it is: therapeutic *work* – as in: *not play*. There's something about the process of crystallizing thoughts into words and then going through the physical action of putting them down on paper (or on a computer screen) that really helps a person pull out and organize his or her thoughts.

But before we dive in, let us share a few "rules:"

- Before you begin to write, spend a few moments in prayer, asking God to direct your thoughts and your writing. Ask Him to reveal any memories that will be useful in your healing process.

- If this exercise seems especially difficult for you, tell God that He will need to help you with it. He will. *The Lord is near to the brokenhearted and saves those who are crushed in spirit.* (Psalm 34:18).

- Spend a few minutes getting relaxed and "centered" – that is, concentrate on eliminating thoughts and concerns that might crowd into your mind and keep you from thinking deeply about your past experiences. Take a few, deep, calming breaths, close your eyes, and let your thoughts drift back to that place and time.

- Imagine you are watching a television show about your traumatic experience.

- Don't get upset if you can't remember all the details. Memory loss is a common symptom of PTSD; so just do your best and don't worry about the rest. It could be that God knows that you're not quite ready to handle certain memories.

- Meditate on the following comforting facts from Dr. Aphrodite Matsakis' *I Can't Get Over It:*[3]

  - You will not die, explode, disintegrate, or cease to function if you dare to remember.

  - Remembering will not result in the memories recurring as real-life events.

  - The memories will eventually diminish in intensity.

  - Safety valve: You can always go back to dissociation, denial, numbing, or whatever methods you used before to keep from remembering. But for now, give this a shot.

- You don't have to try to do this all in one sitting. If you feel overwhelmed, take a break.

- We would like to help you better grasp your trauma – not cause *more* trauma. So if you start experiencing any of the following feelings or urges, it's time to STOP for a while:

  - Faintness
  - Uncontrollable shivers
  - Hyperventilation
  - Irregular heartbeat

- Losing touch with reality, flashbacks, hallucinations

- Disoriented, spacey

- Nausea, diarrhea, unexplainable pains

- Rage, violent behavior

- Desire to self-mutilate

- Thoughts of suicide or homicide

- You may choose to write on paper other than this manual, or on a computer. By doing this, you can later add to what you write today. Your memories of what happened to you will continue to sharpen and expand. Keep writing them down as you think of new things.

- Don't worry about the things your junior high English teacher worried about – spelling, punctuation, penmanship, style, etc. Just write. You will not be graded.

- Consider using prompting objects that might help trigger some of your memories, such as photos, objects you carried with you on duty, your badge, commendations or medals, something from the place at which you were traumatized, music you listened to during that period, etc.

- If you just don't think you're up to writing your story, consider recording it.

Warm Up

Let's start off with a warm-up exercise that doesn't have much to do with your first responder experience, but *does* have something to do with trauma, helping you connect with your past feelings and remembering how you coped with them in an earlier time. Think back a few years. Write about one difficult experience you had when you were in high school or earlier. It might have involved the death of a parent, friend, sibling or relative. Maybe your parents divorced, you were assaulted, your house burned down, you were jilted by the love-of-your-life, failed a class …What was it that wounded you so deeply back then?

_____

_____

_____

What were some of the feelings you experienced during and after that experience?

_____

_____

What helped you deal with that experience and the feelings it evoked?

_____

_____

How did that experience help to make you the person you are today (a *positive* observation)?

_____

_____

_____

A Long-Delayed Debriefing

In the past twenty-five years or so, we've learned a great deal about recovering from traumatic stress – whether experienced by first responders, emergency workers after a catastrophe, rape victims, combat veterans, crash survivors – anyone. Two of the breakthroughs that just about all experts are agreed upon are (1) the victim needs to remember and talk about what they experienced, and (2) the sooner the better. As PTSD authority Patience Mason writes:

> "Today in many communities, after a crisis all the rescue workers are debriefed. They get to talk about what happened, what they saw, smelled, heard, felt, what they wanted to have happen and how it all turned out. Debriefing is what trauma work is about. You *don't* have to know every detail or relive every moment of trauma. As you talk [or write] about what happened to you and feel the feelings you had to suppress in order to live, you will relearn the broad variety of human feelings, because they have all been suppressed along with the painful ones. Recovery will help you understand yourself and be understood. This is a very healing experience for people who have felt like no one could ever understand what they have been through."[4]

The goal nowadays is that the trauma victim would experience this debriefing within seventy-two hours of their traumatic event. Well, for most of you reading this manual, that seventy-two hours is long gone. This makes the processing of your trauma a bit more difficult, but by *no means* impossible! With God's help, anything can be accomplished. Trust the Lord, and trust the process.

Writing Your Story

This exercise will have three parts. Each part is crucial to the recounting of your story, so don't skip any of it! In **Part 1**, we'd like you to spend some time writing about what life was like before you became a first responder. Read over the following questions to jog your thinking about what to write (don't attempt to answer *all* of them – just the ones that prompt your thinking):[5]

- Where were you brought up?

- What did you look like?

- What did you enjoy most when you were young? What made you happy?

- How did you get along with your family?

- What was your biggest struggle then?

- What were your friends like?

- What did you like or not like about yourself?

- What did you believe about God then?

- What were you realistic about? Naïve about?

- What were your goals or dreams for yourself then?

Part 1: My Life Before Becoming a First Responder

[Use additional paper if necessary.]

Part 2 will be a little dicier. In this assignment, we want you to write about your traumatic experience – or experiences – as a first responder. If you're like most first responders, you may have many incidents that contributed to your current condition. Write about a couple of the most painful. Or it could simply be that years of stressful work in law enforcement eventually wore you down, and you can't put your finger on a single causative incident. The accumulation of minor events over a long period of time can add up to a mountain of pain. Just describe how and when your Operational Stress Reactions began to bother you, how you responded, and how they grew. As you write, your insights and associated emotions will follow.

In your writing, don't just recount the facts of the incident(s). Let your mind go back and remember the sensual and emotional details as well. What did you smell? What did you hear? What did you taste? Describe the heat, cold, rain, sand. How did the experiences make you feel? What were your emotional reactions to the stress and trauma? Dr. Aphrodite Matsakis writes about the necessity of "feeling" to your recovery:[6]

> For you to heal completely, the trauma must be reworked not only on the mental level, but on the emotional level as well. This necessitates two further processes:
>
> - First, the feelings generated by the trauma that were not felt at the time need to be identified.
>
> - Second, and more difficult, the feelings must be experienced, at least in part, on a gut level.
>
> The feelings trauma generates are perhaps the most powerful feelings known to human beings, among them fear, anger, grief and guilt. If you think you don't have these feelings, think again. Do you still have PTSD symptoms? Are you struggling with an addiction? Do you have headaches, backaches, stomach problems or other physical symptoms of unexplained origin? If so, this suggests that even though you may not want to deal with your feelings, your feelings are dealing with you.

You and your feelings need to get to know each other again. After the nation of Israel had been conquered by the Babylonians and were taken in chains to Babylon (present day Iraq, by the way), their emotions were obviously quite high. But they didn't hold back experiencing and expressing them through their weeping, lethargy and their writing of this lament:

> *Beside the rivers of Babylon, we sat and wept*
> *   as we thought of Jerusalem.*
> *We put away our harps,*
> *   hanging them on the branches of poplar trees.*
> *For our captors demanded a song from us.*
> *   Our tormentors insisted on a joyful hymn:*
> *   "Sing us one of those songs of Jerusalem!"*

—Psalm 137:1-3 (NLT)

As we mentioned, this won't be easy. Emotions that emerge due to loss or trauma are seldom pleasant. It will be uncomfortable and may even be painful. This is why you are to be *commended* for your willingness to do this hard work. You have made many sacrifices up to this point and we're asking you to make yet another one. But this sacrifice will be for your own sake, for your family, for your friends and for the sake of the Kingdom of God. Don't complete this writing exercise just because it was "assigned." Take it to heart, and do it because of how it's going to help you. You'll get out of it only what you put into it.

Part 2: What Happened To Me

_____

_____

_____

_____

_____

_____

_____

_____

_____

_____

_____

_____

_____

_____

_____

_____

_____

_____

_____

_____

_____

_____

_____

_____

_____

_____

_____

_____

_____

_____

[Again, you are encouraged to use additional paper if necessary.]

Sometimes remembering – especially remembering our periods of crisis – can be painful, but it is an emotionally corrective experience, like setting a bone. Are you feeling like someone just wrenched your emotional femur? It's understandable, expected and normal. Sorry to put you through that. But as any orthopedic surgeon will tell you, there'll be no healing without the pain.

Part 3 shouldn't be as difficult. In this section, we would like for you to write a realistic account of your life at present – both the good stuff and the bad. You may be pretty satisfied with your current situation, if so, write down why. On the other hand, if you're suffering from PTSD, your life probably isn't exactly a sweet stroll down a rose-strewn path. Be open and honest – not only about the facts concerning your current status, but *also how you feel about them*. Here are some questions that we hope will stimulate your thinking:

- In what ways are you different from your pre-first responder self?
- What kind of work are you doing now, if any? Is this work satisfying or frustrating? Is it what you expected to be doing?
- How is your relationship with your spouse or significant other? Your children? Parents? Siblings?
- How is your relationship with friends you knew before you became a first responder?
- Do you still have contact with the first responder friends you had during the days of your trauma and/or stress? If so, how is it when you get together?
- Have there been any incidents that really capture your current level of frustration, anger and pain since your traumatic event(s)?
- What are your most frustrating symptoms?
- What triggers you and what happens when you are triggered? How often does it happen?
- What makes you want to weep, pound the table, kick the wall?
- What is the significance of your traumatic experience to you?
- How different is your life now than how you thought it would be when you first became a first responder? How does that make you feel?
- What are some *positive* things that are in your life at present? What gives you joy, hope, energy? What's fun? What do you look forward to doing?

Again, don't try to answer *all* the questions, just the ones you feel motivated to write about. But we *would* like for you to include the last item in the above list for sure.

Part 3: My Life Since My Traumatic Experience(s)

_____
_____
_____
_____
_____
_____
_____
_____
_____
_____
_____
_____
_____
_____
_____
_____
_____
_____
_____

[Again, you are encouraged to use additional paper if necessary.]

✠   ✠   ✠   ✠   ✠

Why?

Why have we done this exercise? Remember in Step 2 (page 29) when we explained that traumatic soul wounds are "episodic memories" – very negative ones, in dire need of processing and integration into our lives, values, beliefs and sense of well-being? The process of healing these memories – and the subsequent reactions and symptoms that surface when they are accessed – involves experiencing them once again in a *safe* environment, and then bringing Jesus Christ into that traumatic event. As you experience this more powerful episode, it overpowers the fear-based, pain-filled memories and opens the door for God's healing to occur. Additionally, if there are spiritual forces at work binding you to that trauma and keeping you from experiencing victory, Christ's presence will break their hold. We'll talk more about that in Step 8: *How Do I Fight?* in the section on "open doors" and "footholds" (pages 116-117).

BATTLE BUDDY. Another element that can contribute to the overall therapeutic value of this exercise is to share it with a fellow first responder – someone you trust, who understands you, and who wants to support you in your struggles. In the military, this person would be called a "battle buddy." In Step 9, we refer to these people as "Bridge people," because they are helping to bridge the gap between you and the Healer. You may want to have him or her right there with you as you are remembering and writing, or you may want to share what you wrote with them later. By sharing your traumatic events with a trusted friend, you're entering into yet another positive episodic experience which will aid your healing process.

Inviting Jesus Into Your Pain

Jesus Christ wants access to every area of your life – not to impose Himself and dominate you, but to bring healing and victory. Like a SWAT team entering a building that hides an armed suspect, checking every nook, cranny and shadow for the suspect, He wants to enter even your darkest, most ominous corners in order to conquer any foes lurking there – whether they are physiological, psychological, philosophical or real spiritual entities.

> *He uncovers deep things out of darkness,*
> *And brings the shadow of death to light.*　　　　**—Job 12:22** (NKJV)

This exercise was designed to help you remember and visualize the trauma you experienced – perhaps deeper than you have ever done before. We know it was probably painful and stirred up a lot of emotions in you. As we've emphasized before, that's not all bad. This would be a perfect time for you to talk with God about how you feel right now, how you felt about what happened to you, and what you would like for Him to do for you. This would be a good time for you to bring Jesus into those dim, shadowy areas of your story, so that He might spotlight your enemies and bring His healing light to bear.

> *Even the darkness is not dark to You,*
> *And the night is as bright as the day.*
> *Darkness and light are alike to You.*　　　　**—Psalm 139:12**

When you were going through your trauma, your brain was dominated with thoughts of panic and self-preservation. You may not have been thinking rationally. You probably had no thought about where God was in the midst of the storm you were experiencing – but Jesus Christ was there, right at your side. Take a few moments alone and invite Him into your pain – He's not afraid of it. Ask Him to open your eyes, ears, heart and mind. Then visualize what you wrote in Part 2 above, and *see Him there.*

- Where is He standing?
- Where is He looking?
- What do you see Him doing?
- Is He touching you?

- Is He saying anything to you? Can you hear anything else?
- Is He giving you any smells or tastes?
- What does He want you to do?

　　　⊞　　⊞　　⊞　　⊞　　⊞

> *He reveals deep and hidden things;*
> *He knows what lies in darkness,*
> *And light dwells with Him.*　　　　**—Daniel 2:22** (NIV)

The Fellowship of His Sufferings

This is a spiritual exercise that you should engage in frequently, if you're up to it. It requires courage, intentionality and optimism. It also requires practice. You may or may not have "seen" Jesus very vividly on your first attempt at this, but as you develop your spiritual muscles, you will experience a stronger connection with Him. Don't neglect the principles we shared in Steps 3A and 3B. They form the foundation for your deepening relationship with Him. And never forget that it is indeed a *relationship*. The story God is writing about you not only says that you know *about* Him, but that you *know Him*. You can know Him as deeply as the Apostle Paul did, in His power and glory as well as in His agony – which He has shared with you:

> *For my determined purpose is that I may know Him; that I may progressively become more deeply and intimately acquainted with Him, perceiving and recognizing and understanding the wonders of His Person more strongly and more clearly, and that I may in that same way come to know the power outflowing from His resurrection which it exerts over believers, and that I may so share His sufferings as to be continually transformed in spirit into His likeness even to His death.*

—Philippians 3:10 (AMP)

Prayer Seed

Father, what I experienced in the line of duty was more than anyone should have to endure. It's affecting me still today. I don't know everything that went on during those traumatic episodes – so much of it is a blur. But I do know by faith that You were there with me. You kept me alive for a reason. You protected me and brought me back home. Jesus, You know what it's like to experience pain, anguish, fear, torture, abandonment and death – at depths even lower than I can imagine. I sense Your brotherhood in that. Nothing I experienced, nothing I did could ever surprise You. I want to bring You into those dark and painful chapters of my story – past and present. Help me open those doors for You. Shine the light of Your presence into those black, horrendous places, and set me free. Amen.

1. Robert Hicks, *Failure To Scream* (Nashville, TN: Thomas Nelson Publishers, 1993). p. 60-61.
2. From Patience Mason's article "Dave Grossman: On Killing" in The Posttraumatic Gazette (www.patiencepress.com), Vol. 4,
3. No. 4 (Nov/Dec 1998).
4. Dr. Aphrodite Matsakis, *I Can't Get Over It: A Handbook for Trauma Survivors, 2nd Edition* (Oakland, CA: New Harbinger Publications, 1996). pp. 154, 155.
5. Patience Mason, The Posttraumatic Gazette (www.Patiencepress.co), Issue 1 (May/June 1995).
6. Some of the questions taken from Dr. H. Norman Wright, *The New Guide to Crisis and Trauma Counseling* (Ventura, CA: Regal Books, 2003). p. 234.
7. Dr. Aphrodite Matsakis, *I Can't Get Over It*, p. 168.

Step 5 How Can I Stand It?
...Processing Your Loss and Grief

Resurrection is preceded by a violent death and a season in the grave.

As a first responder, you probably know something about violent death. So does Jesus. When the physical, psychological and spiritual elements of His death are combined, His was the most violent ever. If you're reading this, odds are good that you have not personally died a violent death ... or have you? Though your body is still functioning, there may be parts of your being that feel *real* dead. And it feels like they were killed violently. The gravestone has "PTSD" on it. And you are experiencing your season in the grave right now.

But there is hope. There is a *resurrection* scheduled for you. As Tony Campolo says, referring to the days of Jesus' crucifixion and resurrection: "It's Friday, but Sunday's coming!"

Understanding Grief

Grief is a normal and natural response to loss. It is the emotional suffering one feels when something or someone the individual loves is taken away.[1] Please note carefully the first two characteristics mentioned: it is *normal and natural.* It's built into us. God invented it. God experienced it. *Everybody* experiences it.

The word "grief" comes from the Latin verb meaning "to burden." That's exactly what grief feels like, doesn't it? A heavy load that you wish you could set down – but you can't.

Grief is always triggered by a **loss** of some sort – losing someone or something we had an attachment to. Grief has different levels and intensities. We grieve a little when our favorite shirt is ruined and we have to throw it away. We grieve a little more when our favorite team has its hopes dashed for championship glory. More profound grief comes when a beloved pet dies, when a cherished relationship ends, when dreams we've held for our futures evaporate, or when someone we love passes on.

But, as grief and trauma counselor Dr. H. Norman Wright tells us "Loss is not the enemy. Not facing its existence is."[2] Loss is the fuse that triggers the bomb. The loss has irretrievably passed – now comes the process of dealing with the crater that's left.

> "Grief is neither a problem to be solved nor a problem to be overcome. It is a sacred expression of love ... a sacred sorrow."
>
> —Dr. Gerald May, M.D.[3]

Name your loss. You have suffered many losses throughout your life – as we all have. Your time as a first responder probably has brought you many rewarding experiences, but it may also have brought some new "lifetime lows" which you may have found difficult to deal with. In Step 4, you invested some hard work putting into words what happened to you. For this exercise, narrow your focus a bit, and write about what you *lost*, specifically. You could write about physical injuries that resulted in lost capabilities, lost friends, ambitions, dreams, self-identity, faith, love ... whatever comes to your mind. By naming your loss, you'll be better able to accomplish the difficult work of grieving over it.

What I lost: _____

_____

_____

The Purpose of Grief

God built the grief response into us for the purpose of mentally, emotionally and spiritually *processing* loss-producing events, integrating those events into our altered world, and helping us move on to a state of greater strength, resourcefulness, resilience and faith. If we are not willing to face the grieving process, or if we try a short-cut, we're left adrift in our sea of pain, never reaching the shores of strengthening that the Lord intends for us.

As coaches love to remind their athletes, "Pain is simply weakness leaving the body!" In a similar fashion, "Tears are a way God has provided for sadness to leave our body."[4] If we resist this mechanism, our sorrow may never lose its intensity.

When we grieve:

- We're authentically engaging the emotions that come with loss – rather than stuffing or denying them. As many grief experts say, **"You can't heal what you can't feel."**

- We're protesting the injustice of the loss, which we are truly convinced of – rather than acting like it was OK with us.

- We're expressing that we deeply wish that the loss had never occurred – rather than minimizing it.

- We're facing the devastating impact of the loss head on, absorbing it and eventually mastering it – rather than running from it, deflecting it or pretending it didn't happen, only to have its effects hit us again and again.

- We are allowing our right brain to replay the tapes of our traumatic episodic memories in a safe environment, thereby robbing them of their terror and integrating them into our rebuilding life.

- We're inviting Jesus to enter the dark forest of our pain, experience it with us, comfort us in the midst of it and walk us out the other side of it – rather than sitting passively alone and paralyzed at the edge.

When we refuse to grieve:

- Unresolved grief has been found to be a factor in the development of a wide range of psychological problems, including outbursts of rage, restlessness, depression, addiction, compulsion, anxiety and panic disorders.

- Unexpressed grief has been linked to the development or worsening of medical problems such as diabetes, heart disease, hypertension, cancer, asthma and a variety of allergies, rashes, aches and pains.[5]

- We are at odds with our body's built-in physiological processes to deal with a traumatic event.

- We are at odds with God's spiritual intentions to meet us in the midst of the fire of our trauma, missing out on His plans to deepen our faith and strengthen our relationship with Him.

What You Can Expect To Experience – "Normal" Grief

C.S. Lewis, one of the greatest Christian philosophers and teachers of the past century, had his own trek through the dark forest of grief after his beloved wife Joy died of cancer. He kept a journal for many months after her death, and in it wrote the following:

> "Grief still feels like fear. Perhaps, more strictly, like suspense. Or like waiting; just hanging about waiting for something to happen. It gives life a permanently provisional feeling. It doesn't

seem worth starting anything. I can't settle down. I yawn, I fidget, I smoke too much. Up till this I always had too little time. Now there is nothing but time. Almost pure time, empty successiveness.[6]"

⊕   ⊕   ⊕   ⊕   ⊕

As you read through the following list of symptoms, check any that you are experiencing (some items will have additional explanation, others are pretty self-explanatory).

- ❑ **Fear.** You may fear that your loss will occur again, that you won't be able to care for yourself, that you'll be alone, that your friends will reject you. If your loss involves the death of someone you were close to, you may have fears about where they are. You may fear that your current level of pain won't improve.

- ❑ **Anger.** It doesn't have to be logical. You could be mad at yourself, your circumstances, your friend who died, at dispatch or your commander who assigned you to a certain traumatizing call, at God for allowing your trauma, at the paperboy for bringing more bad news, at your neighbor for being intrusively helpful and caring, etc. Your anger might always be seething just below the surface.

- ❑ **Rage.** You may yell, scream, slam doors, kick the trash can, kick the dog, punch the wall, punch your best friend, throw things, yank things off walls or out of the ground. Sometimes you feel better afterwards. Sometimes you don't.

- ❑ **Weeping.** You may cry. Then cry some more. And more. And just when you think you couldn't possibly have any more tears to cry, you cry some more. You may wail, scream, or just sit in a chair with your tears flooding down your shirt.

- ❑ **Guilt.** *If only I'd… What if… I should have…* Hindsight and Monday-morning quarter-backing could occupy all your thoughts for a while. You may blame yourself for what happened, even though you didn't cause it and couldn't do a thing about it.

- ❑ **Loneliness.** You may feel that no one can understand what you're going through now – and that no one wants to, either. People may indeed avoid you for a while – not because they don't hurt deeply for you, but because they just don't know what to do or say. So they choose the typical default setting: do nothing.

- ❑ **Blaming.** *This is so unfair! Where's the justice? Who's going to pay for this? Somebody has to be held accountable!*

- ❑ **Running away/numbing.** You may look desperately for an escape hatch. *There must be a way out of this!* You may try drugs, alcohol, work, travel, ministry, sex, food, shopping – anything to get you away from your difficult environment.

- ❑ **Loss of appetite**

- ❑ **Loss of sexual desire**

- ❑ **Dehydration**

- ❑ **Memory lags, mental short-circuits**

- ❑ **Unexplained aches and pains**

- ❑ **Sleepiness, fatigue, lethargy**

- ❑ **Sleeplessness**

- ❑ **Nightmares**

- ❑ **Hyperactivity**

❑ **Feeling abandoned**

❑ **Frustrated**

❑ **Overly talkative**

❑ **No desire to talk**

❑ **Feeling out of control**

❑ **Emotionally overloaded**

❑ **No feelings at all**

❑ **Others?** _____

Engaging Your Grief

This might sound strange to you, but the more boxes you checked, the better! It means that you are more fully engaging your grief. If you could only check a few of them you might be either denying your grief or deferring it – putting it off until later (of course, one other possibility is that you've already worked through a lot of your grief issues – if so, great!). In any case, healthy grieving will probably involve a number of the above symptoms simultaneously. If they persist for a long, long time (many months or years) it means something has "hung up" the process. But for now, it's *OK!* What you feel is normal and you need to welcome these feelings, not try to fend them off!

What About "Loss of Faith?"

In Step 1, we examined the question of how a loving, all-powerful God could allow His creatures to experience so much pain. A person may know the answer to that question. And yet, when your world is crashing around you, and you're one, huge tangled ball of emotions, excellent theology isn't always the greatest comfort. How we *feel* often dictates what we believe. As psychologist, counselor and educator Dr. Larry Crabb writes in his book *Shattered Dreams:*

> In our shallow, sensual way of looking at life, we tend to measure God's Presence by the kind of emotion we feel. Happy feelings that make us want to sing, we assume, are evidence that God's Spirit is present. We think a sense of lostness or confusion or struggle indicates His absence.[7]

Consider the paragraph written below by C.S. Lewis not long after his wife died. He didn't hesitate to communicate his disappointment with God as he tried to come to grips with the most shattering experience of his life:

> Meanwhile, where is God?…Go to Him when your need is desperate, when all other help is vain, and what do you find? A door slammed in your face, and a sound of bolting and double-bolting on the inside. After that, silence. You may as well turn away. The longer you wait, the more emphatic the silence will become. There are no lights in the windows. It might be an empty house. Was it ever inhabited? It seemed so once.[8]

? How closely can you identify with Lewis' "crisis of faith" expressed above?

_____

_____

_____

✠ ✠ ✠ ✠ ✠

How Long?

C. S. Lewis' crisis didn't last forever. By the end of his journal, we read how he had come out the other side of the dark forest, with more clarity, more love, and stronger faith than ever before:

> Turned to God, my mind no longer meets that locked door; turned to Joy, it no longer meets that vacuum … There was no sudden, striking, and emotional transition. Like the warming of a room or the coming of daylight. When you first notice them they have already been going on for some time.[9]

God's Secret Work

As Dr. Larry Crabb has written: "When God seems most absent from us, He is doing His most important work in us. He vanishes from our sight to do what He could not do if we could see Him clearly."[10]

Remember when Jesus Christ hung on the cross, and cried out to His heavenly Father in confusion and despair, *"My God! My God! Why have You abandoned Me?"* (Matt 27:46 (NLT)). God was silent. But it was at that exact moment that God the Father was closing the transaction that was the *number one reason* the Son had come to earth – reckoning His death as payment for our sins. And this is what brought Jesus the greatest joy of His eternal existence![11]

Pastor Ron Mehl describes what God is doing in your life while He seems absent:

> God is aware of your circumstances and moves among them.
>
> God is aware of your pain and monitors every second of it.
>
> God is aware of your emptiness and seeks to fill it in a manner beyond your dreams.
>
> God is aware of your wounds and scars and knows how to draw forth a healing deeper than you can imagine.
>
> Even when your situation seems out of control.
>
> Even when you feel alone and afraid.
>
> God works the night shift.[12]

What You Can Expect From Others

When you have experienced a great trauma or loss and your grief is assumed and evident to all those around, you will be treated differently for a while. This is to be expected – but some treatment we receive is helpful and some we could do without. As C.S. Lewis expressed in his journal, "Perhaps the bereaved ought to be isolated in special settlements like lepers."[13]

The Less-Than-Helpful Things

Especially in the Western world, social taboos have been invented that make us try to avoid or deny any discomfort from loss. We look with disdain at the outpouring of grief in other cultures and accuse them of "lack of control." We don't realize that *we* are the foolish ones, holding in something that would better be let out.

But it's important to remember that your friends mean well. Their insensitivity is not because they intend to hurt you or prolong your grief – it's just that they're uninformed about what to do and how to help. When the following comments are shared, it's best to see the good hearts behind them. Smile if you can, say thanks and move on. But *don't follow their advice!* Check the ones you've heard…

❑ You need to put it behind you. Time to move on.

❑ Don't dwell in the past.

❑ You just need a good distraction.

❑ Think happy thoughts!

❑ Haven't you prayed about this yet?

❑ Don't "cave in" to your sorrow. Keep a stiff upper lip!

❑ You should be over this by now.

❑ What would Jesus do? (Counseling by cliché.)

❑ It's not as bad as it seems.

❑ Keep a grip on your emotions. Don't cry in front of *anyone*.

❑ Since you're a Christian, you shouldn't be grieving. Don't you know that God works everything out for the good?

❑ You'll feel better tomorrow.

❑ Hey! How 'bout those Seahawks? (In other words, let's talk about anything else but your grief.)

❑ Be strong for your kids – don't let them see you cry.

❑ How are you? (But they don't *really* want you to tell them too much.)

❑ You think *that's* bad? Let me tell you what happened to *me*...

❑ If you just had a little more faith, this wouldn't seem so bad.

The Helpful Things

There are going to be a few of your friends who are wise in the ways of grief – either because they've experienced it themselves, have been trained, are particularly intuitive or have read a lot of books! When you find these people, do whatever it takes to keep them around!

- When they ask, "How are you?" they really want to know, and they stick around for the answer.

- They're willing to give you their time, available when you need them.

- They'll sacrifice for you.

- They take the initiative with you; they reach out to you by calling you up, asking you out, including you in their lives.

- They're good listeners, non-judgmental, won't interrupt you to talk about themselves.

- They find out what you need and then go get it for you.

- They'll pray *for* you and pray *with* you.

- They won't mind if you cry, in fact they'll end up crying with you.

- They've got your back.

 Who do you have in your circle of friends like this?

_____

_____

Prayer Assignment: If you can't think of anyone, start asking God to send someone like this to you or to open your eyes to a current acquaintance who can be that kind of a friend. Make this request of Him daily – keep on knocking![14]

⊕   ⊕   ⊕   ⊕   ⊕

How NOT To Grieve

We humans will sometimes do *anything* rather than to undertake the hard work of grief – then think we're accomplishing something. These actions may make us feel a little better temporarily, but it doesn't move us out of our despairing state. Following is a list of ways people attempt to cope with their situation without actually facing their grief – check any that you think you might do from time to time.[15]

- ❑ **Act out** – giving in to the pressure to misbehave.
- ❑ **Aim low** – to what seems more achievable.
- ❑ **Attack** – beat down what's threatening you.
- ❑ **Avoid** – stay away from anything that causes you stress.
- ❑ **Compensate** – make up for weakness in one area by gaining strength in another.
- ❑ **Deny** – refusing to acknowledge that the event occurred.
- ❑ **Displace** – shifting an intended action to a safer target (like kicking the dog).
- ❑ **Fantasize** – escaping reality to a world of unachievable wishes.
- ❑ **Idealize** – playing up the good points of a desired action and ignoring downsides.
- ❑ **Identify** – copying others to take on their desirable characteristics.
- ❑ **Intellectualize** – avoiding emotions by focusing on facts and logic.
- ❑ **Passive aggression** – an indirect expression of hostility by avoiding responsibilities.
- ❑ **Project** – seeing your own undesirable characteristics in others.
- ❑ **Rationalize** – creating logical reasons for bad behavior.
- ❑ **Regress** – returning to a child state to avoid problems or responsibility.
- ❑ **Suppress** – consciously holding back unwanted urges while ignoring the root cause.
- ❑ **Trivialize** – making something small when it is really something big.

If you recognize any of these behavior patterns in yourself, you first need to see them for what they are: hoped-for shortcuts to restoration which won't get you there at all. **Suggestion:** show this list to a friend and ask them if they see you engaging in any of these behaviors.

Then, make it a matter of prayer. Ask God to help you realize when you're avoiding your grief work by falling into these habits, and to help you partner with Him in the process.

⊕   ⊕   ⊕   ⊕   ⊕

How To Grieve

Be Aware of the Process

It is a process, for sure. But it's not a *precise* process. Everyone will process their grief a bit differently than the next person. However, there are some generalized descriptions that are useful – kind of like milestones along a journey – to let you know that you are making progress. Or not.

Elizabeth Kübler-Ross was a Swiss physician who did groundbreaking research in the area of grief. Her book *On Death and Dying* has been a classic for decades. In her studies she found that there is a pattern that most people experience after a life-changing trauma or crisis.

This cycle of emotional states is shown on the chart below. It demonstrates the roller-coaster ride of activity and passivity as the hurting person wriggles and dodges in their desperate efforts to cope with the trauma, avoid change and finally be reconciled to it.

The person starts out in a state of relative stability and then the bomb goes off. Over unspecified periods of time, he or she progresses through these stages:

- **Immobilization stage** – Shock; initial paralysis after being exposed to the crisis or trauma. It takes a while for the enormity to register and sink in. Jaw drops, breath catches, can't decide what to do next.

- **Denial stage** – Trying to avoid the inevitable. *No! This can't be happening!* Or, *It didn't affect me; it wasn't that bad.* Or even, *It never happened. You just imagined it.*

- **Anger stage** – Frustrated outpouring of bottled-up emotion. *Life sucks!!* Rage seething below the surface at all times; lashing out at anyone for the slightest reason; blaming others; sometimes cold, icy anger; self-isolating to avoid blowing up.

- **Bargaining stage** – Seeking in vain for a way out. Making promises to God if He'll fix things; setting conditions for healing, like: *When the perp that raped and killed that little girl is behind bars, then I'll get well.*

- **Depression stage** – Final realization of the inevitable. A very sad time, but also the turning point, because the griever is finally resolved to the fact that he or she won't be able to restore life to the way it was. It's the staging area for victory.

- **Testing stage** – Seeking realistic solutions. *Maybe I should try getting out more. Maybe I should talk with someone about my situation. Maybe I should start exercising again. Maybe I should join that Bible study I heard about.*

- **Acceptance stage** – Finally finding the way forward. They are now fully acknowledging the trauma or crisis. *It was bad – real bad – but I survived. I'm going to make it. My world changed, but I can live in this new world. I could even prosper.*

The Kübler-Ross Grief Cycle:

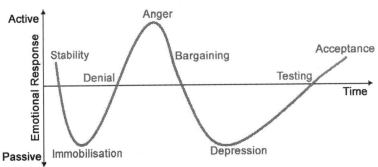

? After you have read the descriptions of the above stages, think about where you might presently be in the Grief Cycle, and place an "X" on the appropriate place on the line. Two questions: How do you feel about where you are in the process currently? What do you think it's going to take to move you beyond your present stage?

_____

_____

_____

A Few Words About the Process

As mentioned before, it's not precise. You may not hit all of these stages. You may skip a stage and then go back to experience it later. You may whiz through one stage and sit in another stage for a long time. You may find yourself going back and forth between a couple of stages, or looping around to various stages willy-nilly. No one can say for sure how you will deal with your unique trauma, given your unique wiring. For you it may be less of a nice, neat "cycle" and more of a "scribble."

Therefore, don't give in to the temptation to compare your grief process with someone else's. If you will keep your connections with God strong during this process, He will take you through it in a way that will maximize every stage and bring you through to the final stage as soon as possible.

How long will it take? Honestly, probably a lot longer than you'll like. In fact, if the trauma you experienced is severe enough, some grief will always be there. It won't be dominating your life like it currently is, but there will always be that hole where the lost person or thing or dream used to be. That ache won't go away completely. But that's not all bad – consider it a memorial to the depth of the love, attachment and value it (or they) held before the loss. And God will use it.

> _Blessed be the God and Father of our Lord Jesus Christ, the Father of mercies and God of all comfort, who comforts us in all our affliction so that we will be able to comfort those who are in any affliction with the comfort with which we ourselves are comforted by God._
>
> **—2 Corinthians 1:3,4**

⊕ ⊕ ⊕ ⊕ ⊕

How To Have A Good Mourning

Blessed are those who mourn, for they shall be comforted.

—Matthew 5:4

When we've experienced a traumatic event, grief is what we _feel_. Mourning is _what we do about it_. It is the action side of grief, the externalizing of our internal pain. And Jesus Christ – who knows _everything_ – says that when we do it we are blessed and _will be_ comforted. Here are eight principles to keep in mind as your work out your grief through mourning.

1. Remember where God is.

> _The Lord is near to the brokenhearted,_
> _And saves those who are crushed in spirit._
>
> **—Psalm 34:18**

Because of your soul wound, you hold a special attraction to the Lord. You've got His attention. He is a compassionate God, always pulling for the underdog, ready to aid anyone who will let Him. _Count on that!_ You can expect

Him to be present and responsive to your needs during this time. He is like your best friend who says, "If you need anything, don't hesitate to ask!" And He means it.

Ask Jesus to enter your pain with you. Close your eyes and feel Him coming up behind you, wrapping His big arms around you and holding on tight. Let Him pull the pain out of your body, soul, and spirit into His.

2. Remember the past and remain optimistic.

> How hopeless the naked wood of a fruit tree would look to us in February
> if we had never seen the marvel of springtime.

—Lilias Trotter[16]

Though what you are currently enduring may be the worst experience you've ever had to slog your way through, it's not the *only* trauma you've known. Think back to all the times God has sustained you in the past. Elisabeth Elliot whose missionary husband was murdered by primitive natives in Ecuador wrote, "The death of wintertime is the necessary prelude to the resurrection of springtime."[17] Spring will come – as it always has for you.

We can make a distinction between the cliché, "Think happy thoughts!" and the admonition from the Apostle Paul to keep our minds focused on positive things:

> *Finally, brethren, whatever things are true, whatever things are noble, whatever things are just, whatever things are pure, whatever things are lovely, whatever things are of good report, if there is any virtue and if there is anything praiseworthy—meditate on these things.*

—Philippians 4:8 (NKJV)

3. Aim steadily at faith's target.

Ask yourself this question: "What do I have faith in?" How did you answer? Assuming you didn't say, "Nothing," perhaps your response was like one of these:

- "That God will bring me out of this depression."

- "That my leg will heal."

- "That my husband won't leave me."

- "That I could quit drinking so much."

- "That I can get past my anger."

These are all great faith *goals* and excellent requests to make to God, but they aren't what you put your faith in. If you do – and they don't come about – what happens to your faith? The only answer to the question, "What do I have faith in?" should be "God." Whenever we tie our faith to our circumstances or to a particular desire, we take God off the throne of our life and set ourselves up for great disappointment. We are *lousy* at playing God! David Shepherd is a man of God who had suffered great setbacks when he wrote this letter to his friend Larry Crabb:

> Faith, as I am growing to understand it more, is about looking beyond my circumstances to a Person. To have faith in better circumstances, even in God creating better circumstances, is not true faith. I want to be the kind of man who can watch every dream go down in flames and still yearn to be intimately involved in kingdom living, intimately involved with my friend the King, and still be willing to take another risk just because it delights Him for me to do so. And my flesh shivers to think about it.[18]

As Thomas Merton wrote: "The real hope is not in something we think we can do, but in God, who is making something good out of it in some way we cannot see."[19] The essence of mature faith is to boldly express our fervent desires to God, and then leave them in His wise and benevolent hands – no matter what. He'll always do what's best.

4. Don't try to be the Lone Ranger.

Grief is hard on a person and mourning is difficult work. Effective grief work is not done alone. Don't try to be the pillar of strength to everyone around you. You'll crumble. Be sure to find a few people that you know you can count on to be there for you when you need them. As Dr. Harold Ivan Smith, death and grief expert writes:

> Grievers cannot extricate themselves from their cistern called grief. They need a rope. Grievers need someone on the other end to pull. But they really need individuals to pad the ropes – not with pat answers or spiritual clichés or even Scripture promises but with hope.[20]

5. Do something with your anger.

When anger is bottled up indefinitely it morphs into bitterness. And as we learned earlier, that bitterness will spread beyond the borders of your life. It's OK to be angry. It is a normal, reasonable emotion when we are confronted with unjust, hurtful or grievous events. It is recorded in the Bible that Jesus Himself became angry on a few occasions (Mark 3:1-5; Mark 10:14; John 2:13-16). But it's what we *do* with that anger that can lead to sin.

The Bible says in Ephesians 4:26 (NIV), "In your anger do not sin." When you feel the anger rising up within you, first remove yourself from the physical cause of your anger if you can (i.e., if it's a person, leave the room; a locational trigger, go somewhere else). It's like removing fuel from the fire. No fuel, no fire. Go out for a run; go to the gym and pound the heavy bag for a while; lift weights; dig a garden; chop down a tree; plant a tree; swim a few hundred laps. Or if you're able, do something truly constructive: go help someone who needs it; build something; go down to the church and see if they need help with anything.

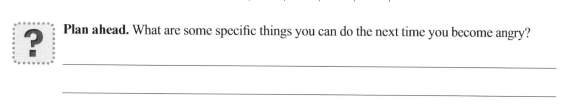

? **Plan ahead.** What are some specific things you can do the next time you become angry?

_____

_____

6. Go with the flow (of tears).

Men normally find this harder than women, because – as many wives would testify – they tend to be right-brain-challenged! They seem to be reluctant to engage the strong emotions associated with grief. It has a lot to do with our society's programming: "Big boys don't cry." Maybe not – but big men *should* when it comes to grief.

King David beat a 9'8" giant in a fair fight, killed a lion and a bear in hand-to-hand combat as a boy, and collected the foreskins of two hundred Philistines as a dowry for his bride. He had a man under his command who single-handedly killed eight hundred men in one battle (that's in the days before automatic weapons, by the way); another who successfully defended a strategic position against the entire Philistine army; another who killed three hundred men in one battle with a *spear*. And David was *their boss*. We can rightfully assume he was "all man."

And yet, David did not hesitate to fully engage his emotions during times of grief:

> *I am worn out from groaning; all night long I flood my bed with weeping and drench my couch with tears.*

—Psalm 6:6 (NIV)

> *I went about mourning as though for my friend or brother. I bowed my head in grief as though weeping for my mother.*

—Psalm 35:14 (NIV)

I am exhausted from crying for help; my throat is parched. My eyes are swollen with weeping, waiting for my God to help me.

—Psalm 69:3 (NLT)

For I have eaten ashes like bread, and mingled my drink with weeping.

—Psalm 102:9

My soul weeps because of grief; strengthen me according to Your word.

—Psalm 119:28

✠   ✠   ✠   ✠   ✠

7. Keep a grief journal.

Crisis care authority "Chaplain Ray" Giunta and his wife Cathy have assembled a very practical tool for those recovering from trauma called *The Grief Recovery Workbook*. In it they say, "To journal is to heal," and they urge their readers to regularly – daily – record their thoughts. "This may be the biggest favor you do yourself," they say.

He urges mourners to make this promise to themselves:

> I'm going to get my feelings out. I'm not going to be scared. I'm going to write down how I feel each day. I'm going to express what I'm discovering, how I'm responding to each new idea, how it helps or doesn't help, and where I am right now on the journey. I'll write at least a sentence or two each time I re-read the earlier entries and chapters, because each day is a new day and a new place on the road.[21]

In your journal, you could answer these three questions:

- This is how I feel (or what I need) right now.

- This is what I've discovered today.

- This is what I still question today.

C.S. Lewis' grief journal, published as *A Grief Observed,* turned out to be extremely therapeutic to him and immensely helpful to all those grievers who have read it down through the years. And King David's grief journal – scattered throughout the Psalms – has been a comfort and a guide to millions for centuries. Two great examples!

8. Write a Lament.

A lament is a special kind of entry that you might find in a grief journal, or you might find it as a literary work all by itself. You find many laments in the Bible – in fact the whole book of Lamentations is a series of long laments by Jeremiah, the "Weeping Prophet."

When a mourner writes a lament, they pour all of their emotion, frustrations, venom, vitriol, sadness, curses – everything *including* the kitchen sink – onto a piece of paper. They rail against their present circumstances. They don't hold back. Like Job (3:11-13 (MSG)):

> *Why didn't I die at birth, my first breath out of the womb my last?*
> *Why were there arms to rock me, and breasts for me to drink from?*
> *I could be resting in peace right now, asleep forever, feeling no pain.*

Or like Jeremiah (Lamentations 1:12):

> *Is it nothing to all you who pass this way? Look and see if there is any pain like my pain which was severely dealt out to me, which the Lord inflicted on the day of His fierce anger!*

Or even like our prime example of a griever, King David (Psalm 22:1,2 (NLT)):

> *My God, my God, why have You abandoned me?*
> *Why are You so far away when I groan for help?*
> *Every day I call to You, my God, but You do not answer.*
> *Every night You hear my voice, but I find no relief.*

Hey! This is the Bible! So apparently it's OK to talk like that to God! In a lament, it's "no holds barred." It's your opportunity to express your despair and anger, knowing that no one – not even God – is going to judge you. So let 'er rip!

And when you're done, read it over again. Read it to Jesus, giving Him all that anger, hurt, hate and despair. And He'll thank you for your honesty, absorb your anger and love you just as fiercely as He ever has.

Signs That Your Mourning Is Working

As the magnitude of trauma and its effects sink in, a person in crisis asks a lot of *"Why"* questions. *Why did this happen? Why did this have to happen to me? Why now? Why did I do that? Why did he/she do that? Why did God let this happen? Why won't this pain quit? Why must I suffer so deeply?* These questions are all normal, typical and expected. No one faults you for asking them.

? What were (or are) some of the "Why" questions you've asked?

_____

_____

_____

As universal as they are, the frustration of the "Why" questions is that most of them will never be answered this side of heaven. We don't ask those questions lightly and we really do expect answers. But they just don't come.

When you start asking the *"How"* questions, that will be a good sign that you are making good progress. *How can I build new dreams? How can I move on? How can I deal with my pain and loss? How can I get back into the swing of things? How can I learn through what I've experienced?* These are all questions that *can* be answered. They look to the future, rather than the past. They spark action, rather than mere contemplation. They invite help from God and from others.

? How can you change some of those "Why" questions you wrote above into "How" questions? What other "How" questions should you be asking?

_____

_____

_____

✠　✠　✠　✠　✠

Grief Memorials

Researchers in the field of grief and mourning have learned that memorials play a very important role in starting the grief process and facilitating continued healing. That's why we have funerals and memorial services. That's why we have gravestones. That's why the National Law Enforcement Officers Memorial in Washington, D.C. and the

IAFF Fallen Fire Fighter Memorial in Colorado Springs are so sacred and meaningful to all who visit them. Every community has similar, local tributes to first responders who have died in the line of duty. These things are tangible experiences and symbols of our grief. We humans need them.

How can you memorialize the grief that's attached to your trauma? What can you do or construct that will provide a touchstone for your pain, something that will symbolize your loss? We're not talking about erecting a shrine in your dining room or anything – or maybe we are. This needs to be a personal gesture that you and God decide upon It could be as subtle as a smooth stone in your pocket from the site where your trauma occurred, a poem that you write and put up on the wall, or as obvious as the Taj Mahal. You and God decide.

Prayer Assignment: Ask God to give you a creative idea of how you could memorialize your grief and trauma in a positive, healing way.

Prayer Seed

Father, sometimes my grief is so burdensome I think it's going to crush me into the ground. I want to be rid of it! It's like my worst enemy. But I need You to help me make it my friend. Help me to embrace it as part of my healing balm from You. Don't let me run from it or try to take shortcuts. Help me to face it head-on. But I cannot go there if You won't come with me. Please enter into my pain with me. Walk me through it. Take me out the other side whole, wiser, stronger and more like Jesus. Amen.

1. Melinda Smith, J.S. (2012, January). *Coping with Grief and Loss*. Retrieved March 15, 2012, from helpguide.org: http://helpgide.org/mental/grief_loss.htm.
2. Dr. H. Norman Wright, *The New Guide to Crisis & Trauma Counseling* (Ventura, CA: Regal Publishing, 2003). p. 64
3. Quote from Dr. Gerald May found in *Ibid*, p. 87.
4. Margaret Hill, Harriet Hill, Richard Baggé, Pat Miersma, *Healing The Wounds of Trauma* (Nairobi, Kenya: Paulines Publications Africa, 2005). p. 37.
5. This point and the one before it are from Dr. Aphrodite Matsakis, *I Can't Get Over It: A Handbook for Trauma Survivors, 2nd Edition* (Oakland, CA: New Harbinger Publications, 1996). p. 202.
6. C.S. Lewis, *A Grief Observed* (New York: HarperCollins Publishers, 1961). p. 33.
7. Dr. Larry Crabb, *Shattered Dreams* (Colorado Springs, CO: Waterbrook Press, 2001). p. 109
8. C.S. Lewis, *A Grief Observed*, p. 5, 6.
9. C.S. Lewis, *A Grief Observed*, p. 61, 62.
10. Dr. Larry Crabb, *Shattered Dreams*, p. 157, 158.
11. Hebrews 12:2 (NIV) – *"Let us fix our eyes on Jesus, the author and perfecter of our faith, who **for the joy set before him** endured the cross, scorning its shame, and sat down at the right hand of the throne of God."*
12. Written by the late Pastor Ron Mehl, who died in 2003 after a 23-year-long battle with leukemia. He was well-acquainted with the night shift. Quoted by Dr. H. Norman Wright, *Experiencing Grief* (Nashville, TN: B&H Publishing Group, 2004). p. 22.
13. C.S. Lewis, *A Grief Observed*, p. 11.
14. Matthew 7:7,8 (NLT) – *"Keep on asking, and you will receive what you ask for. Keep on seeking, and you will find. Keep on knocking, and the door will be opened to you. For everyone who asks, receives. Everyone who seeks, finds. And to everyone who knocks, the door will be opened."*
15. This partial list of coping mechanisms was taken from www.changingminds.org under the "Explanations/Behaviors/Coping" tab.
16. Elisabeth Elliot, *A Path Through Suffering* (Ventura, CA: Regal Publishing, 1990). p. 29. Quote by Lilias Trotter, missionary to Africa from 1888 to 1928.
17. Ibid, p. 41.
18. Quote by David Shepherd in Dr. Larry Crabb, *Shattered Dreams*, p. 161.
19. Quote by Thomas Merton in a letter to Jim Forest, director of the Fellowship of Reconciliation, quoted by Henri Nouwen in *Turn My Mourning Into Dancing* (Nashville, TN: Thomas Nelson Inc.,2001). p. 60.
20. Dr. Harold Ivan Smith, *When Your People Are Grieving* (Kansas City, MO: Beacon Hill Press, 2001), p. 38. Dr. Smith speaks widely on the subjects of grief and death, and conducts "grief gatherings" around the US.
21. Ray Giunta, *Grief Recovery Workbook* (Brentwood, TN: Integrity Publishers, 2002). p. 15.
22. Robert Hicks, *Failure To Scream* (Nashville, TN: Thomas Nelson Publishers, 1993). p. 187.

Step **6A** # How Do I Move On?

...Forgiveness Received and Given

[This Step is covered in two parts: 6A and 6B.]

> "Every saint has a past,
> every sinner a future."
>
> —Oscar Wilde

Though your sins are as scarlet, they will be as white as snow;
Though they are red like crimson, they will be like wool.

—Isaiah 1:18

A big mistake. I was the newest hire at the station, and had been off probation for about four months. The heavy training was over, but it had taken a toll on me and my family. Two years to get my Fire Suppression degree at the community college, the application and interview process, Fire Academy… My little family and I were running on fumes emotionally, physically and financially. Nevertheless, I was starting to fall into a rhythm as a firefighter/paramedic.

One afternoon we responded to a call at the home of an elderly man in medical distress. When we entered the residence, it became obvious we were going to be placing him in a care facility. He lived alone. Dirty dishes were heaped on the counter and soiled clothes were scattered everywhere. Piles of mail sat on almost every horizontal surface. A film of dust covered everything. But what really caught our attention were the envelopes of cash laying randomly here and there. The man would apparently cash his pension checks at the bank, set the money packets down when he got home and forget about them. Some were opened, and bills were scattered everywhere among the rest of the clutter.

The Captain immediately called dispatch requesting police presence to deal with the cash. We stabilized the man, and waited for the medic unit to arrive for transport. I couldn't believe all the money that was just laying around.

When the unit arrived and the patient was loaded and out the door, the engine crews followed. As I was leaving, the Captain asked me to go back in and make sure nothing was left behind. Then we were to lock up the residence and wait for the PD.

I went back in and everything looked good… especially those money envelopes laying around. "There's two month's rent," I thought. "There's four car payments. There's a month of groceries. Who's going to know? This old guy obviously doesn't need it – and my family does." I quickly glanced around, then grabbed two fat envelopes and jammed them in my pocket.

The Captain shouted for me to hurry up, so I quickly headed for the front door. That's when I noticed the surface of a bookshelf. One of us must have jostled it, and a small statue had tipped over, leaving a perfect dust-free circle where it had been.

"What's going to be left where I picked up those envelopes?" I thought in a panic. "Are the cops going to see where they had been? Are they going to put two-and-two together and nail me?" It was too late to put them back now – the Captain was right there.

I haven't been able to sleep for four days. They *must* be on to me. The Captain looks at me funny. Things were bad before, but what happens if I get arrested? Will I go to jail? Will I lose my job? How will I support my family? How can I look at myself in the mirror?[1]

✚　✚　✚　✚　✚

Why Is Forgiveness Crucial To Moving On?

Our sins usually seem inconsequential when we first commit them – otherwise we wouldn't do them. And the immediate results often seem relatively harmless. But something is *always* going on behind the scene that isn't apparent. These issues will have effects that will linger for a long time if not dealt with.

What is happening is *separation*.

Every time we make the decision to go against one of God's laws, three separations potentially occur:

- A separation between you and God
- A separation between you and another person
- A separation between you and you

Between You and God

When we switch places with the Holy Spirit on the throne of our life in order to do something we know is wrong (page 36), we are "quenching" and "grieving" Him (1 Thessalonians 5:19; Ephesians 4:30). Isaiah 59:2 says *"But your iniquities have made a separation between you and your God, and your sins have hidden His face from you so that He does not hear."* This does not alter your eternal connection with God – you were born into His family when you received Christ as your Savior, and you can't get "unborn." The eternal life He gave you is indeed *eternal* and He loves you with an everlasting love (Jeremiah 31:3). But in terms of your experiential *relationship* with Him, it is strained. Much like when a husband and wife have a fight – they're still married, but their communication is clipped, awkward and cold. They live together, but their hearts are separated. This is how it can feel between us and God.

Between You and Another Person

When we do something that injures another person in some way, this too results in alienation – like the couple in the previous paragraph. In Matthew 5:22-26, Jesus describes this split between people, and urges us to set everything else aside and be reconciled to our offended brother or sister – for our own good (read the above passage in Matthew if you have a moment).

This works the other direction, too. When you are hurt by someone, you don't want to hang with them much anymore. You avoid them. Once burned, twice smart.

Between You and You

Sin also brings about a separation between who you are and who God is making you. In Ephesians 4:22-24, the Bible talks about our "old man" – corrupt, lustful, deceitful – and your "new man" – righteous, holy and honest. In Romans 7:14-24, no less a man than the Apostle Paul describes the war that rages between these two "men" in his soul. It's like having two dogs fighting inside of you – a good one and a bad one. The one you feed wins. And sin feeds the bad dog.

These separations are counter-productive to your healing. You *need* those life-giving connections to God and to other Spirit-filled friends. Without them, you're like that redwood tree growing in the open field (page 50), or like a sheep wandering alone through the woods – vulnerable. And you need that unified, Christ-oriented control internally, so that you can receive and respond to His healing touch and direction.

What's needed is *reconciliation* – to God, to others, and to yourself. This is accomplished through forgiveness – received and given.

Accepting God's Forgiveness

One of the greatest transactions that occurs in the universe is forgiveness from God.

God runs a tight ship. There are absolutes. There is right and wrong. There are laws which keep the universe and society running properly. If you break a law, it will break you. Example: there is a law (gravity) that says if you jump out of an airplane you will go down fast, land hard and hurt all over. Every time. That is, unless there is another law operating that supersedes the law of gravity, such as the law of the *parachute*.

Another example: With regard to eternity, the Bible says that if you sin, you will experience eternal death (Ezekiel 18:20). Why? Because in your natural, sin-prone state, you are separated from God, and if you step into eternity in that separated condition, you stay that way forever. That is, unless *that* law is superseded by the law of *forgiveness*.

What Do You Need To Be Forgiven For?

Most people are prompted to seek God's forgiveness because they feel *guilty*. But there are two kinds of guilt, and you need to know which kind you are feeling, because one needs forgiveness and the other *doesn't*.

1. False Guilt

Dave was excited about the bust that was going down tonight. Narcotics officers (a male and a female) had worked a dealer and wanted to keep using him. This night they decided to arrest him, hoping to get info about his supplier.

The male narc had a quick meeting with Dave and his partner (both uniformed officers) and two other narcotics officers in the back of a van close to where the deal was to go down. They discussed the plan of giving a signal after they saw the dope. The van would then move in, arrest the suspect and the two undercover narcs. However, Dave and his partner were not given a description of the suspect nor the other undercover narcotics officer – not even their genders. There hadn't been time.

The target vehicle arrived and shortly thereafter the signal was given. The van roared up blocking the car's escape. Dave, his partner and the other two narcotics officers exited the van, drew their weapons and surrounded the car – Dave took the passenger side. The suspect and an associate were in the back seat, the female narc in the front passenger seat, and the male narc was driving.

As Dave went to remove the female narcotics officer from the passenger side, she tried to make a good show and pulled out her pistol. She assumed all the officers knew who she was. Dave saw the gun and ordered her to drop it. It was pointed directly at him. She didn't immediately drop her gun, so Dave fired once.

At this point, the other narcotic officers screamed at Dave who she was – but it was too late. She died instantly from Dave's shot.

No one in the department blamed Dave for this tragedy – it was a breakdown in communication. But Dave couldn't get past it. His conscience hammered him relentlessly about killing another human being, a woman, and – worst of all – a fellow officer. He knew he had done everything "by the book" given the conditions at the moment, but that didn't matter to him. He couldn't forgive himself.[2]

We have an enemy who is seeking to devour us (1 Peter 5:8). One of his methods of doing this is to counterfeit the things of God, twist them, and use them for his destructive purposes. Guilt is good, invented by God. It is meant to let us know when we are doing something that's leading to separation of one sort or another, prompting us to go back to God for forgiveness and restoration. But Satan likes to give us guilt trips that have nothing to do with God's laws. This is why one of his names in the Bible is "The Accuser" (Revelation 12:10). His accusations of guilt do nothing but produce frustration and depression. This happens because there's no way to rid ourselves of the effects of that kind of guilt – unless we recognize it for what it is: *false*. Here are some examples of **false guilt:**[3]

- **Survivor's Guilt** – "I shouldn't have survived when others died." "If I'd suffered more, others would have suffered less." "If I had died, others might have lived."

- **Survivor's Euphoria Guilt** – "I feel so ashamed about it, but I can't help thinking, 'I'm so glad I didn't get killed!' How can I feel *good* when others died?"

- **Guilt Over Involuntary Flight/Fight/Freeze Response** – "I always thought I was so brave, but I just froze in my tracks! I couldn't move!" "When that guy jumped me in the alley, I went berserk. I killed him, but couldn't stop beating him until his face was an unrecognizable pulp."

- **Guilt By Association** – "I'm a cop; cops sometimes abuse their authority; I am among the authority-abusers. That's how people probably see me."

- **Competency Guilt** – "If only I had acted quicker, more skillfully or smarter, people wouldn't have suffered and died."

- **Catch-22 Guilt** (Forced to make a lose/lose choice) – "The young woman was high and waving a handgun. I wasn't sure it was real. I kept yelling at her to put it down, but she wouldn't. Suddenly she took aim at a bystander. If I shoot she dies; if I don't shoot maybe the bystander dies. I shot. Her gun was a toy. How do I live with that?"

- **Helplessness Guilt** – "I saw the child in the fourth floor window, smoke swirling around him. I was powering the ladder up to him as fast as I could. He panicked and jumped for it. It was still too far away. I should have thought of *something*."

- **Role and Responsibility Guilt** – "Job #1 is for me to keep my men safe. Some of them died, so I didn't do my job. It's all my fault."

In each case listed above, there is *no guilt* as far as God's laws are concerned, no immoral factor in any of the decisions that were made. The *felt* guilt was always based on a false premise.

- You can't blame yourself because you lived while others died – you had nothing to do with that. There's no way you could have controlled all the conditions surrounding your traumatic events. The conclusions drawn are illogical and inaccurate.

- The euphoria over your survival is an involuntary function of your lower brain, as was your fight/flight/freeze response – *involuntary.* As in: they are uncontrollable reflexes. They're *not* moral choices that you should be held accountable for.

- Guilt by association? As long as you didn't participate in authority abuse, it's a huge thinking-error for you to punish yourself for it. You didn't do the crime, so why do the time?

- The "if onlys" of Competency, Catch-22 and Helplessness are irrelevant. In hindsight we may be able to see other options, but in the moment of crisis, *no one* can see them all. You did your best, and *no one* – at that moment under those conditions – should judge you for it. You could wish that some magical solution would have presented itself at the last moment, but it didn't. That's reality – not your fault.

- And leaders simply *can't* protect all those under their command all the time. When first responders put themselves in dangerous situations (as is required by their jobs), there is always potential for disaster and thousands of moving parts. Are you God, that you could control all of those variables simultaneously?

In all of these cases, it's normal to feel sad, angry and frustrated about how things turned out – but don't turn that emotion in on yourself. You weren't meant to take the hit for those very unfair and unfortunate events – so don't take it. Remember that you have a spiritual enemy who will try to manipulate the memories of those events in order to weaken and destroy you. Also, remember what you heard all the time growing up: "Life isn't fair." It won't be until we get to heaven.

? Read over the list of false guilts above. Can you identify with one or more of them? If so, write them down below. Do you still feel it's legitimate to feel as you do? If so, why?

_____

_____

_____

The only way to deal with false guilt is to recognize its illogical, irrational basis, shine a spotlight on its source (Satan), and ask God to remove it from you. The guilt feelings may or may not lift immediately, but keep bringing it before God and let Him take that burden off your shoulders. False guilt is not accomplishing anything. God doesn't mean for you to carry it – and *no one else* wants you to either.

2. Real Guilt

For everyone has sinned; we all fall short of God's glorious standard.

—**Romans 3:23** (NLT)

As you look back to your experiences as a first responder, you may have done some things that were real, definite, no-kiddin' sins – not like the fake ones listed above. You may have broken some of the Top Ten found in Exodus 20:1-17. You may even have broken all ten and many more. There are two bits of good news you need to hear:

1. If you are feeling guilty about *those* sins, then it's because you are currently *not* quenching the Holy Spirit; you're sensitive to His conviction – that's *good!*

2. You're not alone – *all* of us have sinned; *every one of us* has done things that have set up separations between us and God. It's a fact of the human condition. And it's fixable.

   All of us like sheep have gone astray,
   Each of us has turned to his own way;
   But the Lord has caused the iniquity of us all to fall on Him.

   —**Isaiah 53:6**

Here's where we come to the greatest transaction in history. No matter how heinous our sins are, even "red like crimson" (Isaiah 1:18) God can forgive them, and no longer hold you accountable for them – because Jesus was willing to be held accountable for them on the cross in our place. He was willing to exchange His perfect righteousness for our sins. He took them upon Himself, and then suffered the ultimate punishment for them: death. But then, to demonstrate His power over death and His eternal nature as God the Son, He rose again from the grave in strength and victory.

In order to have Jesus' sacrificial death apply to *your* sins, you need to take **two steps**:

1. Confess

As mentioned earlier, the word "confess" is from a Greek word that means "to say the same thing as." God has told you what you did wrong, as in, "John, you stole that money." You confess by saying the same thing: "Yes, it's true. I stole that money and I agree it was wrong. Please forgive me." The Bible gives us a great promise concerning this:

If we confess our sins, He is faithful and righteous to forgive us our sins and to cleanse us from all unrighteousness.

—**1 John 1:9**

Math Test. What percentage of our unrighteousness has God promised to cleanse us from if we confess our sins to Him? _____ Which leaves how much *not* taken care of? _____

Memorial Project #1

Grab a glass jar with a lid that can be screwed on tightly. Take a few minutes alone and present yourself before God. Ask Him to reveal to you any sins that are creating a separation between you and Him. Ask Him to be very specific about it. On a separate piece of paper (*not* in this manual), make a list of all the sins that He reveals to you.

When you're done with this, take your list and agree with Him regarding each thing you wrote down. When you're done, write "1 John 1:9" across the top of it in big, bold letters and numbers.

Then, take the paper and stuff it in the jar. Take it to a safe place (with no smoke alarms!) and light the paper on fire. Watch it burn and thank God as it symbolizes what He's doing to the list of sins that were being held against you.

After it's out and cooled down, screw the lid on, and put a piece of tape on the front. Write "1 John 1:9" and the date on the tape. Then put the ash jar somewhere to remind you of the "great transaction" God has accomplished for you. Whenever Satan tries to remind you of your sinfulness, bring out the "Memorial Jar" and remind *him* of what Jesus Christ did with your sins.

If you've been struggling with false guilt, write those on a list as well and burn them at the same time. Tell Satan he can't use those counterfeit accusations against you any more.

⊕　⊕　⊕　⊕　⊕

2. Repent

The word "repent" comes from the Greek word that means, "to turn around and go the other direction." While "confess" has to do with a transaction that takes place in the spiritual realm, "repent" has to do with action that needs to take place in *this* dimension. It's not enough to say, "Oops, sorry. I blew it. Forgive me," and then repeat the same act again and again. That's not true confession anyway, because if you were really agreeing with God that it was wrong, you would at least make the attempt to stop doing it.

Bottom line: God's not merely looking for your agreement with Him about your sins. He's interested in changed *action*. Your actions will validate your intentions. When this happens, it clears the way for God to bring His healing unhindered.

> *Therefore repent and return, so that your sins may be wiped away, in order that times of refreshing may come from the presence of the Lord.*
>
> **—Acts 3:19**

Confession and **repentance** won't be a once-and-for-all thing. The Memorial Jar you made commemorates a day when you drew a line in the sand and said, "From today on, I *know* that my sins are eliminated, and I am clean before God." It's going to make it a lot easier for you to do the maintenance necessary to keep Christ on the throne of your life, through regular "spiritual breathing" as needed (see page 39).

Restitution. In some cases, you may need to make restitution as part of your repentance. If you stole something, you need to return it or reimburse the victim for their loss. If you told a lie that damaged someone's reputation, you need to try to fix it. If you fathered a child through adultery, you need to support that child. If you broke a law, you may need to talk with God about turning yourself in. Forgiveness doesn't mean you are absolved of all responsibility attached to your sin. It means that it no longer separates you from God and clears the way for Him to work in your life. But part of your healing process may involve taking steps to make things right with other people.

But You Don't Know What *I've* Done...

Some people look at their sins and come to the conclusion that they are unforgivable. These poor souls live under a load of shame and self-condemnation that will eventually crush them. They're under that load *not* because God wants them there, but because their enemy does. This is "Industrial Strength False Guilt." Don't misunderstand – there is sin and therefore there is guilt, but the lie that it is *unforgivable* sin is what makes that guilt crushingly false.

To have the opinion that God is not willing or able to forgive their particular sin is a bit audacious, don't you think? How can we decide for God what He can or cannot do? In fact, we're saying that Jesus' death on the cross wasn't enough to pay for our sin. He's already told us in the Scripture at the beginning of this Step (Isaiah 1:18 - paraphrased): *"No matter how bad your sins are, I can make you pure. No matter how low you've gone, I can go there and get you."* Do you really feel tough enough to say to the Almighty God of the universe, "Oh, no, you can't!"? If so, then you've either got "Industrial Strength Courage" or "Industrial Strength Foolishness." Probably the latter.

World Record Holder

The Apostle Paul referred to himself as "chief among sinners" (1 Timothy 1:15). Here's why: Before he became a Christian, he had broken every one of the Ten Commandments – even though he was one of the greatest (non-Christian) religious leaders of the day. He threatened, chased, kidnapped, imprisoned, tortured and killed Christians, just because they were Christians. If he'd had the opportunity, he would have considered it a great honor to do the same to Jesus Christ Himself. But then he met the resurrected Christ, and everything changed. That's why he could write with confidence:

> *Because of the sacrifice of the Messiah, His blood poured out on the altar of the Cross, we're a free people—free of penalties and punishments chalked up by all our misdeeds. And not just barely free, either. Abundantly free!*

> **—Ephesians 1:7,8** (MSG)

If God could forgive Paul, the world record holder of sinners, He can certainly forgive *you!* If you haven't done the Memorial Jar exercise yet, do it now with the "unforgivable sins" that have been weighing you down. Thank Him for setting you "abundantly free!"

 Can you think of any sin that would be unforgiveable? If so, write it down here. If you aren't going through this study with a mentor of some sort, ask someone who knows God and the Bible real well if they would agree with your assessment.

_____

_____

Seeking Forgiveness From Others

Hal was surprised when he was introduced to his new partner – Gail. Although he wasn't worried about being partnered with a woman, he knew his wife wouldn't be too thrilled with it. But what could he do?

The first few weeks were strictly professional, but as the weeks turned into months and they ran out of shop-talk topics, conversations gradually drifted towards more personal areas: family, hobbies, childhood memories, future dreams. Hal was careful not to get intimate in their discussions.

The Accident

That all changed one rainy afternoon. A family – father, mother, and three kids all under the age of seven – had been T-boned by a semi. None survived the impact. The resulting carnage shook Hal to the core, haunting his dreams and his daytime thoughts. He couldn't talk to his wife about it – how could he expose her to the horrific details of body parts and the innocent, lifeless open eyes he'd encountered? His wife was a young mother herself. No, he'd just have to man up and move on. But try as he might, the images, sounds, and smells just wouldn't go away.

About three weeks later, Hal and Gail had taken a Code 7 for a quick bite to eat. Out of nowhere, she started to tear up. Initially alarmed by her distress, he inquired and quickly found it had to do with what had happened three weeks prior. The memories were eating her alive. Slipping out of the restaurant and back into their patrol unit, Gail's emotions poured out. She couldn't shake off the sadness, the images that relentlessly plagued her, the increased anxiety she now felt for her own children. It all spilled out amongst the tears and crying.

Before he realized it, Hal was pouring out his own raw emotions, identifying with the same struggles Gail had been wrestling with. He had never been so vulnerable with another person before – not even his wife.

Unintended Consequences

That was the beginning. As time went on and difficult incidents were encountered, they knew they weren't alone. There was someone there who truly understood; someone they each could talk to, laugh with, even cry with. And as the emotional barriers fell, so did the physical ones. A comforting arm around the shoulder, a brief, reassuring hug, the covert grabbing of one another's hand after experiencing something particularly disturbing. Before either of them knew it or intended it they shared the ultimate comfort and oneness found in sharing a bed.

It didn't take long for Hal's feelings of guilt to knock him for a loop. He didn't love Gail, he loved his wife and kids. But he had blown it badly. With Gail's agreement, they cut off the affair and requested different partners. But it wasn't enough for Hal. The emotional hurricane in his heart was worse than anything generated by the accident. His wife was sensing it. Hal knew he needed God's forgiveness, but also his wife's. Was that even possible?[4]

When we sin against someone, our relationship with that person suffers harm – directly proportional to the severity of the sin. Hal's betrayal of his wife pretty much buries the needle, and we don't mean to suggest that a simple request for, and granting of, forgiveness will cure *that* wound. It will take time, work, grace, mercy and the intervention of God Himself. But in addition, we also do great harm to *ourselves*. Both wounds require intentionally seeking the forgiveness of the one wounded.

For some people, the idea of admitting a wrong to another person and asking for their forgiveness would produce more anxiety than going on foot patrol through the roughest part of town in your underwear with no weapon. But Jesus makes the point that this issue is so important that you should even put worshipping God on hold until you settle things:

> *This is how I want you to conduct yourself in these matters. If you enter your place of worship and, about to make an offering, you suddenly remember a grudge a friend has against you, abandon your offering, leave immediately, go to this friend and make things right. Then and only then, come back and work things out with God.*

> **—Matthew 5:23,24** (MSG)

Here are six steps you can take to help you in the process of seeking forgiveness from another.

1. Ask God to show you who you have hurt.

Consider praying the prayer that David prayed:

> *Search me, O God, and know my heart; test me and know my anxious thoughts. Point out anything in me that offends you, and lead me along the path of everlasting life.*

> **—Psalm 139:23,24** (NLT)

If you're filled with the Holy Spirit, and if there *is* someone you've hurt, God will bring it to your mind pretty quickly. Be open to whatever He has to say to you.

 Has God brought one or more people to your mind? Write their name(s) here:

_____

2. Ask God to forgive you for the pain you inflicted

This is like a "double sin." You've sinned against the person, but also against God for breaking one of His laws. Go through the process of confession and repentance regarding this incident. Get right with God first. *[**Note:** you don't have to fire up a Memorial Jar every time you confess a sin, by the way! That was a one-time symbolic act that depicts an on-going process in your life.]*

3. Pray for the one you've hurt

If you've wounded someone either physically or emotionally, how do you think they feel toward you? You're probably not their favorite person on earth. So spend some time praying for that person, asking God to heal the wound that you caused. Ask Him to perform a miracle: that the hard feelings your wounded acquaintance probably holds toward you would be mitigated by God's supernatural love. Ask God to make a way for you to meet with him or her with a minimum of misunderstanding and vitriol. And ask God to make him or her receptive to your request for forgiveness.

4. Take the initiative and go to the one you've hurt

Here comes that walk through the rough part of town in your underwear! But God will give you the courage to do it. He'll be right by your side in this, because He will be *very* pleased about what you're doing. It'll probably start with a phone call or an email. Let them know you want to talk to them about something, and try to get an appointment with them. If you can't get face-to-face, you'll have to deal with it over the phone, but talking in person is the best way to go. They will probably know from the tone of your voice what it's about and that you feel bad about it.

 When will you take steps to contact each person whose name you wrote above?

_____

5. In humility, recount to the person what you did and ask for forgiveness

You could say something along these lines: "Joe, remember that time that…Well, I've thought a lot about what happened since then, and I want tell you that I'm sorry for what I did. I was wrong. Do you think you could forgive me?"

Don't try to put yourself in a better light, or try to explain or defend your actions. "I want you to know that the reason I said those things was because of what you said to me first." No. Now you're taking the spotlight off of *your* responsibility and pointing out theirs. That's between them and God, and you don't need to do God's job for Him. Just take responsibility for what *you* did. Go to them totally unarmed.

And don't say, "If what I did offended you, I'm sorry." No "ifs" about it. You did. God said so, and so did the damaged relationship. To say "if" is to say, "My actions may or may not have been wrong and offensive." That's no confession. You already know they were offensive.

6. Work on rebuilding trust with that person

They may or may not say they forgive you at that time. In either case, you can't expect your relationship to go immediately back to how it was before. You broke trust with that person. It's going to take some time to re-establish it. And it's going to take some initiative on your part to demonstrate that you meant what you said, and that you've changed. Ask God to give you some creative ideas about how to do that.

What are some things you could do to rebuild a person's trust in you?

_____

_____

Realistic and Unrealistic Expectations About Forgiveness

Can They Forget?

Deep hurts can rarely be wiped out of one's memory. In all likelihood, the person you wounded will always remember the wound – but they *can* look past it. Your hope is for their forgiveness, not their forgetting.

Can They Forgive?

They may not even be willing to forgive you at this point. Maybe later. But this is something you have no control over. As Nazi concentration camp survivor Simon Wiesenthal wrote, "Forgetting is something that time alone can take care of, but forgiveness is an act of volition, and only the sufferer is qualified to make the decision."[5] But if you obey God and take care of *your* obligation in this matter, it releases you from any further condemnation. You've done the right thing.

Realize that it might take the offended person a while to really forgive you from their heart. In fact, they may have to forgive you at deeper and deeper levels over a long period. Give them time, and in the interim continue to work at rebuilding trust. Don't let yourself resent the person as they slowly process your wound and confession. "Why can't they just get over this? I said I was sorry!" Healing takes time. The deeper the wound, the longer the convalescence. Whenever you start to feel impatient, just remember: You put that wound there.

Can We Be Reconciled?

You may have done your best to mend fences between you and the one you hurt, and they may have forgiven you the best they could. But that doesn't mean that the two of you are going to be best pals from now on. You can only control what happens on your side of the ledger. Keep reaching out to them in love, keep praying for them and perhaps the Lord will do a miracle.

Semi-Conclusion

In this first half of Step 6, we've learned some important principles about forgiveness – seeking it from God and seeking it from people we have hurt. In the second half of Step 6, you'll be venturing into a realm that may be one of the most difficult you've ever entered, but one that holds enormous promise. It will examine how and why we should forgive those who have harmed us. Seem ridiculous? Hold your judgment until you've seen what we – and God's Word – have to say on the subject. You may just be blown away – in a *good* sense!

·····Prayer Seed·····

Father, thank You for being willing to forgive me for my many sins. Jesus, thank You for being willing to die on the cross and experience death in my place – purchasing life for me. I can never repay you for that. You say in Your Word that even while I was still a sinner – running from You, disobeying You, with no interest in You whatsoever, You were willing to die for me.[6] Amazing! And even while belonging to You, I still sin – and You still love and forgive me, and draw me back to Yourself. I know I don't deserve it – no one does. That's what makes Your gift so incredible. Thank you. Father, give me the courage I'll need to seek forgiveness from others whom I have hurt in the past. Give me grace and favor in their eyes. Help me rebuild their trust. Amen.

---

1. Fictitious story from Michael Anderson based on actual events. Mike is a 35-year firefighter/paramedic, having served in Eugene, Coos Bay, Florence and Albany, Oregon. He also served four years as a police officer and four years with the Navy.

2. Fictitious story from Terry Bratton based on actual events. Terry is a 39-year Houston (TX) Police Department veteran.

3. Dr. Aphrodite Matsakis, in her book *Trust After Trauma* (New Harbinger, 1998) has an excellent section that goes into great detail about these different types of false guilt, and offers exercises that will help a PTSD sufferer recognize them as false guilt and be released from their influence. Chapter 6 on "Guilt," pages 164-180.

4. Fictitious story from Chaplain Bret Truax based on actual events. Brett is a 55 year old pastor who has served throughout the Midwest and who currently serves in Salem, Oregon. He also is a nine-year volunteer law enforcement chaplain with various agencies in Michigan and Colorado.

5. Quote by Simon Wiesenthal, survivor of Nazi concentration camp in Lemberg, Poland, from his book *The Sunflower*. Quoted by Os Guinness in Unspeakable (HarperCollins, 2005), page 172.

6. Romans 5:6-8.

Step 6B How Do I Move On?

...Forgiveness Received and Given

[This is the second of two parts.]

In Step 6A we studied two important aspects of forgiveness: accepting God's forgiveness and seeking forgiveness from those we have hurt. There is one more major component to this study that needs to be considered...

Forgiving Those Who Have Wounded You

Trust is a rare commodity, but essential between first responders who work together. You need to know that your partner has your back at all times and that you can depend on him or her no matter what. If that trust is broken, it's very difficult to repair it.

Sam and William met at fire academy. They became fast friends – helping each other study, pushing each other to their limits in the physical training elements, cheering on each other's successes.

Upon graduation they were fortunate enough to be picked up by the same municipality. They continued and deepened their mutually-beneficial friendship, each helping the other make it through the critical calls and the daily shift routine.

As time went on, promotions were in order. Both made engineer, but before long William moved on to officer level.

Soon after, changes crept into their relationship. Sam found himself assigned by William to other stations, which meant they were no longer working together. Their families socialized less and less. When they did happen to be at the same event, Sam picked up that William was uncomfortable talking with him. His responses to Sam's friendly banter were clipped and cold, and he'd find any excuse to end the conversation and leave.

It depressed Sam that he had apparently lost his best friend and partner for reasons that were not clear. His career had lost the excitement it once had. It began to effect his home life as well – the warmth between Sam and his wife was fading, arguments spun up quickly, hurtful words spilled out too often.

"I guess this is just part of life," Sam thought one day. "Nothing stays the same. People change. Situations change. No big deal. Just need to roll with the punches and move on."

If only it had been that simple. Sam's world came crashing down the night his wife announced to him that she was having an affair with William. She would be moving out that weekend while he was on shift.

Betrayed by the two most important people in his life. Anger crowded out every other emotion Sam had, and a sense of helplessness began to overwhelm him.

"Trust?" Sam thought. "I'll never trust anyone again." This became a major theme in Sam's life. Forgiveness was not even on his radar screen.[1]

Sam tells you his story, then says, "What do you think? Got any advice for me?" What would you say?

_____

_____

_____

Definition

What does it mean to forgive someone who has brought crippling pain, trauma and difficulty into your life? The Greek (Biblical) word for "forgive" is *aphiemi,* which means "to release or set free." Here are some of the components of The International Forgiveness Institute's definition:[2]

- A merciful response to a moral injustice.

- The foregoing of resentment or revenge when the wrongdoer's actions deserve it and giving the gifts of mercy, generosity and love when the wrongdoer does not deserve them.

- A freely chosen gift (rather than a grim obligation).

- The overcoming of wrongdoing with good.

Think you can do that? Set somebody free who deserves punishment? If we're honest, the first response from most of us would be "No" – especially if you are an LEO whose full-time *job* is to make sure that those who deserve punishment receive it. The notion of forgiveness seems to negate justice, fairness and righteousness and to give a pass to those who break the laws of God and man. The fact is it will take a miracle in the hearts of any of us to choose the route of forgiving. Good news: we belong to a miracle-working God!

 "Fight fire with fire." You've heard that one before, right? Before reading any further, write down whether or not you agree with that philosophy and why.

_____

_____

It probably depends on what real-life scenario you're applying it to. In wildland firefighting, strategically placed back-fires rob a larger, advancing fire of fuel and bring it under control. Law enforcement officers fight fire with fire all the time. For instance, if a criminal with a gun is barricaded in a house with a hostage, match him with a SWAT team, snipers, stun grenades and semi-autos. Meet force with force – it's the only language aggressors seem to understand. If we back off, the bad guys often fill the vacuum and evil triumphs.

But when it comes to interpersonal relationships, it does not apply. Fighting fire with fire only yields more fire.

"I don't get mad, I get even."

"Go ahead, make my day."

"Do ya feel lucky, punk? Well, do ya?"

I know, I know. Those lines *do* get the adrenalin pumping in many of us who like action movies. And they may suggest an appropriate philosophy when dealing with an armed criminal, bully or terrorist (as long as you have superior firepower!). But in the unarmed world of normal human interaction it leads to needless escalation of tension and no resolution of the problem. And it makes things worse for you.

What alternative strategy does the Bible give us?

Do not be overcome by evil, but overcome evil with good.

—Romans 12:21

Setting backfires is an effective firefighting technique only under certain conditions. Firefighters generally prefer to use a substance that is the *opposite* of fire: *water.* "Put the wet stuff on the hot stuff." That principle holds true here. If there's enough of it, water always puts out most kinds of fires. Likewise, if there is enough *good* and it's empowered by the Spirit of God – it is always going to be stronger than evil.

> Darkness cannot drive out darkness; only light can do that.
> Hate cannot drive out hate; only love can do that.

> —Dr. Martin Luther King, Jr.

⊕   ⊕   ⊕   ⊕   ⊕

Against a simplistic approach...

There are different "intensities" of harm and woundings, and therefore different intensities of forgiveness required. When Sally makes a snide comment about how frumpy Janie looks in her new dress, that's one level. But the intensities take several quantum leaps when the offending incident involves a gang-banger who ambushes an undercover cop in downtown Los Angeles, severely wounding his leg – which leads to an amputation. And in the same ambush his partner is shot and dies. How easily will the ability to forgive come to that cop?

The truths contained in this Step are foundational in helping a first responder work through forgiveness issues attached to *that* level of pain and trauma. But the process might be augmented with the help of a PTSD support group or trained Christian therapist who can facilitate a deep-valley walk for him and Jesus Christ. In Step 9 we'll be giving you some input regarding how to seek out "bridge people" who could assist in this.

⊕   ⊕   ⊕   ⊕   ⊕

What Forgiveness is NOT

1. Exoneration

When someone breaks the law, they need to be brought under the corrective actions of the state – for the victim's, the public's, and their own good. Law-breaking has consequences. This Step isn't about letting criminals skate free, but about how to keep those who harm you personally from dragging you down.

2. Forgetting

Deep hurts can rarely be wiped out of one's awareness. We can't just make-believe that the evil never happened. Forgiveness isn't a plastering over of wrong. Forgive and *forget?* Won't happen.

3. Reconciliation

Reconciliation requires agreement between two parties. An injured party can forgive an offender without reconciliation. You can only control what happens on your side of the ledger.

4. Agreeing with your abuser

"If I don't take the opportunity to even the score, I'm letting them get away with their abuse." Forgiving isn't a sign that they've won, it's a sign that they're *wrong,* and you've finally figured it out.

5. Dismissing

It isn't trivializing the wrong, it's canceling the debt that is owed because of the wrong. When Jesus forgave us, it wasn't a simple dismissal of all charges. It was a very expensive transaction that cost the Forgiver far more than it cost us who were being forgiven. He paid *our* debt.

6. Pardoning

A pardon is a legal transaction that releases an offender from the consequences of an action. Forgiveness is a personal transaction that releases the one offended (you) from the on-going torment of the offense.

7. Emotion

A loss of anxiety and gaining of joy may or may not be immediate products of forgiveness. Over time most people see this change, but it's not automatic.

8. Justice

Justice involves reciprocity of some kind – reaping what one sowed. Forgiveness is an unconditional gift given to somebody who does not deserve it. That's not just, that's loving.

Why Forgive Those Who Have Wounded Me?

1. For your own good

Poison oak thrives in the Pacific Northwest. If you don't deal with it, it will take over acres of fields and forests, making it virtually impossible to enjoy that land. No picnics, no football games, no hide-and-seek – you dare not even walk through it without long pants on. Mowing it down won't help, because as long as its roots are left in the ground, it will always come back within a few months, stronger and more widespread than ever.

That's the spiritual target of this passage of Scripture:

> *Look after each other so that none of you fails to receive the grace of God. Watch out that no poisonous root of bitterness grows up to trouble you, corrupting many.*
>
> **—Hebrews 12:15** (NLT)

> "Not forgiving is like drinking rat poison and then waiting for the rat to die."[3]
>
> —Anne Lamott

When we have been wounded in some way and feel helpless against the consequences, conditions are ideal for bitterness to grow. Our hatred for our attacker deepens, our frustration mounts, which makes us more angry and hate-filled, until finally nobody wants to be around us anymore. The bitterness spreads, just like the poison oak. The irony is that all this anger and poison does absolutely nothing to the guilty one – only to the one who was wounded. It makes him or her worse and worse.

Christian educator, counselor and behaviorist Dr. Bill Gothard says,

> In our counseling of troubled youth nowadays, we initially don't even bother about most of the other issues. The first thing we do now is to look for a root of bitterness in the person. In 90% of the cases, we find that's the primary reason the person is having psychological, emotional or spiritual problems.[4]

The only way to deal with bitterness is to pull out its root – and that can only be done by forgiving the offender. When we remove that poisonous root with God's help, the useless escalation of hatred and anger toward our offender stops, allowing us to move on to more constructive pursuits.

Spend a few minutes alone in prayer. Ask God to reveal to you whether or not you are harboring a "root of bitterness" in your heart toward someone who hurt you and has contributed to your PTSD. If the answer is "yes," ask Him to let you know what you can do about it. Then keep your spiritual ears open. He may give you an immediate answer, or the solution may become apparent over the next few days or weeks. Once you have an action plan from God about this, write it down here:

_____

_____

_____

2. It's a God-like Characteristic

We are sons and daughters of a forgiving God. His desire is that we grow up to be like Him.

He has not dealt with us according to our sins, nor rewarded us according to our iniquities. For as high as the heavens are above the earth, so great is His lovingkindness toward those who fear Him.

—Psalm 103:10,11

The main point here is that God doesn't treat us the way we deserve. He forgives. When you forgive, you're acting like God. The next time you decide to demand your rights, realize that you *really don't want* your rights. If you got your rights, you'd be in hell today! Instead, God is asking us to do for others what He has done for us: not count their sins against them:

God was reconciling the world to himself in Christ, not counting people's sins against them. And He has committed to us the message of reconciliation.

—2 Corinthians 5:19(NIV)

 The fact that you may feel deep anger toward someone who has caused you great pain is perfectly understandable. How do you think Sam felt toward William in this Step's opening story? You probably wonder, "Why should they suffer no negative consequences when I have suffered so greatly?" When you consider forgiving that person, how hard do you think it will be? Put an X on the line:

Piece of cake. I could do it easily.										Absolutely, positively impossible.
1	2	3	4	5	6	7	8	9	10	

What is your level of confidence that God can perform a miracle in your heart and enable you to forgive your attacker(s)?

I'm absolutely confident that He can do this.										Absolutely no way ever.
1	2	3	4	5	6	7	8	9	10	

Prayer Assignment

We weren't kidding when we said it may take a miracle for you to come to the point of being able to forgive the ones who have hurt you. This level of love and mercy is indeed "supernatural". If you placed your X's toward the "10" end of the two scales above, begin asking God for that miracle. You won't be able to generate it on your own – but He can build it into you, if you're open to it.

3. It's a Christ-like Characteristic

The most monstrous, unjust wounding in history occurred when the sinless Son of God was crucified by brutal Roman soldiers at the behest of corrupt Jewish leaders. The ironic thing is that Jesus could have ended the procedure at any time by calling in His Quick Response Team of 10,000 angels – but He was willing to go through it for our sakes. During that six-hour period of agony on the cross while He was waiting to die, He made this incredible request of His heavenly Father:

Father, forgive them; for they do not know what they are doing.

—Luke 23:34

Rather than demand justice, He extended mercy to his killers. That's supernatural.

A few months later, one of Jesus' disciples named Stephen was being stoned for being a Christ-follower (Acts 7). His final words as his body was being crushed by the stones was, *"Lord, do not hold this sin against them!"* He released his killers from their penalty before him and before God – just as Jesus did. It's interesting to note that one of those released was young Saul of Tarsus – the famous Christian Killer – who eventually was transformed into the Apostle Paul, one of the greatest Christians ever. This is the effect we have on the world around us when we act like Christ.

4. Unforgiveness blocks God's blessings to you

What did Jesus Christ say we should do when others have harmed us?

Forgive us our sins, as we have forgiven those who sin against us.

—Matthew 6:12 (NLT)

He presupposes that we would forgive them. And why would we want to do this? Two verses later, Jesus shares a rather disturbing commentary on what He just said:

If you forgive those who sin against you, your heavenly Father will forgive you. But if you refuse to forgive others, your Father will not forgive your sins.

—Matthew 6:14,15 (NLT)

We humans – not just LEOs, but *all* of us – are big on justice, aren't we? Especially when *we're* the ones who have suffered injustice. We generally think, "Lord, forgive me my debts… but as for those who owe debts to me – *whack 'em!"* We prefer to receive grace, but everybody else should have judgment. That would definitely qualify as hypocrisy.

God wants us to apply the same standards to others that we expect from Him. He wants us to be like Him. When we are, it facilitates His blessings to us. When we aren't, it staunches the flow of His grace and mercy to us. Again – it doesn't affect our standing with Him or our eternal destination. But as far as what God wants to do in and through us, we're going to be stuck here for a while.

 Do you feel you are being blocked from some of God's blessings right now? If so, describe what you feel you're missing as best you can.

_____

_____

_____

Do you think it's possible they are being blocked because of unforgiveness in your heart?

_____

⊕ ⊕ ⊕ ⊕ ⊕

5. It allows God to bring perfect justice

Never take your own revenge, beloved, but leave room for the wrath of God, for it is written, "Vengeance is Mine, I will repay, says the Lord.

—Romans 12:19

The Bible is full of laws. Jewish scholars count 613 commandments in the Old Testament. A great number of them have to do with penalties imposed when one person does something wrong to another person. They address murder, rape, assault, theft – all the usual issues. These are meant to be universal standards for all the kingdoms of earth.

When you are the victim of someone breaking those laws, God has given you a legal, moral, and civic right to expect the appropriate punishment to be administered to the perpetrator. They owe you. You are in a position of superiority. You are due your pound of flesh.

A Different Way

But then Jesus Christ steps in and says, in effect, "That's all true. But in My kingdom, we do things differently. You have been sinned against, and you are entitled to justice. But how would you like it if I take care of it personally? If you'll step aside, give up your right to restitution and vengeance, and let Me handle it, I'll take care of you and your abuser *perfectly.* Vengeance is Mine, I will repay. But I'll do it in a way that will free you of your bitterness, bring your abuser to justice, and move *both* of you closer to My righteousness. So what do you say?"

This is what happened when Stephen asked God to release his executioners from the penalty of their murderous sin. Stephen stepped aside. At that moment, heaven went into action for Saul of Tarsus and Jesus Christ dealt directly with the Christian Killer. (Extra Credit: read about it in Acts 9:1-22). For Saul, it involved punishment, condemnation, pain, guilt, torment and probably intense fear for his eternal future. But in the end, Stephen gets heaven (not a bad deal!) and an entire chapter-and-a-half in the Word of God (Acts 6&7), and Saul gets transformed into the greatest missionary for Christ in history: Paul. Stephen wins, Saul wins, and the Kingdom of God wins. That is an *exceptionally* good outcome!

[?] When the Apostle Paul finally died and entered heaven, how do you think Stephen greeted him – his murderer? Imagine their reunion and describe it as best you can.

_____

_____

_____

_____

_____

_____

⊕ ⊕ ⊕ ⊕ ⊕

How Do I Forgive Those Who Have Wounded Me?

1. Ask God to give you His supernatural mindset for this

Satan wants you to add more fire to the fire. We often go along with that because of our desire for vengeance – whatever the cost. Here's our natural mindset, which Satan encourages:

- I'm hurt,

- He's hurt,

- Nobody wins,

- But at least the score's even.

But as you read earlier in this Step, the Bible says that – rather than fighting fire with fire – the best way to overcome evil is with good (Romans 12:21). By making the decision to forgive, you are not condoning their sin. You are not minimizing what happened to you. You're making a direct assault against your true enemy (Satan) who will use your bitterness and righteous indignation to destroy you.

> "There is no revenge so complete as forgiveness."
>
> —Henry Wheeler Shaw

Your mindset needs to become: "I know there is evil here, and I choose to break the cycle of pain and violence. Rather than add to the evil, I will contain it, starve it out, and kill it – with good." God can give you that heart.

2. Make a list of your points of pain and trauma, and who caused each one

If you don't know their name, just describe them ("That dude that threw the brick off the bridge and shattered my windshield."). Make this list on a separate sheet of paper – not in this manual. Put *all* those points of pain down – not just the big ones. Don't say, "Oh, it doesn't matter. That wasn't really *that* big a deal." It may take you a while to accomplish this step, but that's okay. It's important.

3. Make an act-of-your-will pronouncement of forgiveness for each person

This is an act of obedience, and may or may not involve your emotions. You might pray something like this:

> "Lord, as an act of obedience I choose to forgive _____. I don't feel like it, but I love You, and I know You love me, and I want to obey You. So I hereby release _____ from my judgment. Forgive me that I may have hindered Your work in me and in him/her by my unforgiveness. Now I step out of the way so that You can go into action for _____ and for me."

It's best to pray this prayer out loud, rather than to just think it silently. Your spoken words have unique power.

4. Stop at difficult places and ask God what He wants you to do

Like what? It's hard to say. That will depend on what's in your heart and in your past. God will work uniquely with each person, according to what they need. He may want you to go and talk to somebody, write a letter, go back to "the scene of the crime," deal with something in your heart … Just keep your ears open and be willing to do as He directs. It will be for your *good*.

5. Begin to act toward your offender the way Jesus said to

But I say to you who hear, love your enemies, do good to those who hate you, bless those who curse you, pray for those who mistreat you… Love your enemies, and do good, and lend, expecting nothing in return; and your reward will be great, and you will be sons of the Most High; for He Himself is kind to ungrateful and evil men.

—Luke 6:27,28,35

When you come to the point that you can do what Jesus has directed in the above Scripture, you can know that you are really beginning to forgive someone. It's not an easy process. The following graphic demonstrates that the path to forgiving is uphill, difficult and involves a series of choices – it's not a one-shot deal. To follow our natural reactive tendencies is easy: downhill all the way.[5]

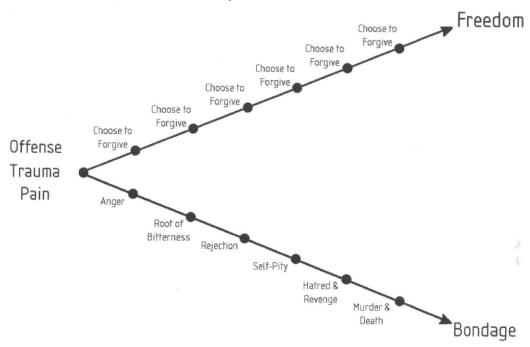

6. Make a memorial of remembrance

Memorial Project #2

This will be very similar to the Memorial Jar you made in Step 6A. Except this time, rather than enumerating and destroying *your* list of sins, you'll be destroying the list of sins of others against you.

When you feel you have worked through the list that you made in Point #2 above and have followed the directions in Point #3 about pronouncing forgiveness, it's time to offer up that list as a sacrifice to God.

Across the top of the list, write "Forgiven – Romans 12:21." That's the verse about overcoming evil with good.

Just like before, stuff the paper in a jar and burn it. As it burns, think about how you are releasing these people to God, asking Him to go into action for them as He sees fit. Also, thank Him for releasing *you* from the bondage of your unforgiveness.

When the jar is cool, put a piece of masking tape on the bottle and write "Romans 12:21" and the date on it. Screw the lid on with the ashes inside and set this Memorial Jar next to your first one. Whenever the anger starts to well up inside you again, and your thirst for vengeance starts to strengthen, take the jar out and remember the day you released your abusers – and yourself – from bondage through forgiveness.

If you find that difficult, pick up Jar #1, and remember what God did for you.

✠   ✠   ✠   ✠   ✠

Think again

Go back and re-read what you wrote at the bottom of the second page of this Step (page 92) where you were asked what kind of advice you might offer Sam after he had been betrayed by his wife and his best friend. After having worked through this Step, would you change your answer at all? If so, what would you tell him now?

_____

_____

_____

_____

⊕　　⊕　　⊕　　⊕　　⊕

Prayer Seed

Father, I have been deeply wronged and hurt. Everything within me cries out for justice and retribution. Your Word says I should be forgiving, but I find it difficult. In my own strength, I cannot do it. That's why I'm asking you to perform the miracles in my heart that will be necessary to accomplish this. Fill me with Your Spirit and supply in me that which I do not have right now. You were willing to forgive all of my offenses against You. Give me a heart to do the same for those who have sinned against me. Show me what it's like to be free of the bondage of unforgiveness. Amen.

1. Story from Michael Anderson, 35-year firefighter and paramedic in Eugene, Coos Bay, Florence and Albany, Oregon. Also served four years as a police officer and four years with the Navy.

2. From the International Forgiveness Institute's "About Forgiveness" page on their website: www.forgiveness-institute.org.

3. Anne Lamott, *Traveling Mercies: Some Thoughts on Faith* (NY: Pantheon Books, 1999).

4. Shared during an informal talk by Dr. Gothard at Campus Crusade for Christ headquarters in Orlando, FL at a "Prayer and Fasting Summit" in 1995. Dr. Gothard is the Founder and retired President of the Institute in Basic Life Principles in Oak Brook, IL. www.iblp.org.

5. Original illustration by Wanda Fisher, *Finally Free* (Eugene, OR: Pine Hill Graphics, 2011). p 41. Used by permission.

Step **7** # Who Am I Now?
...Rebuilding Your Identity

During World War II, a near-disastrous incident occurred off the coast of Newfoundland. A US Navy destroyer was operating without running lights and under radio silence, because they'd received intelligence that a German sub had been prowling that area. They also knew there were other allied ships nearby, so they had to exercise caution navigating on that moonless night.

Around 0100 hours, the ship's captain saw some small lights directly ahead. Due to the elevation of the lights, he knew it couldn't be the sub, so he directed his signalman to send the following flashing light message to alert the other vessel that they were on a collision course.

"Advise you to alter course ten degrees west."

Right away, they received this message back. "Negative. Advise you to alter course ten degrees east."

Now, very few commanding officers like to be countermanded. So he ordered his next message with a little pepper: "I am a US Navy Commander. Alter your course ten degrees west."

"I am a Lieutenant. Alter your course ten degrees east."

The captain was fit to be tied. The air turned blue in the wheelhouse and the captain ordered this final message be sent: "I am a US Navy destroyer. Alter your course ten degrees west or else!"

In a few moments came this final response: "I am a lighthouse. Your call."

Perception and Self-Perception

We don't usually think very deeply about who or what we are or how other people see us. But as the above story illustrates, our identity is extremely important – not something that either we or those around us should be confused about. It is crucial that both perception and self-perception is accurate. Not many things deter a destroyer, but going head-to-head with a lighthouse is a really bad idea.

Trauma and Identity

When a person experiences severe trauma or long-term stress, their self-perception is often shaken to the core. While they used to see themselves as rational, self-sufficient, adaptive, strong and worthy, *that* destroyer was torpedoed. Those characteristics are replaced by feelings of fear, confusion, powerlessness and helplessness. And that's not all. As trauma and victimization authority Dr. Ronnie Janoff-Bulman writes:

> In addition, victims are apt to experience a sense of deviance. After all, they have been singled
> out for misfortune and this establishes them as different from other people. This self-perception
> of deviance no doubt serves to reinforce negative images of oneself as unworthy and weak.[1]

The effects of this negative transformation of your self-image don't remain in the psychological realm. They bleed into your behavior too – your plans, activities, priorities, reactions, values, hopes, dreams, ambition, social interaction ... the list goes on and on. Pastor, educator, counselor and spiritual warfare expert Dr. Neil Anderson states:

> No person can consistently behave in a manner that is inconsistent with the way he sees himself.[2]

It can't be done. You can't hold one set of opinions about yourself and try to live according to a different set. You may succeed for a while, but the energy required to keep up that front is enormous. Eventually exhaustion sets in, the mask comes off and meltdown occurs. No matter how emphatically you command that lighthouse to move, it won't. And unless you alter *your* course, you'll end up wrecked on the shoals.

While trauma started your self-identity ball rolling downhill, there are three other factors that keep it rolling and spin it faster: Satan, the world around you, and negative self-talk.

Self-Perception Assessment

Dr. Steven Stosney,[3] an international authority on trauma and victimization, has developed a very useful template that will help assess your current self-perception – how positively or negatively you view yourself. Dr. Stosney's normal approach goes much deeper than we'll be able to apply in this manual, but some of the components will be very useful here. There are eight dynamics of self-perception listed below – the positive side on the left and the negative side on the right. Place an "X" somewhere on the line that indicates how you currently see yourself.

Regarded. . . . . Disregarded
Important . . . . Unimportant
Forgiven . . . . Accused/Guilty
Valued . . . . Devalued
Accepted. . . . . Rejected
Powerful . . . . Powerless
Lovable. . . . . Unlovable
Connected. . . . . Separated

Obviously, your adversaries want your "Xs" as far to the right side as possible, which keeps you in a vulnerable position. If that's where they are at this point, it's because you have been fed compromised intelligence that has no credible independent verification – in other words **LIES!** Here's what the Son of God says about Satan:

He was a murderer from the beginning, not holding to the truth, for there is no truth in him.
When he lies, he speaks his native language, for he is a liar and the father of lies.

—John 8:44 (NIV)

At this moment, you are probably not being shot at, but you *are* in a war. And as the great Chinese warrior Sun Tzu wrote, *"All warfare is based on deception."* Satan has been honing his undercover tactics for thousands of years. He and his network of minions have been observing you since you were a kid, and they know just what to say and how to say it to deceive with maximum effect. Their objective is your destruction, which will diminish the Kingdom of God and grieve the great heart of the King.

Exposing Your Enemy's Deception

In this Step, we're going to expose as many of Satan's lies as we can. When deception is exposed, it gives an advantage to the previously deceived. We want you to be able to say with the Apostle Paul, "We are not ignorant of his schemes." (2 Corinthians 2:11) This is most definitely "actionable intelligence."

These lies were spawned by Satan himself. He'll whisper them in your subconscious at your most vulnerable moments. You'll be reminded of incidents in your childhood that validate them. He'll contextualize them in your traumatic events. He'll reinforce them with messages bombarding you from the world system that surrounds you. He'll be sure you're listening when your friends mimic and verify them accidentally or on purpose. And before long, he'll have you telling *yourself* the lies. And we all know how closely we listen to our own opinions.

Following are **eight deceptive traps** Satan and the world have laid for you. Consider whether or not you've heard them before. Each lie will be followed by the countering **TRUTH** that God wants you to hear.

Deception #1: Disregarded

Lies of the enemy:

- You are a nobody.
- No one cares about you. Why should they?
- No one wants to know you.
- You don't deserve the respect that others get.
- You are *such* a jerk.
- Who do you think you are, anyway?

Have you heard any of those comments before? Have you made them to yourself? Maybe those exact words weren't used, but after their world has been turned upside down, many trauma victims hear and swallow that devilish sentiment. "You've proven to be someone who should and must be disregarded." You hear that, you look at your situation, you look at how people respond to you, you consider your own "deviancy" and you resign yourself to the "truth" of those lies.

Spiritual explosive devices

To be effective, every lie must have an element of truth. No good deception ever *looks* like a deception. It must appear plausible, rational and believable. The explosive devices used by terrorists that are so hellishly effective at wounding and killing so many look harmless: a backpack, a parked van, a trashcan. That's why they work. And if we don't have some information to the contrary, we assume that the lies we perceive are the truth.

Well, God wants to give you *true* information that counters Satan's deceptions. Your stress and trauma *have* changed you – that's the kernel of truth. But to say, "Because I've changed and I'm not functioning as I used to, I am worthy of disregard" is an absolute lie and needs to be opposed by God's truth.

Not only is God's Word *true*, it is *living and active* according to Hebrews 4:12. That means that it's not just words that some ancient prophet scribbled on papyrus twenty or thirty centuries ago. It continues to be vitally relevant and applicable today. As you read those words, and as the Holy Spirit energizes and breathes life into them, they become the words of God being spoken directly to *you*, right here in the twenty-first century.

The above facts hold true for all eight of the lie-countering truths that we'll be examining below…

Your TRUE Identity: REGARDED

After each verse, answer the questions which highlight who you *really* are.

> *[Jesus speaking:] I no longer call you servants, because a servant does not know his master's business. Instead, I have called you friends, for everything that I learned from My Father I have made known to you.*
>
> **—John 15:15** (NIV)

Jesus Christ, the Son of God, calls you His _____

> *So now Jesus and the ones He makes holy have the same Father. That is why Jesus is not ashamed to call them His brothers and sisters.*
>
> **—Hebrews 2:11** (NLT)

Jesus Christ is not ashamed to call you His _____

> *Even before He made the world, God loved us and chose us in Christ to be holy and without fault in His eyes.*
>
> **—Ephesians 1:4** (NLT)

How long ago were you known, loved and chosen by God? _____

> *Now you are no longer a slave but God's own child. And since you are His child, God has made you His heir.*
>
> **—Galatians 4:7** (NLT)

You are God's child and also His _____

These Scriptures describe *you* as a friend, brother (or sister), child and heir of the King of the Universe! He has had plans for you even since before He created Adam and Eve. And you can be sure He's *really* excited that you finally showed up! In God's opinion, you are *loved* and ***highly regarded!***

Deception #2: Unimportant

Lies of the enemy:

- Your input is unnecessary.
- You're a little fish in a big pond.
- Go sit on the sidelines.
- Don't call us, we'll call you.
- What have you *ever* accomplished?

Your TRUE Identity: IMPORTANT

After each verse, answer the questions which demonstrate who you *really* are.

> *But as many as received Him, to them He gave the right to become children of God, even to those who believe in His name.*
>
> **—John 1:12**

Since you have received Christ, you have rightly been named as what? _____

When you consider all of eternity and all the other animals and angels that God created that are *not* considered His children, how important would you say it is to be called a child of God?

_____

> *You're here to be salt-seasoning that brings out the God-flavors of this earth.*
>
> **—Matthew 5:13** (MSG)

God has made you His *what* on the earth? _____

What do you think that means? _____

> *You're here to be light, bringing out the God-colors in the world.*
>
> **—Matthew 5:14** (MSG)

God has made you His *what* in the world? _____

In what ways can we be "light?" _____

_____

For God so loved the world, that He gave His only begotten Son, that whoever believes in Him shall not perish, but have eternal life.

—John 3:16

What kind of life have you been given? _____

How significant do you think it is to be an eternal being? _____

Not only do you hold important positions as an eternal child of God, His seasoning and His light, you have been trained and qualified for unique future leadership in Christ's Kingdom on earth. He was wounded, and all those who follow Him also receive wounds, as you have. Down through the ages, the men and women who were significantly used by God were wounded in some severe way. You've been through the refiner's fire. There are evil forces doing their best to propel our cities and towns into chaos. The Bible predicts that in the end times society will crumble and treacherous times will ensue – and those times may be very close. Who better to lead us through those traumatic times than someone like you? As a first responder, you have been to hell and back. It is hated but familiar territory for you. You're *important* now. But as you are more fully restored to health and the "chaos factors" in our society ramp up, you will prove to be *increasingly valuable*.

Deception #3: Accused/Guilty

Lies of the enemy:

- You really blew it.
- You're unforgivable.
- You need to be punished.
- You can't be trusted.
- Everyone knows what a hypocrite you are.

Your TRUE Identity: FORGIVEN

 We've already spent an entire Step (6A) on this subject, but a little more input shouldn't hurt. After each verse, write what each says about who you *really* are.

Therefore there is now no condemnation for those who are in Christ Jesus.

—Romans 8:1

Assuming you're a Christian, what will you *not* experience? _____

Therefore, having been justified by faith, we have peace with God through our Lord Jesus Christ.

—Romans 5:1

What happened to you by faith? (Hint: the word means "declared not guilty.")_____

So you are no longer at war with God, now you have peace with Him. The war is over. You and God are no longer enemies. Your crimes are no longer being held against you.

Their sins and lawless acts I will remember no more.

—Hebrews 10:17 (NIV)

What does God think about your sins and lawless acts? (watch it – trick question!)

Deception #4: Devalued

Lies of the enemy:

- We don't need you.

- You're not good enough.

- You don't have what it takes; you're worthless.

- You really *suck!*

Your TRUE Identity: VALUED

After each verse, observe why your true designation is "Valued By God":

The Lord appeared to us in the past, saying:

> *"I have loved you with an everlasting love; I have drawn you with unfailing kindness."*

> **—Jeremiah 31:3 (NIV)**

Who loves ya, baby? ＿＿＿＿＿＿ How long has this been going on? ＿＿＿＿＿＿＿＿＿＿＿

How valuable do you think being loved eternally by God and wooed into an everlasting love relationship with Him makes you?

＿＿＿

> *Don't you realize that your body is the temple of the Holy Spirit, who lives in you and was given to you by God? You do not belong to yourself, for God bought you with a high price. So you must honor God with your body.*

> **—1 Corinthians 6:19, 20 (NLT)**

What has your physical body become? ＿＿＿＿＿＿＿＿＿＿＿＿＿＿＿＿＿＿＿＿＿＿＿＿

When Israel was strong, and before Christ came, the Temple in Jerusalem was the one place on earth where God was manifested and represented. It was the most magnificent and expensive building on the planet at the time for that reason. Since Christ's resurrection, *we* have become the Temple of God. Now *we* are where God is manifested and represented. Valuable or not valuable?

＿＿＿

Additionally, this verse says we were bought with a high price. What was the price that God the Father paid to buy us?

＿＿＿

> *For God knew His people in advance, and He chose them to become like His Son, so that His Son would be the firstborn among many brothers and sisters. And having chosen them, He called them to come to Him. And having called them, He **gave** them right standing with Himself. And having given them right standing, He gave them His glory.*

> **—Romans 8:29,30 (NLT)**

So, we were known by God, chosen by Him to become like Jesus Christ, called by God to come to Him, given right standing with Him, and finally given *what*?

＿＿＿

Conquering generals are given glory by their countries. How valuable, then, is glory given by God?

Deception #5: Rejected

Lies of the enemy:

- You're a failure.
- You're such a loser.
- No one wants you.
- You're not qualified.
- Everyone else is better than you.

Your TRUE Identity: ACCEPTED

After each verse, observe why your true designation is "Accepted By God":

> *To the praise of the glory of His grace, by which He made us accepted in the Beloved.*
>
> **—Ephesians 1:6 (NKJV)**

God's grace made you *what* in the Beloved (Christ)? _____

> *As you come to Him, the living Stone – rejected by men but chosen by God and precious to Him – you also, like living stones, are being built into a spiritual house to be a holy priesthood, offering spiritual sacrifices acceptable to God through Jesus Christ.*
>
> **—1 Peter 2:4,5 (NIV)**

The "living Stone" is Jesus Christ, who was rejected by mankind (when He was crucified), but always chosen and precious to the Father. In the same way, you were selected by the Master Stonemason to be part of His spiritual construction, and you are therefore shown to be *what* to God through Jesus Christ?

> *Let us therefore come boldly to the throne of grace, that we may obtain mercy and find grace to help in time of need.*
>
> **—Hebrews 4:16 (NKJV)**

How are we allowed to approach God's throne of grace? _____

Would this indicate that we are *barely* acceptable or *totally* acceptable to God? *(Circle one.)*

Deception #6: Powerless

Lies of the enemy:

- You are weak.
- You are damaged goods.
- Can't you do *anything* right?
- How helpless can one person be?
- Someone's always got to take care of you.

Your TRUE Identity: POWERFUL

After each verse, answer the questions which indicate your power as a son or daughter of the King.

For God has not given us a spirit of fear, but of power and of love and of a sound mind.

—2 Timothy 1:7 (NKJV)

What kind of a "spirit" has God given us? _____

You are from God, little children, and have overcome them; because greater is He who is in you than he who is in the world.

—1 John 4:4

"*He who is in the world*" refers to Satan and his allies. Between us (plus God) and them, which one is the more powerful?

_____

_____

For everyone born of God overcomes the world. This is the victory that has overcome the world, even our faith. Who is it that overcomes the world? Only the One who believes that Jesus is the Son of God.

—1 John 5:4,5 (NIV)

As a Christian, you are "born of God." "The world" referred to is the world system that is ruled over by Satan. When you and the world mix it up, who has the power to win?

_____

If you are currently suffering from PTSD, you probably don't *feel* particularly "powerful." You may still be nursing physical injuries. You may feel powerless to accomplish basic goals, control your anger, sleep, and conquer your depression. But your weakness is only temporary. When Jesus was taken into custody, flogged, tortured and crucified, He seemed *very* weak. But it was only temporary. In fact, He had massive *latent* power during that entire ordeal. The power was there, just not being used – and for good reasons. You have that same latent power, but the odds are good that it's not being used for *no* good reason!

Prayer Assignment:

Begin asking God to help you release the latent power that He has placed within you. He wants to! Just ask Him!

⊕   ⊕   ⊕   ⊕   ⊕

Deception #7: Unlovable

Lies of the enemy:

- Who would ever love you?

- You're so ugly and boring.

- You are beyond being loved, by God or by people.

- You really have no redeeming qualities.

Your TRUE Identity: LOVABLE

 You are of infinite worth. God was so much in love with you that He was willing to sacrifice His Son to redeem you from your sins. Even if you were the only person on earth, He would have done it for you. Obviously, there is *something* about you that is *infinitely* worthy of God's love!

> *For I am convinced that neither death, nor life, nor angels, nor principalities, nor things present, nor things to come, nor powers, nor height, nor depth, nor any other created thing, will be able to separate us from the love of God, which is in Christ Jesus our Lord.*
>
> **—Romans 8:38,39**

From the above passage, make a list of the things that God would fight through in order to get to you because of His love for you.

_____

_____

_____

> *Greater love has no one than this, that one lay down his life for his friends.*
>
> **—John 15:13**

Jesus made this statement shortly before He was crucified. Who were the "friends" He was referring to, for whom He was about to lay down His life?

_____

_____

> *But God showed His great love for us by sending Christ to die for us while we were still sinners.*
>
> **—Romans 5:8 (NLT)**

How much love would it take for you to be willing to die for someone else? Would you do it for your mother? For your daughter or son? How about for your best friend? You may have had an experience as a first responder where a friend got in harm's way to shield you from injury or death. *That* was a supremely unselfish, loving act. But have you heard of a first responder who gave up his or her life for someone they didn't even know? It happens from time to time and it always amazes us. How could someone be *so* selfless? But would you be willing to die for someone who had betrayed you the night before, spit in your face, punched you in the stomach, stole your wallet, your car and your girlfriend or boyfriend? You would have to hold incredible love and forgiveness to die for *that* person. And yet, that's who we were, when Christ died on the cross for us. That's how much He loves us.

Deception #8: Separated

Lies of the enemy:

- You are alone and you should stay that way.

- No one wants you on their team.

- You shouldn't bother other people so much.

- People wish you weren't here.

- You don't need anybody else anyway.

Your TRUE Identity: CONNECTED

You are connected in two realms…

1. Connected to God:

[Jesus speaking:] I am the vine, you are the branches; he who abides in Me and I in him, he bears much fruit, for apart from Me you can do nothing.

—John 15:5

What picture of "connectedness" did Jesus use to show how attached we are to Him?

_____

For you are all children of God through faith in Christ Jesus.

—Galatians 3:26 (NLT)

What are some deep, meaningful ways that children and parents are connected?

_____

_____

I have been crucified with Christ; and it is no longer I who live, but Christ lives in me.

—Galatians 2:20

This verse indicates that Christ lives *where?* _____

2. Connected to the Body of Christ – other Christians:

All of you together are Christ's body, and each of you is a part of it.

—1 Corinthians 12:27 (NLT)

What are all Christians a part of? _____

What do you know about how connected various cells and organs of a body are?

_____

_____

You are no longer foreigners and strangers, but fellow citizens with God's people and also members of His household.

—Ephesians 2:19 (NIV)

This verse gives us two pictures of "connectedness" with other people. What are they?

_____

_____

As you work through the difficulties of your service-related stress and trauma, there will be times when you feel alone, rejected, unlovable, devalued and unimportant. That's when Satan will pile on and do all he can to affirm those thoughts. It's at that time that you need to recognize his tactics. He's using deception to move you closer to defeat. He is **lying**. How can you tell when Satan is lying? Whenever his mouth moves. Counter his lies with the truth.

Right now, and at least once a day for the next 21 days, make the proclamation found below based on what you just learned from God's Word. Do it out loud if possible…

This Is Who I Am

Regarded

I am a friend of the Almighty God of heaven and earth. (John 15:15)

Jesus is not ashamed to call me His brother (sister). (Hebrews 2:11)

I am chosen by God, holy and without fault in His eyes. (Ephesians 1:4)

I am an heir to the riches of the Creator of the universe. (Galatians 4:7)

Important

I have been rightly called a child of God. (John 1:12)

God has made me His salt and light in the world. (Matthew 5:13,14)

I am an eternal being. (John 3:16)

Forgiven

I am no longer condemned. (Romans 8:1)

I have been justified before the righteous Judge. (Romans 5:1)

I am at peace with God. (Romans 5:1)

God no longer remembers my sins. (Hebrews 10:17)

Valued

God loves me with an everlasting love. (Jeremiah 31:3)

I am God's temple, bought at a great price. (1 Corinthians 6:19,20)

God knows, chose, called, justified and glorified me. (Romans. 8:29,30)

Accepted

I am accepted in Christ. (Ephesians 1:6 NKJV)

I am a chosen, costly, living stone in God's building. (1 Peter 2:4,5)

I have bold, unrestricted access to God's throne of grace. (Hebrews 4:16)

Powerful

God has given me the spirit of power, love and a sound mind. (2 Timothy 1:7)

God's Spirit in me is greater than any unholy spirits in the world. (1 John 4:4)

I am born of God and believe in Jesus – I'm a world-overcomer. (1 John 5:4,5)

Lovable

I am loved by God and *nothing* will keep us apart. (Romans 8:38,39)

I am loved supremely – enough for God to die for me. (John 15:13)

I am loved unconditionally, *even* when I sin. (Romans 5:8)

Connected

I am intimately attached to Christ and bearing fruit. (John 15:5)

I am a member of God's eternal family. (Galatians 3:26)

Christ is as close to me as my heart and lungs. (Galatians 2:20)

I am part of Christ's body with millions of brothers and sisters. (1 Corinthians 12:27)

I am an eternal member of God's Kingdom and household. (Ephesians 2:19)

Follow-up

Write today's date here: _____ One month from today, re-take the "Self-Perception Assessment" that you completed at the beginning of this Step. If you have been regularly thinking about and proclaiming the above truths concerning your true identity, you should notice that your "Xs" have traveled a considerable distance to the left!

⊕   ⊕   ⊕   ⊕   ⊕

Prayer Seed

My Father, thank You that Your truth drives out lies like light rids a room of darkness. I wasn't aware of the lies and deceit that had been infiltrating my mind. But now I am. Sharpen my defenses. Help me to be aware every time my enemy tries to deceive me and help me to counter his attacks with Your truth. I am not a victim – I am a victor! I want to live like one! Enable me to incorporate Your truths about who I am into my daily thought life. Amen.

⊕   ⊕   ⊕   ⊕   ⊕

---

1. Quote by Dr. Ronnie Janoff-Bullman in "The Aftermath of Victimization: Rebuilding Shattered Assumptions," Nashville, TN: Thomas Nelson Publishers, 1993). pp. 28,29.

2. Dr. Neil T. Anderson, *Victory Over The Darkness* (Minneapolis: Bethany House Publishers, 2000). p. 43.

3. Opposed pairs of core values/core hurts are found in Dr. Steven Stosny's *Manual of the Core Value Workshop* (Copyright 1995, 2003 Steven Stosny) and in other publications of his. For a fuller explanation, consult his website: www.compassionpower.com.

Step ⑧ How Do I Fight?
...Rebuilding Your Defenses

> "Know the enemy and know yourself.
> In a hundred battles you will never be in peril."
>
> —Sun Tzu in *The Art of War*[1]

He may or may not have known God, but this Chinese warrior of the sixth century B.C. knew warfare. After completing Step 7, you should have a much clearer concept of "yourself." In this Step, we will follow Sun Tzu's good advice and inform ourselves about "the enemy." The Apostle Paul expressed the same sentiment regarding our need for preparation in 2 Corinthians 2:11: *"We are not ignorant of his schemes."*

First responders must never lose site of the fact that – despite the absence of bullets and bombs – we are all locked in a desperate war against a deadly enemy. It doesn't seem like it sometimes, because Satan is a master of deception. But the spiritual war our souls are engaged in is as real as the ones involving geography, steel and blood – and just as consequential. As Arthur Mathews, English WWII vet and missionary wrote, "In Eden, God decreed enmity between the serpent's seed and the seed of the woman. Because of this, the *law of strife* became the *law of life* for the human race."[2] Unfortunately, the Kingdom of God is taking heavy casualties because so many of its soldiers don't know their enemy, and aren't convinced there is even a war! We've engaged the enemy in much more than "a hundred battles," but won precious few victories. Peace in our souls is elusive, though we desire it desperately. Our top General during the Revolutionary War tells us how to win it:

> "There is nothing so likely to produce peace as to be well-prepared to meet the enemy."
>
> —George Washington

⊕ ⊕ ⊕ ⊕ ⊕

Preparing To Meet Your Enemy

? What do you already know about Satan? Do a little brainstorming and write down anything you can think of regarding his nature, his strategies, his likes, his dislikes, his motives, his destiny, etc.

_____

_____

_____

His Origin

As we mentioned earlier in this manual, Satan started out as Lucifer, one of the most powerful angels in God's command. The prophet Ezekiel[3] describes him as having "the seal of perfection; full of wisdom; perfect in beauty; covered with every precious stone – ruby, topaz, diamond, emerald..." well, you get the idea. He must have been an amazing being, because at some point he looked at himself, looked at the all-powerful God of the universe, and thought, *I think I can take Him.* Pride was born in his heart and he made five pronouncements about the coup he intended to accomplish:

I will ascend to heaven;
I will raise my throne above the stars of God;
I will sit on the mount of assembly;
I will ascend above the heights of the clouds;
I will make myself like the Most High.[4]

—Isaiah 14:13,14

Revelation 12 indicates that one-third of the angels believed he could do it, and so they joined his rebellion. Why they made such a foolish choice, we're never told. But this left two-thirds still loyal to God, who triumphed. The rebels – including Satan – were banished from God's heaven, no longer free to roam the universe, confined to one planet: Earth.

His Objectives

Some time after this, God created man and woman and gave them authority over all the earth. Satan saw this as his grand opportunity to continue his rebellion. Four objectives formed in his mind:

1. Use deceit to steal some or all of their authority and use it against the Kingdom of God.

2. Afflict these objects of God's great affection and thereby afflict Him – and if possible, get them to blame their afflictions on God.

3. Turn the humans against God – as he did one-third of the angels – and recruit them to his army.

4. Use them to stage a second coup attempt – which he feels certain will succeed this time.

Most of the book of Revelation contains prophesies about how that second attempt will play out. All the evil we've seen down through history, all the wars, all the pain, all the ungodly ways in which humans treat other humans is all part of Satan's staging of that final push to wrest control of earth from God's hands, and take His place. By the way, he won't succeed in this – we've read the last chapter of the book!

His Tactics

 Here is a little more detail about how Satan uses deceit to weaken and overcome us. Read each Bible passage below and in the space provided after each selection **record what you observe about Satan's tactics**. The first one is completed for you, so you'll get an idea of what we're looking for.

Then Jesus was led up by the Spirit into the wilderness to be tempted by the devil.

—Matthew 4:1

Satan takes the initiative and intentionally tempts people to do wrong - especially when they are isolated. He'll tempt anyone - even the Son of God! So we should all expect it.

But I am not surprised! Even Satan disguises himself as an angel of light. So it is no won-
der that his servants also disguise themselves as servants of righteousness.

—2 Corinthians 11:14,15 (NLT)

_____

_____

_____

The Devil took Him [Jesus] to the peak of a huge mountain. He gestured expansively, pointing out all the earth's kingdoms, how glorious they all were. Then he said, "They're Yours—lock, stock, and barrel. Just go down on your knees and worship me, and they're Yours."

—Matthew 4:8,9 (MSG)

_____

_____

_____

This is the meaning of the parable: The seed is God's word. The seeds that fell on the footpath represent those who hear the message, only to have the devil come and take it away from their hearts and prevent them from believing and being saved.

—Luke 8:11,12 (NLT)

_____

_____

_____

⊞　⊞　⊞　⊞　⊞

Breaking The Code

Satan's lies and temptations are very subtle – and they haven't changed much in thousands of years. They haven't needed to – they continue to work excellently. Examine the Genesis passage below in which the temptation of Adam and Eve are recorded. Draw a line from the underlined words of Satan on the left to what he's *really* saying on the right. This will help you recognize your enemy's voice…

And the Lord God commanded the man, "You are free to eat from any tree in the garden; but you must not eat from the tree of the knowledge of good and evil, for when you eat of it you will surely die."

—Genesis 2:16,17 (NIV)

Now the serpent [Satan] was more crafty than any of the wild animals the Lord God had made. He said to the woman, "Did God really say, 'You must not eat from any tree in the ⊙ *garden'?"*

The woman said to the serpent, "We may eat fruit from the trees in the garden, but God did say, 'You must not eat fruit from the tree that is in the middle of the garden, and you must not touch it, or you will die.'"

"You will not surely die," the serpent said to the woman. ⊙

"For God knows that when you eat of it your eyes will be ⊙ *opened, and you will be like God, knowing good and evil."* ⊙

—Genesis 3:1-5 (NIV)

⊙ "Do you mean that God – that restrictive old meanie – won't let you eat from *any* trees in the garden? I can't believe it!"

⊙ "Don't you see what's going on here? God doesn't want you to experience new, mind-expanding things! He wants you to stay ignorant – blind! He's *limiting* you!"

⊙ "Oh, don't get excited. God tends to misrepresent the facts a lot. Let me straighten you out: you won't *really* die. He was just saying that to keep you under His control."

⊙ "God doesn't want you as competition – He wants to keep you ignorant and oppressed. He doesn't want you to know the things He knows."

Anatomy of a Temptation

The framework of most of Satan's temptations contains these five elements. Can you see them implied in the Genesis interchange we just looked at?

> **Major Premise**: Restrictions are bad.
> **Complementary Major Premise**: Freedom is good.
> **Proposition**: God's plans are restrictive.
> **Conclusion**: God's restrictive plans are bad and *should not* be followed.
> **Corollary**: My non-restrictive plans are good and *should* be followed.

Notice how logical and true the two Major Premises seem? How can people who appreciate their independence argue with them? No one likes to be restricted, and freedom *is* good. That's the kernel of truth. But we also know that some restrictions are good and some freedoms are bad. If we skate over that fact and accept the Proposition, we find ourselves nodding in agreement with the Conclusion and Corollary.

? Name a few restrictions that are good. _____

_____

Name a few freedoms that are bad. _____

_____

⊕   ⊕   ⊕   ⊕   ⊕

Satan's Primary Tactic – Doorways & Footholds

Doorways

Genesis 4:1-12 records the birth of Adam and Eve's first two sons, Cain and Abel. Unfortunately, it also records the first homicide in history – inspired by The Murderer himself. Cain and Abel had made offerings to God, and for some reason Cain's was not acceptable. We're not sure why – perhaps it had to do with Cain's heart attitude as he presented it. At any rate, Cain became very angry and resentful. God could see what was in Cain's heart and confronted him about it, giving him some very valuable advice – which Cain didn't take.

In verse 7, God tells Cain,

> *You will be accepted if you do what is right. But if you refuse to do what is right, then watch out! Sin is crouching at the **door**, eager to control you. But you must subdue it and be its master. (NLT)*

Control?

What? I thought Satan was offering me freedom! Anyone who has given in to the "freeing" temptations of Satan knows they eventually lead to bondage. It's interesting that in the last book of the Bible, Jesus also talks about standing at the door: *Here I am! I stand at the door and knock. If anyone hears My voice and opens the door, I will come in and eat with that person, and they with Me.* (Revelation 3:20 NIV). The door that is being spoken of at both ends of the Bible represents our **will**. Whatever we allow to come through that door will influence our choices, our life and our destiny – for good or for evil. And in both verses, *we* have control of the door. We decide who comes in, and who doesn't.

God describes sin (Satan) as crouching just outside the door of your will, trying to convince you to hold it open for him – because he wants to master you, little by little. You've got two options. You can slam that door shut, sending a loud and clear message to both him and God that you're not interested in his propositions … or you can leave it open a crack. By doing that, you're saying, "Satan – I'm open to suggestions. How would you meet my needs?" He'll make his proposals. You'll listen. They will sound *very* good. As Eugene Peterson wrote, "Every temptation is disguised as a suggestion for improvement."[5] Improvement is good, right? So usually, after a short period of deliberation, you'll swing the door open.

Footholds

The principle is presented again in Ephesians 4:26,27 (NIV):

> *In your anger do not sin. Do not let the sun go down while you are still angry, and do not give the devil a **foothold**.*

Anger is not sin, as was mentioned in Step 7. But what we *do* when angry *can* be sin, or our anger can eventually *lead* us to sin if we don't deal with it in a timely manner. If we let negative attitudes – sinful or not – dwell in us un-addressed, we run the risk of giving the devil a "foothold."

When rock climbing, you need to find a series of footholds to make progress. One foothold will not conquer the pitch – each one enables you to make it to the next. This is a key point to remember about how Satan will try to influence your life. He won't blast in and take over all at once. He can't – such an obvious move would alert you. But if he can gain a little foothold – get you to agree to letting him have just a tiny bit of control in a small area, he's gotten just a little closer to conquering you in larger areas. God's advice to you: Don't give him even the first foothold! Once you've given it to him, it will be difficult to get it back!

One other important point: How does Satan get a foothold? **We give it to him**. He cannot seize it by force. He can't overrule our will. But he can deceive us into thinking that we will benefit by agreeing to his suggestions. So we give him that itty-bitty foothold in exchange for something we think will be of more value. We're always wrong.

Exploiting Vulnerabilities

"To be certain to take what you attack, attack a place the enemy does not protect."

—Sun Tzu in *The Art of War*[6]

When it comes to targeting our open doors and footholds, Satan has stolen this stratagem from Sun Tzu's book —or vice versa. Each of us has areas of weakness, vulnerabilities and undefended places in our lives. Satan is aware of them, and *that's* where he waits. He won't waste time in your areas of strength—he's a skilled strategist patiently scoping out your soft spots and looking for an opportunity to strike.

 You will demonstrate *your* skill as a defensive strategist if you'll take the time to assess where your vulnerabilities are. Spend a few moments right now and ask God to reveal to you where they might be. Where are your areas of chronic defeat? Which temptations are no match for your resolve? Where have you fallen before?

_____

_____

For a list of *potential* doorways, see Appendix B. You'll notice we emphasize "potential." Just because you have encountered one of these events, habits or experiences, it doesn't necessarily mean they have provided an open doorway or presented a foothold. But it's possible. If you have had experience with one of the items on the list, spend some time with God asking Him if there is an open door there that needs to be shut.

Closing Doorways

"You must subdue it and be its master." (Genesis 4:7) Whenever you become aware of an open door in your life, there are three steps you need to take in order to shut it:

1. **Confess and repent of opening the door.** If it was due to a willful choice on your part, this step is obvious. See Step 6A for a refresher on confession and repentance. But some doorways may have begun to be opened when you were in a passive state, and not disobeying God at all – like when you were under anesthesia or traumatized on a call. It may be that you later made a willful choice due to something that began then. It could be something like becoming psychologically addicted to pain meds after surgery (pain is no longer the problem, the desire to be "floating" all the time is), or an insatiable urge to kill developing sometime after a firefight. In those cases, you should confess the sin, but also intentionally close the original door.

2. **Take action to demonstrate repentance and purify your life.**

   - Release resentment and bitterness.

   - Seek forgiveness of anyone you offended or hurt.

   - Pay restitution if it's owed.

   - Renounce occultic involvement.

   - Destroy any offending objects (occultic amulets and games, pornography, books, satanic music, DVDs, drugs, alcohol, etc.).

   - Break off any harmful relationships.

   - Put yourself back under God's authority.

3. **Reappropriate the filling of the Holy Spirit.** (Step 3A)

Suggested Prayer

Father, I confess that I have opened a door to my enemy. I have given him a foothold. I was vulnerable and deceived when I made the decision, but I'm still responsible for it. I confess to You that I [describe what you did to open the door]. I agree with You that it was sin, and I'm sorry for it. Please forgive me. On the basis of Your promise in Your Word, I accept your forgiveness of my sins. Thank You.

And now, Father, before You and before all the forces of darkness, I renounce my decision and renounce my opening of that door. I shut that door and take back that foothold. Satan, I remove your authority and ability to influence me in that area any longer. I bind you back from it in the name of Jesus Christ, who is my Lord, Savior and King.

Father, please strengthen that area of vulnerability. May it no longer be an undefended place. I commit to taking any further action You tell me to regarding this matter.

I relinquish the throne of my life to You once again. Please fill me, control me and empower me with Your Holy Spirit. Amen.

Our Weapons

The weapons of our warfare are not physical weapons of flesh and blood, but they are mighty before God for the overthrow and destruction of strongholds.

—2 Corinthians 10:4 (AMP)

Weapon #1: Authority

Being one of the most powerful beings God ever created, and honing his warfare skills for centuries, Satan is an adversary more powerful and deadly than anything we can imagine. If we were to go head-to-head with him in our own strength, he'd squash us like bugs.

But the Bible talks about the authority we have been given as servants and soldiers of Jesus Christ. The Greek word for it is:

> EXOUSIA: *"Right, power, authority, ruling power, a bearer of authority."*[7]

It's more than *just* power – it's power *plus authority.* It's like in football. There are twenty-two men on the field with awesome power. They are strong, fast, and can inflict pain in a multitude of ways, but they aren't in authority. There are five or six other guys down there with striped shirts and whistles who have *exousia.* The players can put people *down,* but the refs can put people *out.*

It's like a cop having a gun and a criminal having a gun. Both have power, but only one has the *badge.*

Ephesians 1:19-23 has a lot to say about Jesus Christ's *exousia.*

> *That power is the same as the mighty strength. He exerted when He raised Christ from the dead and seated Him at His right hand in the heavenly realms, far above all rule and authority [exousia], power and dominion, and every name that is invoked, not only in the present age but also in the one to come. And God placed all things under His feet and appointed Him to be head over everything for the church, which is His body, the fullness of Him who fills everything in every way. (NIV)*

 In the above passage, whose (plural) authority does Christ's authority exceed?

_____

Colossians 2:9,10 states that someone else besides Christ *also* is in possession of this same fullness and *exousia.* Circle who that is in the passage.

> *For in Christ all the fullness of the Deity lives in bodily form, and in Christ you have been brought to fullness. He is the head over every power and authority [exousia]. (NIV)*

Your Place of Warring

There is no authority in the universe higher than Jesus Christ's. No king, no general, no president, no demon, no angel – not even Satan himself can stand before His exousia. And since we are now His children, God has equipped us to operate in that same authority as we deal with the forces of darkness. As the verse to the right says, we are positioned with Christ in the heavenly realms – a position of immense power and authority over our spiritual adversaries. Christ – and we – have this authority because of Christ's willingness to die on the cross and rise again, thereby defeating Satan, sin and death once and for all.

> *God raised us up with Christ and seated us with Him in the heavenly realms in Christ Jesus.*
>
> **—Ephesians 2:6**

You have the upper hand, superior firepower, tactical advantage, and a well-protected command post. The outcome is assured:

> "It is not for us to fight *for* victory, because "we are more than conquerors through Him that loved us." (Romans 8:37) Our fight is *from* victory: and from this vantage point, empowered with Christ's might, and completely enclosed in the whole armor of God, the powers of evil are compelled to back off as we resist them."
>
> —Arthur Matthews in *Born For Battle*[8]

We fight from victory and authority, seated with Christ in His heavenly command post. If we try to fight from any other vantage point, we will be defeated. Spiritual warfare expert Mark Bubeck writes in *Overcoming The Adversary*:[9]

> "No believer who willfully walks in the sins of the flesh and world can hope to escape Satan's hurt and bondage. Can you imagine what would happen to a soldier who took a little stroll into his enemy's territory during the heat of war? If not killed, he would soon be surrounded and taken captive. Yet there are believers who think they can carelessly engage in sin without being vulnerable to Satan."

Weapon #2: Our Spiritual Kevlar

In football, basketball and war, we have learned that without a good defense, we have no offense. It doesn't matter how skillful we are with our offensive weapons, if we take one in the chest, we're done. That's why – if you're in law enforcement – you almost always wear ballistic vests.

God gave us spiritual armor for our spiritual battles as well. The Apostle Paul writes about it in **Ephesians 6:13-17 (NIV):**

> *Therefore put on the full armor of God, so that when the day of evil comes, you may be able to stand your ground, and after you have done everything, to stand. Stand firm then, with the **belt of truth** buckled around your waist, with the **breastplate of righteousness** in place, and with your **feet fitted with the readiness that comes from the gospel of peace**. In addition to all this, take up the **shield of faith**, with which you can extinguish all the flaming arrows of the evil one. Take the **helmet of salvation** and the **sword of the Spirit**, which is the word of God.*

Consider briefly each element of the armor God has given us:[10]

Belt of Truth. Satan's chief tactic is deceit. Our only counter is truth. Any structure fire assault, police action or medical procedure is only as good as the information and intelligence that guides it. Jesus said that He *is* the truth (John 14:6), and He describes the Holy Spirit as "the Spirit of Truth" (John 14:17). As we strap on this Belt of Truth, it alerts us to the lies and deceitful tactics of the enemy and helps us fight with efficiency.

Breastplate of Righteousness. The breastplate is like your flak jacket. Its main function is to protect the organs that are vital to your life. You can function without a hand or a leg, but if you lose a heart – no spares. God urges you to *"Guard your heart above all else, for it determines the course of your life."* (Proverbs 4:23 NLT) Our hearts are guarded by the righteousness of Jesus Christ that was given to us when we were saved. Righteousness is everything that Satan is not, so it repels him like WD-40 does water – only better!

Boots of the Gospel of Peace. Boots protect your feet and give you traction and stability. Without them we tenderfeet would move too slowly and fearfully – ineffective in an emergency. You know that the Gospel brings peace to those who hear it. But don't forget that it also brings peace to *you*. Sometimes, when the world is so difficult to deal with, we become slow, unsteady and unstable. It's easy to lose traction and stumble in that condition. Strap on those Gospel boots of peace, so that you can negotiate the rugged terrain before you. Jesus said in John 16:33, *"These things I have spoken to you, so that in Me you may have peace. In the world you have tribulation, but take courage; I have overcome the world."* Let His victories bring you peace and stability.

Shield of Faith. The particular shield talked about here is a *thureos* – a very large shield. It could protect a soldier from *anything* that his adversary launched his way. Faith is our shield – or more accurately, the *object of our faith* is our shield. As we believe in and count on His power and authority to protect us, our shield will hold. If we shift our focus to our enemy and his strength, our faith can waiver. The Warrior-King David knew this well, as he wrote in Psalm 3:3, *"But You, O Lord, are a shield about me, my glory, and the One who lifts my head."*

Helmet of Salvation. As the breastplate protects our torso's vital organs, the helmet protects our other vital organ and the command center of our lives: our brain. If the head is injured, the rest of the body will malfunction. Satan's *main* attacks won't target our feet or our houses or our jobs – though he may hit them as a diversion. His ultimate objectives have to do with our *minds*. If he can turn our wills to do his bidding, he's turned us completely. This is why, upon salvation, God gave us this helmet to protect our minds from Satan's influence.

Sword of the Spirit. This is a unique implement, because it can be both a defensive *and* an offensive weapon. The sword is the Word of God, and as such, it can serve us both defensively and offensively. When Jesus was attacked by Satan in the wilderness (Matthew 4:1-11), He parried every thrust of His adversary with a verse of Scripture, and eventually sent him on a hasty retreat. As the Apostle Paul affirms, *"For the word of God is living and active and sharper than any two-edged sword."* (Hebrews 4:12) More about this in the next section.

If you're a law enforcement officer, you never venture into gang territory without first putting on your body armor, right? Very smart. In our conflicts with *Satan's* gang, there are no territorial boundaries. Every step we take is behind enemy lines. So it is also smart that we *intentionally* put on our *spiritual* armor each day before we venture out into the world. If you do, you will notice a much higher degree of effectiveness in your ability to cope, be a resource, and even to minister to others – whether you are currently experiencing PTSD or not. You'll take a lot fewer hits, too.

Armor up!

Following is a suggested prayer you could pray each morning. This is not a "magical prayer" – the words aren't important. God looks at the heart, so to the degree these words reflect what your heart wants to express, God will hear them. Visualize each piece of armor as you put it on.

> *Dear Father, I stand before You this morning in order to receive the armor You have for me today. I receive from Your hand and wrap around my waist your belt of truth. May I receive, believe, and speak only Your truth. I receive from Your hand and strap to my torso the breastplate of righteousness – the righteousness of Jesus Christ given to me the day I was saved. Guard my heart with it. I receive from Your hand and put on my feet the boots of the gospel of peace. May these boots give me stability and speed in my warring. And may Your peace fill my being and flow out to those around me.*

> *I receive from Your hand and take in my [left/right] hand the shield of faith, with which I will deflect the missiles of my enemy, except for the ones You want to use for my purification and Your glory. I receive from Your hand the helmet of salvation, bought for me almost two thousand years ago when Jesus Christ died on the cross for me, and rose again. Guard my mind with it. Finally, I receive from Your hand and take in my [right/left] hand the sword of the Spirit, which is Your Word. Give me skill to use it to defend myself and attack my enemy. So clothed in this armor, equipped with this sword and backed by Your authority, may I this day push back the kingdom of darkness and expand the Kingdom of Light. I pray this in the name of Jesus Christ, my Savior, Redeemer, God, and King, Amen.*

Weapon #3: The Word of God

How Things Get Done In the Kingdom of God

In each of the following passages, something is being accomplished by God or by representatives of God. At the end write down what is common to each passage. What is it that is "making it happen?"

Then God said, "Let there be light"; and there was light.

—Genesis 1:3

Then Jesus said to him, "Go, Satan! For it is written, 'You shall worship the Lord your God and serve Him only.'"

—Matthew 4:10

Jesus said to the paralytic, "Get up, pick up your bed and go home." And he got up and went home.

—Matthew 9:6,7

Jesus said to the man, "Stretch out your hand!" He stretched it out, and it was restored to normal.

—Matthew 12:13

Jesus rebuked him, saying, "Be quiet, and come out of him!" The unclean spirit cried out with a loud voice and came out.

—Mark 1:25,26

Jesus rebuked the wind and said to the sea, "Hush, be still." And the wind died down and it became perfectly calm.

—Mark 4:39

Jesus cried out with a loud voice, "Lazarus, come forth!" The man who had died came forth, bound with wrappings.

—John 11:43,44

Peter said, "I do not possess silver and gold, but what I do have I give to you: In the name of Jesus Christ the Nazarene – walk!" With a leap he stood upright and began to walk.

—Acts 3:6-8

Paul said to Elymas the magician, "You who are full of deceit and fraud... now, behold, the hand of the Lord is upon you, and you will be blind and not see the sun for a time." And immediately a mist and a darkness fell upon him.

—Acts 13:8-11

Paul turned and said to the spirit, "I command you in the name of Jesus Christ to come out of her!" And it came out at that very moment.

—Acts 16:18

What does each passage have in common, in terms of what was done just before the supernatural event occurred?

_____

_____

Hopefully you were able to see that the way things are accomplished in the spiritual realm is not through muscle-power, electricity, computers, bulldozers or bombs. It gets done by *the spoken word.*

In the listing of your spiritual armor, the Sword of the Spirit is clearly equated with God's Word. When God wanted to create, He commanded matter into existence. When Jesus wanted to neutralize Satan, heal, calm a storm, raise the dead, control a demon, He spoke a word of commandment. When Jesus' disciples needed to heal or do spiritual warfare, they followed His example and spoke commands as representatives of their Master.

This is also how Jesus wants *you* to fight your enemy. As mentioned earlier, you have position, overwhelming firepower, righteous authority and allies that are out of this world. You accomplish your offensives by *speaking* your commands to your enemy, just as Jesus did when He fought Satan in the wilderness in Matthew 4.

Spiritual Ammo

Each time Jesus was attacked, He came back at His enemy with Scripture. Follow His example! Suppose your enemy is coming at you with a temptation to go to bed with someone other than your spouse. He or she is available and willing – what are you going to do? Grab some spiritual ammo, lock and load! Recall what God's Word says on this subject and use it against your tempter (Satan, not the one you're lusting after), just as your arms instructor – Jesus Christ – showed you. Here's a suggested confrontational pattern:

"Father, Satan is tempting me to sin against You. He wants me to commit adultery. But I desire to master him. *Please fill me with Your Holy Spirit. I take my position seated with Christ at Your right hand in the heavenly realms above all forces of darkness. With Your blessing and protection, and in Your authority, I ask You to help me resist my enemy, and thereby defeat him.*

"Satan, I address you in the name and authority of the Lord Jesus Christ, King of kings and Lord of lords – who has bought me with His blood and made me a child of the Most High God. I am aware of your attempts to cause me to sin. In doing so, you have transgressed the commandment of God, for He has said in His Word, 'You shall not commit adultery.' You are trying to get me to commit this sin, so you are in the wrong. Therefore, in the authority given to me by God Himself, I command you to cease your activities directed at me, remove yourself from my area and go where Jesus Christ tells you to go.

"Thank you, Father, for this victory. Just as your angels ministered to Jesus after His fight with Satan, I ask that You would minister to me as well, and strengthen that vulnerable area in my life. Amen!"

In doing this, you are following a very clear pattern that God has set up in His word. You see it in James 4:7,8. Compare each component of the verse with each of the three paragraphs above.

> *Submit therefore to God. Resist the devil and he will flee from you. Draw near to God and He will draw near to you.*
>
> —James 4:7,8

First paragraph = ***Submit to God.***

Second paragraph = ***Resist the devil and he will flee from you.***

Third paragraph = ***Draw near to God and He will draw near to you.***

Advance or Retreat?

Here's an important distinction that all God's spiritual warriors need to be aware of. You may have heard it said, "Resist temptation" and "Flee the devil." This is a good example of how Satan twists the truth in order to engineer our defeat, because God tells us to do the *exact opposite.*

When it comes to temptation, we are to *flee!* As Proverbs 4:14,15 says:

> *Do not enter the path of the wicked and do not proceed in the way of evil men. Avoid it, do not pass by it; turn away from it and pass on.*

When it comes to eyeball-to-eyeball confrontation with the devil, we are to *resist!* Don't back down, don't run, *fight.* If we do, *he'll* run, as we just read in James 4:7 – *Resist the devil and he will flee from you.*

Here's the fun part. It doesn't say we have to engage him and beat him to a pulp or try to pull off some overwhelming victory in order to make him retreat. All we have to do is resist. That's it! He'll see our *exousia*, recognize our training, and run for the hills!

Need some ammo? Check out your very own *Spiritual Warfare Ammo Bunker* found in Appendix C of this manual. There's plenty there! But if you come up against an attack of the enemy and don't see the exact cartridge you need in the bunker, do some searching of the Scriptures on your own and add it to your supplies.

? Would you like to try out your new weaponry? Ask God to show you an area in which Satan has been attacking you lately. Select your "ammo" verse, and then engage the enemy! Use the prayer pattern suggested above. Then, sometime tomorrow come back to this manual and write down what happened.

Prayer Seed

Give me victory, Father! I've suffered so many defeats over the past months. I need to win some! Just as I was trained to function at maximum efficiency as a first responder, I need you to teach me to fight in the spiritual realm. I know that in my own strength I am useless against such a formidable enemy as Satan. But in Your authority, I am more than a conqueror. Help me to put on my spiritual armor every day. Give me the intelligence and discernment I need to counter the deceitful moves of my adversary. Equipped with your mighty weapons, may I secure victory for myself, my family, and for Your Kingdom. Amen.

1. Sun Tzu, *The Art of War*, translated by Samuel B. Griffith (Oxford University Press, 1963), p. 84.

2. Quote from R. Arthur Matthews in *Born For Battle*, p. 11

3. Ezekiel 28:12-19. In this passage, the Spirit of God is speaking through the prophet Ezekiel against the King of Tyre – a very devilish king. In this pronouncement He was in essence saying, "King of Tyre, your characteristics are just like Satan's. Now let me tell you his history – and his destiny."

4. Isaiah 14:13,14. Here God speaks to a different king (the King of Babylon – present day Iraq) using the same theme: "You're just like Satan – in these respects..."

5. Quote from Eugene Peterson (translator of The Message) in *A Long Obedience In The Same Direction* (InterVarsity Press, 1980, 2000), p. 127.

6. From *The Art of War*, p. 96.

7. Colin Brown (Ed.), *The New Int'l Dictionary of New Testament Theology* (Regency, 1967, 1971), Vol. 2, p. 606.

8. Quote from R. Arthur Matthews in *Born For Battle*, p. 27,28.

9. Quote from Dr. Mark I. Bubeck in *Overcoming The Adversary*, p. 17.

10. For an in-depth, inspiring, practical six-chapter treatment of our spiritual armor, see Dr. Mark I. Bubeck's *Overcoming The Adversary*, pages 64–120.

Step ⑨ How Do I Get Across?
...Finding Bridge People

When you're weary, feeling small,
When tears are in your eyes,
I will dry them all.
I'm on your side
When times get rough
And friends just can't be found –
Like a bridge over troubled water
I will lay me down.

—Paul Simon[1]

The Necessity of Bridges

Bridges come in all shapes and sizes. Some are permanent, some are portable, some are massive and some are quite simple. They help us get where we need to go, but sometimes they can save a life. Here's a story about a life-saving bridge that was only 17 feet long, buoyant, and equipped with a 60 horsepower Mercury outboard...

It had been a brilliant November day in northeast Ohio. Dusk was descending, painting gold and russet colors over the clear sky. It was the kind of day in which people forget that summer is gone, and winter is right around the corner – unless they check the thermometer.

The tones dropped for "a possible capsized boat on LaDue Reservoir." A local said he saw something unusual on this 1500 acre lake. He wasn't sure what it was, but just thought Auburn Fire Department should check it out. We put LifeFlight on standby and got moving. I was assigned to the first-out squad, and as soon as I jumped on board I started warming up a couple of liter saline bags on the defrost vent, in case we needed to re-warm a victim. The engine and the truck towing our brand new rescue boat were right behind us. If this incident had occurred just a few weeks earlier, we would been pulling an old aluminum rowboat. Fortunately, a grant for a state-of-the-art Zumro had just come through for us. We responded priority one, lights and sirens.

It was a short distance to the scene and we quickly determined that it was indeed a capsized small boat, with one in the water. Air temp was 28 degrees at the time, water temp about 45. We knew that if we didn't get the subject out of the water FAST, he would be a statistic. The engine crew donned their gumby-suits, deployed our rescue boat, and sped to the water-logged victim. It was a young man of about 25, his face barely above water when they reached him. He was carefully put on board, stripped, wrapped in space blankets, and rushed to our waiting squad.

Multiple lines of warmed saline were started as LifeFlight landed nearby. Our patient was delirious and not able to form any intelligible words. He was white and not shivering, obviously very near death. We helped LifeFlight package and load him aboard the bird, and he was soon in the night sky. We prayed as we watched the fading navigation lights speeding him to Metro Hospital in Cleveland. Core temperature when we handed him off: 80 degrees. "Nobody" gets that cold and lives to tell about it.

Except this guy. To our overwhelming joy, Metro let us know that he survived and did exceptionally well! His Mom wrote us a letter, thanking us for "another Thanksgiving with my son... and what a Thanksgiving it will be!" It was a great Thanksgiving for us all, as a department. We were so thankful for our "bridge," our new rescue boat, without which this save would not have been possible![2]

When in crisis, we can't be too fussy about where our help comes from. Normal people in abnormal circumstances need unique transfusions of support. While the Auburn FD's Zumro was the ideal answer in this scenario,

God's preservation and provision can come in many different forms. Sometimes it looks like another person. When it shows up, don't hesitate to make use of that "bridge."

Bridges To Healing

Throughout this manual we have stressed that God is your Healer (Exodus 15:26). But because we live in a fallen world with its various complexities, traps, weaknesses, and land mines, your healing is no easy fix. It will take place when the environment surrounding your woundedness gives God maximum access to your soul. We have shared many practical measures you can take to facilitate this, but one of the most effective – and least used – has to do with people.

The tendency of those struggling with stress and trauma is to self-isolate, which does absolutely nothing beneficial for you. What you need is to be in contact with people who are Spirit-filled, Spirit-directed, unselfish servants of God who've got your back. When we get into trouble, God *expects* us to help each other out. The first responder community exemplifies this principle by recognizing that the ideal work environment involves at least two partners working together. There is safety and strength in numbers – even if it's only one or two others:

> *Two people are better off than one, for they can help each other succeed. If one person falls, the other can reach out and help. But someone who falls alone is in real trouble. Likewise, two people lying close together can keep each other warm. But how can one be warm alone? A person standing alone can be attacked and defeated, but two can stand back-to-back and conquer. Three are even better, for a triple-braided cord is not easily broken.*

—Ecclesiastes 4:9-12 (NLT)

A Systemic Problem

First responder work is a helping profession. Your image of yourself is always to be the "help-ER," not the "help-EE." So it feels unnatural to think of yourself as the one in need of aid. There is an unwritten code that many first responders hold to (either consciously or unconsciously): "It is inappropriate that those mandated with protecting and rescuing others should be in need of protection and rescue themselves." This mindset is one of the main reasons so many first responders remain stuck in their struggles with stress and trauma. Rather than to lance that boil, drain the infection, and expose it to the healing effects of oxygen, they'd rather cover it up with a Band-Aid and hope it gets better.

But when a person becomes intentional about enlisting the aid of others to help them past their stress-induced difficulties, they almost always improve significantly. We're not saying that you should open yourself up to anyone and everyone around you, but there ought to be a few trustworthy, faithful, understanding, God-led friends that you can enlist in your quest for strength, stability and your new normal.

This Step is meant to help you identify those friends and motivate you to engage with them. We call them **"bridge people."**

 To what degree would you say you try to conceal your stress and trauma symptoms from your colleagues and those around you? How much do you seek out "bridge people?"

Friends of Faith

When you get the chance, read **Mark 2:1-12**. This is the story of a paralyzed man and four of his bridge people. The word had gotten around that Jesus was healing people at a certain house in Capernaum. These four men immediately thought of their paralyzed friend. They knew there was no way he could get there, so they rushed to his house, put him on a stretcher, and carried him to Jesus. Unfortunately, they weren't the only ones who had heard about the Healer. The house was crammed full of people and surrounded by hundreds more. The four men cared about their incapacitated friend too much to give up and go home. So they hoisted him up on top of the house, tore up the roof and lowered him through the hole down to Jesus! They would not be denied. Then Jesus – *"seeing the faith of his friends"* – healed the paralyzed man immediately.

There are faith-filled people who want to do that for *you* – if you'll let them. Sure, it goes against the macho first responder image of a man or woman who is self-sufficient and in need of no one's help. But, if your pride isn't getting in the way, you know that you *do* need some help right now – like that Zumro rescue boat provided for that drowning man. There is no shame in needing and seeking help. Every normal person does from time to time. The shame goes to the one who doesn't seek it, preferring to remain proud but forever paralyzed.

Your bridge people may be old friends, or you may not know who they are at this time. You might not even have met them yet. But they're nearby, motivated by their love for God and their love for you.

 The four men in the story did not heal their friend – Jesus did. But would the healing have taken place had the men not taken the initiative and altered their friend's environment so that it included Jesus? What does this fact make you think about your current situation and the potential "roof demolishers" you have in your life?

_____

_____

God Invented Bridges

There is an obvious principle of Bible interpretation that says, "If it's advocated in the Bible, it's in God's will." As you read the following verses, would you say it is God's will that we should be bridge people for each other?

Now we who are strong ought to bear the weaknesses of those without strength and not just please ourselves.
—Romans 15:1

Bear one another's burdens, and thereby fulfill the law of Christ.
—Galatians 6:2

Always be humble and gentle. Be patient with each other, making allowance for each other's faults because of your love.
—Ephesians 4:2 (NLT)

Be kind and compassionate to one another, forgiving each other, just as in Christ God forgave you.
—Ephesians 4:32 (NIV)

Confess your sins to one another, and pray for one another so that you may be healed.
—James 5:16

 Name one or two things that these verses say are true about a bridge person.

_____

_____

What Can We Expect From A Bridge?

The bridge people we're talking about in this Step are people who will help transport us to God so that He can provide healing. In many ways, they are representatives of His, ambassadors, messengers and liaisons. The following six verses will give you some insight as to how a properly-functioning bridge person can help you get closer to God.

A friend loves at all times, and a brother is born for adversity.

—Proverbs 17:17

There are probably a few people – maybe you work with them every day, maybe not – to whom you could say, "For better or worse, I'm on your side. Even if you're wrong, I'm still on your side. I've got your back no matter what." You would consider it an honor to aid them, right? Write down their names:

_____

_____

There are people who feel the same way about you. If you were to list them now, that list would probably be very close to the one you just wrote. If any of your friends were in a jam, you'd come to their aid in a heartbeat, wouldn't you? And wouldn't you be upset with them if they concealed from you that they were having trouble, keeping you from putting yourself out for them?

THE POINT: *Expect* a bridge person to be eager to help you out. They *want to!* Don't hesitate to call on them.

In everything I did, I showed you that by this kind of hard work we must help the weak, remembering the words the Lord Jesus himself said: "It is more blessed to give than to receive."

—Acts 20:35 (NIV)

If you're an unselfish person, you would rather give than receive, right? How do you normally act when you have to be a receiver?

_____

So, if you're reluctant to receive, that means you're reluctant to allow your friends to give – which means you are robbing them of a blessing. Thief!

THE POINT: Don't be a thief! Provide the opportunity for your friends to be blessed by allowing them to give to you.

Understand this, my dear brothers and sisters: You must all be quick to listen, slow to speak, and slow to get angry.

—James 1:19 (NIV)

From this, what would you say a bridge friend should be good at?

_____

As was mentioned in a previous Step (page 61), one of the practices that will help you in your healing is to process your traumatic episodic memories in a safe environment. In other words, you need to *talk* about them. A bridge person will be a good listener. If they're constantly interrupting you in order to tell *their* story, or if they are freaked out by what you share and keep trying to change the subject, then they probably aren't the one to talk to at the deeper levels.

THE POINT: Expect a bridge person to be a good listener.

As iron sharpens iron, so a friend sharpens a friend.

—Proverbs 27:17 (NLT)

What does this verse say a friend – a bridge person – will do for you?

_____

What do you think it means for one person to sharpen another?

_____

Sharpening is an intentional process – a knife doesn't sharpen itself. So a good bridge person will take the initiative, reaching out and proactively helping you improve your healing environment. By the way, sharpening is not always pleasant for the knife – sparks fly, it gets real hot, and some of its best cutting-edge material is ground off. In the same way, your bridge person may not always stroke your ego just the way you'd like. You may have some nicks and burrs that need to be smoothed out. Be ready for it, and receive it in the same manner in which it's offered: in love.

THE POINT: Expect a bridge person to be intentional, looking for ways to help you improve your healing environment – some of which might create a few sparks.

An open rebuke is better than hidden love! Wounds from a sincere friend are better than many kisses from an enemy.

—Proverbs 27:5,6 (NLT)

If you had a cancerous tumor, would you prefer that your doctor use a scalpel in the appropriate area, or just say a lot of nice things to you?

_____

Sometimes it hurts to hear the truth, doesn't it? But truth is like medicine – it often tastes bad but it's *good* for you! Sometimes we get mad at people when they tell us a distasteful truth. But a true bridge person won't care. They are willing to risk their friendship with you, hurting you if necessary, in order to help you in your healing process. Think back to some of the most influential people in your life. Perhaps it was a parent, a coach, a friend, an instructor, a doctor. Write a couple of their names here.

_____

No doubt you felt the love and respect they held for you. But wasn't there another element in each case? Weren't they people who were willing to tell you some hard truths? Didn't they get a little tough on you from time to time? When you needed somebody to bust your chops, weren't they willing to volunteer for the honor?

THE POINT: A good bridge person is willing to risk your friendship in order to open your eyes to a vital truth you may not know.

But encourage one another day after day, as long as it is still called "Today," so that none of you will be hardened by the deceitfulness of sin.

—Hebrews 3:13

Yes, you need to know the hard truths. *But...* you also need that input strongly balanced by a good dose of encouragement. Make sure you surround yourself with people who are positive and supportive – people who "day after day" catch you doing something right. No one has ever died from receiving too much encouragement, and you won't be the first.

What is something that you need to hear? Write down a piece of encouragement that you have not been receiving lately…

_____

Prayer Assignment

Bring this up with God. Let him know that you need for Him to bring others around you who will communicate those encouraging words.

Notice something else about that verse. It tells us two things about sin: It hardens us and it's deceitful. Sin has the same kind of effect on your conscience as an ill-fitting boot would have on your foot. The rubbing hurts at first, but after a while callous forms and it doesn't bother you anymore. Sin works the same way. It'll sting your conscience the first few times, but if you keep at it long enough the discomfort will fade. Then you'll figure it's OK, since you don't feel bad about it anymore. But that's when it's easiest for Satan to slip in his poison daggers.

However, if you've got good, positive, salt-and-light-sharing bridge people around you, God's Spirit in them can throw a spotlight on your errors and sins and draw you back to the Father long after you've turned down the Spirit's volume knob in your life.

THE POINT: Expect massive doses of encouragement from a bridge person, but also be open to their kind, corrective feedback to keep your heart soft to God's conviction of sin in your life.

⊕　⊕　⊕　⊕　⊕

A Formalized Bridge Relationship

It's perfectly alright to carry on a "casual" relationship with people you have identified as bridge people in your life. They might not even know what a "bridge person" is – or that they are one. They may not even be a first responder. On the other hand, if you've become acquainted with someone who is spiritually mature, compassionate, resourceful and insightful, you may want to pursue a more "formal" bridge relationship with him or her.

If they aren't aware of the "bridge" concept, perhaps you could tell them about it or give them a copy of this manual. They may have been the one who gave *you* this manual, and in that case, they probably know a lot about how to be a bridge person for you.

One of the main things that causes any relationship to self-destruct is "uncommunicated expectations." One person has a set of expectations that the other knows nothing about, and when they aren't met, the pin gets pulled on the friendship flash-bang. So if you plan to formalize your relationship, it would be a good idea to ask him or her the following questions:

- ❑ Will you commit to listening to me with your ears, eyes and heart to try to grasp what I'm saying, even if I'm not doing a very good job of communicating?

- ❑ Will you simply accept and not judge me for what has happened to me while on duty and how I am responding?

- ❑ Will you revise your expectations and accept how I work at expressing my responses – even if they involve heightened emotion and profanity?

- ❑ Will you commit to walking with me through the emotions and thoughts this journey reveals?

- ❑ Will you encourage me by reminding me that I am a normal person who has experienced abnormal events?

- ❑ Will you acknowledge that it is normal for a grieving person to express the full array of emotions including anger, helplessness, and frustration?

- ❑ Will you commit to not withdrawing from me because of what I've opened up and shared with you, no matter how painful?

- ❑ Will you understand that at times, all I want is for you to sit with me and wait?

- ❑ Will you commit to listening, even if I am sharing the same experience over again?

- ❑ Do you understand that you don't have to try to fix me?

I know – parts of it almost sound like wedding vows. Sorry about that. Didn't mean for it to. But that's one of the functions of any kind of vow: they help *both* parties understand what is expected, and based on that they *both* make a good effort to live up to the expectations. "You know what I need, and I know that you know. If there are any questions, let's deal with them now rather than later."

> Make a list of people that you would like to start a "formal" bridge relationship with. Then start praying that God will bring it about. As He leads, take the initiative with them.

_____

_____

Group Bridges

Those with extensive experience in research and therapy related to critical incidents, trauma and PTSD almost unanimously sing the praises of group settings to help them work through the difficulties of their past horrific experiences. There are many reasons for this:

- In a group, you are actively countering a trauma survivor's normal tendency to self-isolate.

- You are forging deep friendships with men and women who truly understand what you have experienced, because they have too.

- The depth of your shared experiences opens up communication and support lines that those who haven't experienced trauma could never understand or appreciate.

- As group members get to know each other at deeper levels, they take a more active roll in "watching each other's back."

- They won't be judgmental, alarmed, or abandon you during any "kookin' out" episodes you may experience. They'll be far more motivated than most to stick with you through them.

- You have the option of benefiting from the experiences and insights of several people who are in the same boat you are.

- You are multiplying bridge people in your life – and you are being a bridge to each of them as well, which enhances your own healing environment and sense of honor.

- During periods when you're taking your "two steps back," you can be encouraged and harvest some hope by hearing of another group member's "three steps forward."

- The give-and-take of a group situation is sometimes less threatening than a one-to-one, eyeball-to-eyeball session with someone you don't know very well.

- You're multiplying your prayer power: see Matthew 18:19,20.

 What has been your experience in the past with "therapeutic" small groups, if any? Have they been helpful or not?

_____

_____

Some helpful tips. Here are a few principles to keep in mind as you begin to participate in group sessions. Most of these are taken from support group expert Jody Hayes' book, *Smart Love:*

- Once you're in the right group, you may feel safe, but you may also feel shy. This brings us to another paradox of recovery: The more you reveal yourself, the safer you will feel. The more vulnerable you make yourself, the quicker you can recover.

- Share your experiences. Your problems will become clearer when you give words to them. You will discover how much harder it is to fool yourself when you actually hear yourself saying something that you know is either a partial truth or a full lie. At the same time, when you are describing signs of progress or small victories, you will find their effect amplified when you applaud yourself in the presence of others.

- Acknowledge how you feel at the moment, whatever those feelings are. Remember, you are not speaking to please others or to be graded on your recovery. You are speaking to help yourself.

- Embrace your feelings and accept them, even if you feel momentarily miserable. By honestly describing your feelings, you will get a clearer understanding of the experience you are going through. Moreover, there is a significant chance that your painful feelings will diminish. A side benefit is that you will almost always help someone else who is not yet brave enough to speak.

- When speaking, it is important to avoid long, detailed descriptions of your experiences, going into great, gory detail. This will only feed your problem, not release you from it. In addition, it may frustrate and trigger other group members. Keep the focus on how you feel, how events affected you and what you are doing about it.

- When sharing in the group, avoid comparing yourself with others. Each person is at a different place in their healing. Keep your focus on yourself and on how God is working in *your* life.

 If you aren't already in one, have you considered joining a group of other first responders to intentionally address your stress and trauma issues? What are your thoughts about it?

_____

_____

When Is It Time To Call In the Pros?

You may have done an excellent job of connecting with a number of bridge people, but still experience struggles that seem more than you can bear. Your level of trauma may be such that you need to see a professional counselor or therapist. Following is a checklist that therapist and writer J. Elizabeth Oppenheim[4] devised to help a person determine if they should seek professional help.

If any of these first 4 warning signs are evident, GET HELP NOW!

- ❑ You are thinking that suicide is a plausible, acceptable way to stop your pain.
- ❑ Your concentration is so poor that you are accidentally hurting yourself or others.
- ❑ You are out of control in some way that is endangering your health or the health of others.
- ❑ You have no plans for the future, no hope of your life getting better.

If you don't have a counselor, doctor, pastor or friend you can call, and if you are planning to hurt yourself or someone else right now, call 911, go to an Emergency Room or call a Suicide Prevention Hotline and ask for help. We're serious! ***Right now!*** Put down the manual and ***GO!***

For the next nine signs, if you notice that three or four of them are present, ask friends, your doctor or your pastor for a referral to a counselor or other professional. If you are a veteran, go to a nearby Vet Center or VA Hospital and ask for a counselor. If you have no other leads, use Google or look in the Yellow Pages under Counselors, Therapists or Psychologists and keep looking until you find someone who really helps you.

❑ You are unable to work.

❑ You cannot keep food down or are eating uncontrollably.

❑ You are not sleeping or are sleeping all the time.

❑ You have lost interest in everything you used to enjoy; nothing can make you smile.

❑ It is too much effort to get dressed, shave, put on make-up, etc.

❑ You cannot clean your house to basic sanitation levels or you compulsively clean it late into the night.

❑ You are barely functioning but you have other people depending on you to take care of them (children, elders, disabled).

❑ You have no one you can talk to honestly about what you're going through – or you've worn out all your friends who would listen.

❑ You have a health problem that flares up when you're under stress.

You're not committing to a lifetime of therapy – just hooking up with a well-qualified bridge for a while. This place is only temporary. Get all the support you can as you move through this phase of life.

A key element

Professional therapists can be extremely helpful – or not. Those who come from a strictly clinical/psychological frame of reference can be helpful with coping mechanisms, talking about your past, dealing with triggers, getting you in touch with your pain and your emotions, among other things. But unless they are aware of the spiritual dimensions of trauma, and understand God as the great Healer, they won't be a true bridge for you. Their input will be helpful, but you need more.

By the same token, you may encounter a biblical counselor or Christian therapist who really walks closely with God, but isn't well-versed in the physical and psychological aspects of stress, trauma and PTSD. They may be a less-than-optimal bridge as well.

Following is a list of questions you could ask a potential counselor to get an idea of how effective a bridge they will be:

1. What is your approach to understanding people's problems and helping them grow, change and become whole again through counseling?

2. What education and experience have you had that has most influenced your approach to counseling individuals struggling with stress, trauma or PTSD?

3. Have you had much experience dealing with first responders in the past? If so, how?

4. Are you a Christian? How does your faith influence your perspective and practice of counseling?

5. Is it your custom to bring biblical truth into your counseling practice?

6. Do you pray with those you counsel? Do you invite those you counsel to pray as part of their counseling journey?

7. What are your education credentials for offering to counsel trauma survivors? How has your preparation influenced you?

8. Have you experienced severe loss, crisis or trauma in your own life? How has this influenced how you counsel trauma survivors?

Locating a Christian Counselor

If you aren't sure where to look for a Christian counselor in your area, here are two places to inquire. They are in contact with two nationwide networks of counselors who could be of help:

- **American Association of Christian Counselors** has constructed a Christian Care Network that you can access online. Go to www.aacc.net. At their home page, you will see several tabs across the top – click on the "Divisions" tab. There will be a drop-down menu – click on "Christian Care Network." Follow the instructions to see if someone in their network has a practice near you.

- **Focus On The Family** also maintains a nationwide network of Christian counselors. You can visit their web site at www.focusonthefamily.com or simply call their headquarters in Colorado Springs at (719) 531-3400 and ask for the Counseling Department.

A Few Other Helpful Links

- Alcoholics Anonymous – www.alcoholics-anonymous.org. (212) 870-3400
- Al-Anon – www.al-anon.org. (888) 425-2666
- Narcotics Anonymous – www.na.org. (818) 773-9999

A few closing thoughts about the benefits of surrounding yourself with good friends…

**"Walking with a friend in the dark
is better than walking alone in the light."**

—Helen Keller

**"Think where man's glory most begins and ends,
And say, 'My glory was I had such friends.' "**

—William Yeats

**"It's a whole lot better to go up the river with seven studs
than with a hundred ****heads."**

—Col. Charlie A. Beckwith
Army Delta Force Founder

Find those seven studs – those seven bridge people – and be intentional about hanging out with them!

·········· Prayer Seed ··········

Thank You, Father, that it is Your desire to make me like Your Son Jesus Christ. Thank You also that You have equipped members of Your Body to help me in that process, and have surrounded me with them. Open my eyes so that I might be aware of them, and give me discernment to know who I can count on to be "bridges" in my life. I know that You are my Healer, as You have said in your Word, but I need a bridge to get closer to You. Also, help me to be a bridge to other people, too. Amen.

---

1. From *Bridge Over Troubled Water* by Paul Simon, 1969. Sung by Paul Simon and Art Garfulkle on the album "Bridge Over Troubled Water."
2. Actual event story by Nancy Picha. Nancy is a former Firefighter/EMT for the Auburn, Ohio Fire Department from 2000 to 2010, currently a registered nurse in Dallas Texas.
3. Jody Hayes, *Smart Love* (NY: Penguin Putnam, Inc., 1989). p. 22, 23.
4. From a currently unpublished manual by therapist and writer J. Elizabeth Oppenheim, MA: *A Crash Course In Crisis Management: Useful Life Skills for People Who Don't Want Them.* You can contact her at elizabeth@oppenheimgroup.com

Step ⑩ How Do I Keep Going?
...Dealing With Line of Duty Stress

The legendary professional hockey goalie Jacques Plante once said, "Job stress? How would you like it if every time you made a mistake, a horn blasts, a big red light flashes and 18,000 people boo?"

When a first responder makes a mistake in the line of duty, the consequences could be even worse. One wrong split-second decision, and you could end up on the 6:00 news. You could be disciplined, fired, or sued. People could suffer. People could die. You could die.

No pressure.

Defining the Problem

In Step 2 (pages 20, 21) we looked briefly at **Occupational Stress Reactions** which include:

- **Critical Incident Stress**
- **Cumulative Stress**
- **Derivative Stress**[1]

Sometimes you experience direct trauma during a critical incident, which always has a strong effect. Multiple intense traumatic episodes can be augmented by months and years of low-level stress from various sources, accumulating with increased consequences (Cumulative). But many times a month – perhaps even daily – you deal with others who have experienced direct trauma and are currently in crisis (Derivative). This stress derives its impact from their trauma and the obligatory burden you feel to help them. You are the one they desperately look to for medical aid, explanations, direction, protection, rescue, justice, critical information, comfort, and strength. You're the one whom regular citizens (and your co-workers) depend on when it's all hitting the fan. You are often society's last line of defense against destruction, chaos, and collapse. Again, no pressure.

Add to that tension with co-workers, command, your spouse, media or politicians, and over time this strain has an incapacitating effect. Camel's backs can indeed break when that final straw is added.

This Step's Focus.

Because they are so subtle and insidious, we'll be concentrating on **Cumulative Stress** and **Derivative Stress** in this Step. However, many of the principles here can also be applied to the stress that results from Critical Incidents.

People in dangerous work environments don't often recognize threats to their health and well-being. This is why coal miners can develop black lung from coal dust, and why shipyard workers can develop mesothelioma from asbestos. During their first few years of employment they feel fine. But without safety equipment, their condition worsens gradually until it's too late to correct and it effects their entire life. The stress that exists in your first responder work environment can have the same stealthy effect on you if you aren't proactive about it. Stress is your coal dust, your asbestos.

Here's a quick review of these two forms of stress:

CUMULATIVE STRESS: Negative psychological reaction due to chronic and frequent exposure to stress-producing incidents over an extended period of time. In addition, long-term burdensome shift work, on-going conflicts with co-workers or command, exhausting work tempo, inadequate or interrupted sleep, rapid technological advances, increased specialty responsibilities, position insecurity, and reorganizations can break down a first responder's resiliency.[2]

DERIVATIVE STRESS comes in three forms that are very similar, but have subtle differences:
SECONDARY TRAUMATIC STRESS – The natural consequence of caring between two people, one of whom has been initially traumatized and the other of whom is negatively affected by the first's

traumatic experiences (even though they did not actually experience them) often mimicking their symptoms.[3]

BURNOUT – A negative, chronic emotional reaction created through long attendance in high stress workplaces, characterized by physical, mental and emotional exhaustion, depleted energy, depersonalization, lowered work efficiency, decreased motivation, pessimism, cynicism and apathy.[4,5]

COMPASSION FATIGUE - The emotional residue or strain of exposure to working with those suffering from the consequences of traumatic events; the deep awareness of the suffering of another, coupled with a fervent wish to relieve it.[6] This often results in hopelessness, a lessening of compassion, a pervasive negative attitude, and the development of new feelings of incompetency and self-doubt when the observed suffering cannot be relieved.[7]

A Lethal Cocktail.

Stress releases powerful neurochemicals and hormones that prepare us for action (to fight or flee) even though we are not in direct danger. Prolonged, uninterrupted, unexpected and unmanaged stresses are the most damaging. If not dealt with, this stress will affect you physically and psychologically in ways that are not pleasant. Your immune system will be suppressed, muscle tension and soreness will increase, digestion problems will ensue, fatigue will deepen, you will desire to exercise even *less* and you'll begin spiraling into a depressing, sedentary lifestyle that will rob you of the true *joy* and *life* God wants you to experience. In addition, this stress can lead to poor decision-making abilities regarding safety issues which jeopardize your coworkers and yourself and impact your capacity to help in a crisis situation.

> "Anyone who looks with anguish on evils so great must acknowledge the tragedy of it all; and if anyone experiences them without anguish, his condition is even more tragic since he remains serene by losing his humanity."
>
> —St. Augustine

Isn't it ironic that the doorway to these effects is your empathy – especially with regard to Derivative Stress? This admirable quality is also making you vulnerable to the high cost of caring. In addition, your training reinforces psychological toughness, self-reliance, and quick reactions to danger. You are taught to control, reject, deny or suppress "normal reactions" to abnormal events. These characteristics are crucial on the job, but they can lead to a person's demise if they don't follow an effective self-care plan.

What Causes Cumulative and Derivative Stress?

First responders are exposed to highly stressful events in the normal course of their employment. Here are some issues which are fairly specific to first responders. If encountered frequently, they can contribute to Cumulative and Derivative stress:[8]

- Having no control over the volume of calls.
- Interrupted sleep due to high call tempo.
- Having to continue responding to calls after an especially disturbing call.
- Many years of first responder service.
- Long periods of overtime requirements.
- Being in a situation where one feels helpless in the face of overwhelming demands, such as a prolonged, failed rescue.
- When a partner or peer is seriously injured or killed in the line of duty.
- Suicide of a partner or peer.
- Being at serious risk, such as dealing with armed suspects or running out of air in a working fire.
- Witnessing horrifying things, such as dismembered bodies or severe wounds.
- Experiencing the death of a child while on duty.
- Responding to a call for a victim who is known to the responder.

- Having to inform a victim's family of their death.
- Making a treatment mistake that leads to someone's worsening condition or death.
- Feeling unappreciated by command, co-workers, public.
- Being given new specialty or command responsibilities.
- Moving to a new station or area of responsibility; department reorganization.
- Job or position insecurity.
- Interpersonal conflicts with coworkers.
- Working without the full support of administration, or when command questions one's actions in an investigation.

 Within the past two years, how many of the above incidents have you experienced? Check them off. Do you feel any of them have affected you negatively – individually or cumulatively? If so, how?

_____

_____

Cumulative and Derivative Stress Symptom Inventory

In the professional literature, each type of stress has a fairly well-defined set of symptoms, but there is a lot of overlap between them. For our purposes in this manual, we'll combine the symptoms into the following list. It doesn't matter at this moment that you know which specific "brand" of stress you are experiencing. But it will be useful to know how strongly it is currently affecting you.

We'll organize them according to five general classes of symptoms. Put a check mark next to any that you are currently experiencing.

EMOTIONAL SYMPTOMS

- ❑ Feeling powerless
- ❑ Anxiety
- ❑ Guilt, shame
- ❑ Anger, rage, irritability
- ❑ Survivor guilt
- ❑ Shutting down

- ❑ Numbness
- ❑ Fearfulness, dread, horror
- ❑ Helplessness
- ❑ Sadness, depression
- ❑ Feeling worthless

- ❑ Hypersensitivity
- ❑ Emotional roller coaster
- ❑ Overwhelmed
- ❑ Depleted
- ❑ Bottled up emotions

PHYSICAL SYMPTOMS

- ❑ Shock
- ❑ Sweating
- ❑ Rapid heartbeat
- ❑ Breathing difficulties

- ❑ Aches and pains
- ❑ Dizziness
- ❑ Impaired immune system
- ❑ Chronic lack of energy

- ❑ Sleepy all the time
- ❑ Poor self-care (i.e. hygiene, appearance)
- ❑ Gastrointestinal distress

COGNITIVE SYMPTOMS

- ❑ Diminished concentration
- ❑ Confusion, spaciness
- ❑ Forgotten appointments
- ❑ Chronic lateness
- ❑ Loss of meaning
- ❑ Decreased self-esteem

- ❑ Preoccupation with trauma
- ❑ Nightmares
- ❑ Flashbacks
- ❑ Apathy
- ❑ Rigid, uncompromising
- ❑ Disorientation

- ❑ Thoughts of self-harm
- ❑ Thoughts of harming others
- ❑ Self-doubt
- ❑ Perfectionism
- ❑ Minimization (nothing really matters)

BEHAVIORAL SYMPTOMS

- ❏ Impatient
- ❏ Irritable, moody
- ❏ Withdrawn
- ❏ Regression (reverting to an immature level)
- ❏ Sleep disturbances
- ❏ Appetite changes

- ❏ Nightmares
- ❏ Hypervigilance
- ❏ Elevated startle response
- ❏ Substance abuse (drugs, alcohol, tobacco)
- ❏ Losing/forgetting things
- ❏ Accident-prone

- ❏ Self-harm behaviors (i.e. self-mutilation, cutting, eating disorders)
- ❏ Compulsiveness (i.e. over eating, gambling, sex, spending, workaholic, thrill-seeking, etc.)

INTERPERSONAL SYMPTOMS

- ❏ Withdrawn
- ❏ Feeling vulnerable, unsafe
- ❏ Decreased interest in intimacy, sex
- ❏ Mistrust, suspicious of others

- ❏ Need to control others
- ❏ Loss of personal control and freedom
- ❏ Changes in parenting (i.e. overprotective, abusive, critical, disinterested, etc.)

- ❏ Intolerance
- ❏ Loneliness
- ❏ Isolation from friends
- ❏ Projection of anger or blame
- ❏ Verbally or physically abusive or combative

Obviously, in this manual we will not be able to give you a bona fide diagnosis regarding your level of Cumulative or Derivative stress – that can be accomplished only through an assessment with a professional counselor. But what we are hoping to accomplish in this exercise is to give you a general idea of the severity or mildness of your current level of stress. Based on this, you can make a decision about whether or not to seek help from someone qualified in this area. Besides this, it could be a strong motivation to seek out other "Bridge People" (Step 9) who can help you work through your stress. It should also prompt you to seek God's direct aid and healing through prayer.

 Has this exercise been helpful to you or not so much? In what ways? _____

_____

Recovery and Resilience

The rest of this Step will involve two pursuits: (1) **Recovery**: devising an intentional plan to stabilize some of your more critical areas of stress and (2) **Resilience**: coming up with a long-term plan to provide a general de-stressing of your life and insulate it from the effects of on-going job-related stress.

Motivation for Recovery and Resilience

Most people in the "helping professions" tend to put the needs of everyone else ahead of their own. It's honorable to do so, courageous, the epitome of humility, and also very short-sighted. Combat medics have this philosophy drilled into them throughout their training: **"You MUST take care of yourself first, because you are no good to anybody dead."** Society desperately needs what first responders provide. But if you are sidelined and unavailable due to debilitating stress, what service can you provide?

A man once asked Jesus, "Teacher, what is the most important commandment in the Law?" Jesus gave him two for the price of one – not only the most important, but the second most important too:

"You shall love the Lord your God with all your heart, and with all your soul, and with all your mind." This is the first and foremost commandment. The second is like it, "You shall love your neighbor as yourself." On these two commandments depend the whole Law and the Prophets.

—Matthew 22:37-40

The previous passage mentions three "persons" who are supposed to be loved, not just two. List them here:

_____

What do you think the difference is between loving yourself and being selfish? _____

_____

Note the standard of measurement Jesus placed on *"love your neighbor."* How are we to love them? *In the same way we love ourselves.* For many people, that's not a very high standard – especially for those who are experiencing depression, stress and anxiety. Their self-esteem and sense of worth are often in the toilet. They feel they are failing on many fronts. "Besides," they reason, "The needs of other people are greater than mine. If I don't meet those needs, who will?" So their needs go unmet, and before long they're stressed out, running on fumes, and sitting on the bench.

The solution is that we need to see ourselves and value ourselves as God does. Give yourself the same dignity, worth and respect that God affords you. How worthy does *He* think you are? Worth enough to die for. Worth every drop of blood He shed for you. Worth turning your body into His temple. Worth calling you friend. Worth adopting. Worth living with forever. He wants you to take care of yourself.

Strategy for Recovery

Stress is no simple matter. There is no magic wand, and no simple plan that will restore you to your pre-stress status. It took a great deal of negative experiences to get you where you are, and it will take no less than the direct action of God to get you where you want to be. Never forget that *He is the healer!*

A. Look over your list of symptoms on pages 137 & 138. Which three concern you the most?

1. _____

2. _____

3. _____

B. For each of those three symptoms, write out a goal statement – how you would like to be functioning regarding that issue within the next two to four months. It doesn't have to be something you achieve through your own efforts. What would you like to see happen? What do you want to see God do?

1. _____

2. _____

3. _____

C. Now comes the difficult, but most necessary and helpful part. Copy each of those goals on a half sheet of paper. Put it in your Bible, or somewhere you will see it each morning. Turn those goals into three daily prayers, asking God to reverse your current debilitating symptoms and turn them into strengths. In your times of prayer, ask God to give you insights about anything you need to do to cooperate with Him in the process. Listen for His voice. Trust the impressions that He puts in your mind. Act on them! Don't abandon this plan just because you don't see results right away. Remember Jesus' instructions on getting "Yes" answers to your prayers: keep on!

> *Keep on asking and it will be given you; keep on seeking and you will find;*
>
> *keep on knocking and the door will be opened to you.*

—**Matthew 7:7** (AMP)

 Spend a quiet moment right now, asking God if there is anything you need to do at this time to partner with His Holy Spirit to bring about the transformation you need in each of these three areas. If nothing comes to mind, leave it blank. If God gives you something specific to do, write it down (next page):

1._____

2._____

3._____

If, after praying about these things for a while, God impresses upon you some action you need to take, write it down in the above spaces or on another sheet. By the way, there is no rule against choosing more than three stress symptoms that you're seeking God's help with. As God tells us in James 4:2, *"You do not have because you do not ask."* So ASK!

Strategy for Resilience

Resilient [ri-ˈzil-yǝnt – adjective]: capable of withstanding shock without permanent deformation or rupture; tending to recover from or adjust easily to misfortune or change.

—**Merriam-Webster's Deluxe Dictionary**

It's not enough to recover from your current stress. Realistically, as long as you are among the ranks of first responders you will continue to encounter new trauma and stress. You cannot hope to be *isolated* from stress, but you can become *insulated* from its effects. Firefighters can walk right through flames and experience no negative effects – provided they are fully decked out in their turnouts, boots, gloves, helmet, face shield and oxygen tank. A police officer can be shot in the chest and live – provided he or she is wearing a Kevlar vest.

So, anticipating all of your future shocks, misfortune, and changes, and planning to avoid permanent deformation or rupture because of your *resilience*, it is vital that you gear up for the long-haul – *before* you arrive at the fireground or the active shooter call.

These "gearing up" measures will not only aid your current efforts to recover from stress, they will prepare you for the future. We'll examine them as they apply to three domains: Spirit, Soul, and Body.

Spiritual Resilience Preparation

1. Stay In Your Healing Place

In Steps 3A and 3B we examined how you can cooperate with God to construct an environment that will facilitate your healing. Five important elements of that environment were expanded upon:

1. The Holy Spirit – your divine power source

2. The Word of God – your divine food and weapon

3. Prayer – vital communication with your divine command structure

4. The Christian Community – your divine station house

5. Your Mindset – spiritual themes for divine healing

Those same five elements are also vital to an environment that will facilitate growing resilience. The more time you spend walking in the fullness of the Holy Spirit, taking in God's Word, talking with Him in prayer, hanging out with Spirit-filled, encouraging friends, and developing your spiritual mindset, the more rapidly you'll progress in both your recovery and your resilience.

We won't reiterate the points we made in Steps 3A and 3B – but if you need a refresher, go back and re-read those Steps.

2. Connect With God Daily

The essence of eternal life is *to know God.* We can begin to know Him right here, right now. We can learn things about Him that will deepen our relationship with Him and prove to be vital to our spiritual resilience. How important is this? Read the Apostle Paul's opinion on the subject:

> *More than that, I count all things to be loss in view of the surpassing value of knowing Christ Jesus my Lord, for whom I have suffered the loss of all things, and count them but rubbish so that I may gain Christ.*

—**Philippians 3:8**

Two Main Objectives in a daily "Quiet Time."

1. To build a deeper relationship with God, which requires *communication* (prayer).
2. To learn about the things of God and His Kingdom, which requires *education* (Bible study).

3. Lots of Other Ideas

Without taking the time and space to expand on these suggestions, here is a list of ways you could also think about preparing your spirit for resilience. Read over the list and ask God to speak to you about anything He might want you to pursue further.

> **Jesus praying:**
> *This is eternal life, that they may know You, the only true God, and Jesus Christ whom You have sent.*
> —John 17:3

- Keep forgiveness issues up to date (Steps 6A and 6B). What do you need to forgive others for? From whom do you need to seek forgiveness? What might you need to forgive *yourself* for?

- Meditate on who *you* are in Christ – your *true* identity (refer to Step 7).

- Keep a prayer journal. Ask God to give you Scripture promises, write them down, pray and meditate on them. Write down answers to your prayers, no matter how small or insignificant they might seem.

- Read inspirational books. Ask a trusted friend who has a strong walk with God what he/she has been reading lately, or what they might suggest for you.

- Ask God to show you His perspective, to see things through His eyes.

- Enlist prayer intercessors. Put your best prayer warriors on active duty. Stay in close contact with them and let them know regularly what you need prayer about.

- Find a trusted spiritual mentor. Don't know where to find one? Ask God to bring one along and to let you know when he or she shows up!

- Serve others outside the first responder context. Think about ways God might want to use you to minister to others in new contexts. Your church? Kid's school? Homeless shelter?

My Spiritual Resilience Preparation Contract

Starting within the next five days to two weeks (note when, exactly), I will make the following adjustments to my lifestyle, and/or add the following activities:

1. _____

2. _____

3. _____

Share this plan with your spouse or a Bridge friend. Write down more than three if you'd like to!

Soul Resilience Preparation

Your "soul" is the part of you that involves your will, your intellect, your understanding, and your emotions. It's the essence of *you*. Everyone has a soul – in fact, you could say that everyone *is* a soul, created by God:

> *And the LORD God formed man of the dust of the ground, and breathed into his nostrils the breath of life; and man became a living soul.*

— **Genesis 2:7** (KJV)

Things you do that mold and stimulate your will, expand and challenge your intellect, deepen your understanding and help you to experience and savor your emotions – these are all things that constitute resilience preparation for your soul. Beauty, love, truth, faith, hope, knowledge, wisdom, humility, fun, friendships, challenge, accomplishment, wonder – all these things feed our souls.

Following are some activities that will help you feed and strengthen your soul…

1. Remember your strengths.

God has endowed you with many strengths, skills, talents, blessings and gifts. You are a work of art! In fact, Ephesians 2:10 refers to us as God's "workmanship." The word used in the original Greek is *poiema* from which we get the English word "poem." In the stress, exhaustion and craziness of your life right now, you may forget that you are God's poem – far more eloquent, deep and full of meaning than anything ever written by Shakespeare! Remembering this should renew your focus and sense of worth. List three things that you would consider strengths, skills, talents or gifts that you possess:

1. _____

2. _____

3. _____

2. Set personal boundaries and margin.

Learn how to say "no" to busyness and unnecessary activities that drain your emotional tank. You may be a chronic "joiner" or the world champion of "get-'er-done." People know this about you and might often take advantage. It's admirable that you are so willing to jump in and help out, but if you're constantly running on fumes your body's natural boundary will force you to stop.

Here's an important motto to learn, love, and live: **"THE NEED IS NOT THE CALL."** You are constantly surrounded by needs, but to see a need doesn't automatically mean that you are called to meet it. Ask God for discernment to know which needs you are called to, and which ones you need to leave for others.

3. Schedule personal R & R.

Calendarize some time to re-charge your soul's batteries. If you do, you'll feel better, act better, react better, and be better able to meet the needs to which you *are* called. Set aside personal time on a daily basis – a quarter-hour to spend time reading God's word or a good book, pruning your roses, polishing your Harley – whatever turns *your* crank.

Set aside an occasional half-day or day to do something you love. Sometimes you should schedule a day to do absolutely *nothing*. Once or twice a year, schedule a personal retreat of three to five days, during which you can totally relax, spend hours with your heavenly Father and get your emotional tanks filled and topped off.

4. Check out something beautiful.

God is a creative being and He's put within each of us a profound appreciation of creation and creativity. Schedule some "Beauty Appointments" to places where they keep the beautiful things: art galleries, museums, parks, churches, the ocean side, the mountains. Absorb the beauty, appreciate the uniqueness of each creation, the genius, the detail.

My Soul Resilience Preparation Contract

Starting within the next five days to two weeks (note when, exactly), I will make the following adjustments in my lifestyle, and/or add the following activities:

1. _____

2. _____

3. _____

Again, share this plan with your spouse or a Bridge person. Write more than three if you'd like to.

Body Resilience Preparation

Up to 90 percent of doctor visits in the USA are prompted by stress-related illness, according to the Centers for Disease Control and Prevention.[9] Excess stress is found from sea to shining sea, but add *first responder line of duty stress* to the mix and you've got some *real* stress! Here are four proactive ways you can reduce stress in your body – and since there is such a strong bond between your body and your mind, they will positively affect your mental/emotional state as well. Here are two key elements:

1. Get Some Exercise!

What happens when I exercise? Flexing and stretching your muscles, getting your heart and lungs working a little harder, rising to a physical challenge – these trigger beneficial responses all over your body. Your immune and endocrine systems get fired up; helpful antibodies are released; your white blood cell count increases; extra adrenaline and growth hormone is released; serotonin (a depression reducer) uptake is increased; pleasure-inducing hormones are released in the brain, creating the euphoria most people feel during and after exercise. Testosterone levels rise in both men and women.

Exercise is also a mood-improver, especially for people with major depression. Clinical studies have shown that exercise promotes positive moods, a sense of meaning in life, and improves self-esteem. It will actually lower the concentration of stress hormones in your body.[10]

Choose a variety of exercises. Don't get stuck in a rut. Make exercise fun – not a chore. Mix them up!

Aerobic Exercises	Anaerobic Exercises
Walking	Weight lifting
Running	Sprinting
Race walking	Interval training/Fartlek
Swimming	Jumping rope
Cycling	Fast or uphill cycling
Aerobics/Dancing	Hill walking/climbing
Racquetball/Tennis	Any rapid burst of hard exercise

2. Get Some Sleep!

When a person is deprived of normal sleep, all kinds of difficulties can crop up:

- Aching muscles
- Accident prone
- Blurred vision
- Clinical depression
- Loss of sexual desire
- Decreased concentration
- Digestion problems
- Dizziness
- Headache
- Suppressed growth hormones
- Irritability
- Loss of appetite
- Hypertension
- Memory lapses
- Weakened immune system
- Slow reaction time
- Slurred speech
- Obesity
- Daytime drowsiness

Planning for better sleep. The normal schedules for first responders are abnormal! So you may have difficulty applying this one consistently. But if you can, here are some tips for becoming a better sleeper:[11]

- **A cool, dark room.** Lower temperature and lack of light is a signal to your pineal gland to kick up melatonin production (a natural relaxant your body makes) and ferry you off to slumber land.

- **White noise.** Sounds that cover a broad range of frequencies and negate or drown out other sounds – a river, the ocean surf, wind blowing through the trees, an electric fan.

- **A good rhythm.** Our bodies like rhythms. If your duty schedule will allow it, get into a consistent sleep/wake pattern. Lights off, alarm on – same time each night and morning.

- **Bedtime rituals.** Think of a series of activities you could perform every night to get your body and mind thinking, "Bed… sleep… rest." TV and laptops are counter-productive here.

- **No booze.** Alcohol is a depressant which can increase nightmares and aggravate an already depressed state. Avoid it for a couple of hours before bedtime.

- **No caffeine.** Coffee, some teas, some chocolate – avoid these at least six hours before bedtime.

My Body Resilience Preparation Contract

Starting within the next five days to two weeks (note when, exactly), I will make the following adjustments in my lifestyle, and/or add the following activities:

1. _____

2. _____

3. _____

Prayer Seed

Heavenly Father, I know you originally made my body, soul and spirit perfect. But you and I are both aware of the traumas and stresses I have endured over the years, and how they have affected me. In many ways, my desire to help others has backfired, and now I am struggling. I cannot by my own efforts reverse the damage that these stresses have inflicted. I need your transformation, your redemption. I desire to cooperate with your plans to bring about healing, strength and stability in me once again. Amen.

---

1. "Derivative Stress" is a non-medical, general term coined by the authors, intended to encompass three familiar and medically well-defined conditions: Secondary Traumatic Stress, Burnout and Compassion Fatigue. The term describes the strong, long-lasting emotional reactions which derive their impact from trauma that happened to another person. Others might use the term "Vicarious Traumatization" (Saakvitne, Gamble, Pearlman, and Lev: 2000).

2. Applied research project paper by Suzanne Todd (CA Dept. of Forestry and Fire Protection/Placer County Fire Dept): "Managing Cumulative Stress In Fire Service Personnel: Strategic Management of Change." (National Fire Academy Executive Fire Officer Program, February, 2001).

3. Dr. Charles Figley (Ed), *Compassion Fatigue – Coping With Secondary Traumatic Stress Disorder in Those Who Treat the Traumatized* (NY: Brunner-Routledge, 1995). p. 11.

4. C. Maslach & M. P. Leiter: "Stress and Burnout: the Critical Research," in C. L. Cooper (Ed.), *Handbook of Stress Medicine and Health* (Lancaster:CRC Press, 2005). pp. 155-172.

5. Dr. Leslie Snider, podcast for Antares Foundation: "Stress Management for Emergency Responders: Understanding Responder Stress." 2009.

6. Dr. Charles Figley (Ed.), pp. xv, 2, 3, 14, 15.

7. Article in *St. Petersburg Bar Association Magazine*: "Compassion Fatigue – Because You Care." Retrieved February 2007

8. Many of these observations are from The Trauma Center: "First Responders and Traumatic Events: Normal Distress and Stress Disorders" www.traumacenter.org/resources/pdf_files/First_Responders.pdf. Also drawing from Suzanne Todd's applied research paper, cited above (2).

9. Dr. Joseph Mercola quoting a USA Today article from March 22, 2005 on www.mercola.com.

10. Medical information in this and the previous two paragraphs are from Claire Michaels Wheeler, MD, Ph.D., *10 Simple Solutions to Stress* (Oakland, CA: New Harbinger Publications, 2007). pp. 113-116.

11. Tips came from www.realage.com/stayingyoung/youtoolstips.aspx?tip=1 and Davidson, *The Complete Idiot's Guide to Managing Stress*, pp. 160-167.

Step 11 How Do I Help My Family?
...Leading Your Family Despite Your Stress and Trauma

From Erin's Journal...

I got out of bed this morning, shuffled into the kitchen and poured myself a cup of coffee. My County Sheriff husband Scott had already left for work. What was left in the pot had boiled down to battery acid. I didn't care – I needed a jump start. I sat at the table, opened my Bible, and just stared at it. I didn't feel much like reading or praying.

My head aches from crying myself to sleep last night. Lately, life feels like a scary amusement park. A greasy, snaggletoothed carnival worker laughs at my helplessness, refusing to let me off the rickety rollercoaster. The tracks lock and pull me to the shaky precipice, then release me, plummeting to the bottom again and again. The sharp corners and abrupt stops whiplash my heart and mind. I'm freefalling through my days, unable to focus in the blur of stress Scott brings to our home. I want off this terrible ride! Nauseated, I stumble off, only to be startled by nightmarish clowns and by my own twisted reflections in my un-fun house, a home that's been invaded by posttraumatic stress.

I'm trying to hold it all together for Scott and our kids, but I think I'm losing it. I can't concentrate on anything. My mind wanders and drifts, searching for a safe place to land. It's hard to track conversations. I read the same sentences over and over, with little comprehension. I find joy in *nothing*, not even in my favorite people or places or hobbies anymore.

I feel jumpy, irritable, edgy. I worry that I might say or do something to set Scott off. So the kids and I tiptoe around on eggshells, speaking in hushed tones like people do in hospital waiting rooms. How fitting though. My home has become like a hospital ward. And I am growing weary, waiting for Scott to heal.

I want to go back to bed, pull the covers over my head, and pray this has been only a bad dream.[1]

The Impact of Line of Duty Stress and Trauma On Your Family

You might be thinking, "Wait a minute. I'm the one who goes out and risks my life every day. I'm the one being traumatized and stressed - not her (him). My spouse should understand that, and be more supportive." And though you may not say this consciously, you may also be thinking, "My needs are more profound and critical than hers (his), and they should take priority."

As a first responder, you have chosen an honorable profession which your family and community value and appreciate. You knew going into it that your career would probably expose you to stressful and/or traumatic events, sometimes with the accompanying post-trauma reactions – and you were OK with that. But you may not have understood how it could spill over and affect your family, and rock what you assumed would be a stable, supportive and encouraging home base for your life.

One trauma, two wounds.

You received excellent training which equipped you to work in life-threatening situations, react to violence and danger, and keep yourself and your buddies safe. Despite this, you have been wounded – if not physically, at least in mind and spirit. Now your wounds may be wounding your spouse, who was never trained to defend herself (himself) from this surprise attack. Your symptoms may be showing up in her (him).

Bottom line: your career affects your family in both positive and negative ways. Hooray for the positives, but how can you be intentional about minimizing the negatives?

"Having PTSD doesn't give you license to be a jerk." This is what we often tell men and women who are suffering from line of duty or combat-related stress and trauma. It doesn't release you from your roles and responsibilities as a leader of your household. Everybody doesn't have to focus on you, accommodate you, understand you, serve you, and make sure you end up ok. That kind of environment is counter-productive anyway – it robs you of your ability to regain your sense of honor and usefulness. This Step will focus on how not to be a jerk, despite the difficulties you may be dealing with currently.

? Have you experienced a traumatic incident in the line of duty that may have affected your spouse? In what ways do you think it has it affected him or her?

_____

_____

In what ways has your relationship with your spouse changed since you began work as a first responder?

_____

_____

✦   ✦   ✦   ✦   ✦

Spousal Secondary Traumatic Stress

What Erin was writing about in her journal entry above has only been recently identified by mental health professionals as a common experience. For several decades, first responders, counselors, psychiatrists, doctors, nurses, social workers, pastors, chaplains, and others who frequently deal with the traumatized would sometimes slip into depression and anxiety. They were at a loss to explain why they were being affected so deeply, or how to avoid it. It wasn't until around 1990 that significant studies were conducted, and Secondary Traumatic Stress was identified and defined (see page 135). Now we understand that this Traumatic Stress can also be experienced by the spouses of first responders in two ways:

1. Reacting to hearing about his/her spouse's traumatic experiences (*Secondary* Traumatic Stress)

2. Being traumatized directly by his/her spouse's behavior (*Primary* Traumatic Stress).

For instance, a wife could be experiencing Secondary Traumatic Stress because her husband has shared with her his horrific line of duty experiences, and it was more than she could handle. In addition, her compassion and empathy has been on overdrive as she's watched her loved one struggle and suffer with his symptoms. If this goes on for long periods, she could also experience Burnout and/or Compassion Fatigue (page 136).

But one night the husband may have a vivid nightmare about a criminal trying to overpower him, and he half wakes up and thinks his wife sleeping in bed next to him is that criminal. He attacks her. He comes to his senses before it's too late, but as you can imagine, this traumatizes his wife. She could now develop Primary Traumatic Stress, since she has experienced a traumatizing event directly.

In either case – Primary or Secondary – her symptoms can become as intense and debilitating as her husband's and even develop into the most severe form of Traumatic Stress: Posttraumatic Stress Disorder. A traumatic stressor is worse when the cause is human neglect or human cruelty. Think how much worse the effect is when the neglect or cruelty comes from her beloved partner, the man she married assuming that she could trust him implicitly, that he would be her primary source of care and protection. When that trust proves to be misplaced, how can she *not* be traumatized?

What Your Spouse Wants You To Know

Your spouse may be handling your stress quite well at present. Or she/he may be having grave difficulties. If you're not aware and intentional, the former could become the latter, and the latter could – in the worst case – develop into divorce or suicide. Whatever the case, there are a number of things that she or he wants you to know but doesn't tell you out of fear of your reaction.

We recently conducted an internet survey with first responder spouses all over the world, asking about their challenges, what they wish their spouse knew, how they cope, and thoughts about how to improve their family environment. Following is a condensed and blended list that expresses the most frequently mentioned issues from the survey responses. These aren't valid for ALL first responder couples, but many of them may be true of yours. Check the ones that you think might be…

❑ I pray for you every day as you leave for work, and often throughout the day. This is comforting, but it also has a tendency to increase my anxiety level a little. But I don't care – I'll pray anyway.

❑ I have a hard time shaking the fear I feel every time the phone or doorbell rings. Could it be the Chief or your partner bringing bad news? This wears on me.

❑ Sometimes you tend to get "lost" in your work. Your body comes home, but sometimes your mind doesn't quite make it to our front door.

❑ We need a brief de-briefing every day when you come home. Just a few minutes to connect and say, "This happened today… I feel… I just need… before delving into…"

❑ I understand that you need to be emotionally detached while on duty, but turn that off at the end of your shift. The kids and I need you to be emotionally present at home. The Ice Man needs to thaw.

❑ Something else to turn off before you come home: your command identity! It's fine to order people around at work, but not at home. Don't expect me and the kids to salute. And when things aren't up to snuff, don't interrogate us like criminals.

❑ Anger can be productively channeled when in stressful or dangerous confrontations at work. But it's not nearly as useful at home. It makes the kids afraid of you, and of what you do. Learn to use anger management techniques.

❑ When you blow it at home, acknowledge it and take responsibility. Let your family (especially your kids) know that they are not to blame. Be willing to apologize.

❑ You may make some wrong decisions at work, and there may be consequences. This causes you anxiety and self-doubt. But they don't love you like we do! Please don't worry about making mistakes here at home. *Love covers a multitude of sins!* (1 Peter 4:8). The kids and I are very *proud* of you and what you do!

❑ When you're on an emotional roller coaster, I'm on an emotional roller coaster.

❑ All first responders form strong friendship bonds on the job – and I know that's good! But please work at making sure your strongest bonds are with your family. You're married to *me,* not your badge or your partner!

❑ The kids and I want to share things with you – good days, bad days, frustrations, challenges, etc. We don't necessarily need you to *fix* them. We just want you to listen and be a part of them.

❑ I need you to be an active pace-setter in our family with regard to spiritual issues – attending church, reading the Bible as a family, setting a Godly example for me and the kids, keeping your relationship with God as your top priority, etc.

❑ You are a protector. I understand that you want to protect me, so you often choose not talk with me about what goes on at work. But this doesn't come across as protection; it feels more like you're cutting me off from a major part of your life. I need to know what you experience, so I can better support you and pray for you. You don't have to tell me all the gory details, but I need you to *not* protect me as much. I can probably handle it. I'll tell you if it's too much.

❑ If you share with me the difficulties you have at work, or about how specific calls affected you that day, we will be better able to address them and their effects *together*. It will help us with communication and connection.

❑ I know that certain programs you watch on TV get you amped up, and it translates into more arguments and tension at home. Could you avoid them – for the family's sake?

❑ I don't like spending so many nights alone. I know it comes with the territory, but I just want you to know I don't like it. I like it best when you're in bed beside me.

❑ Frankly, I am afraid of you having an affair. It happens with a lot of first responders. I need assurances from you – not just words, but opportunities for me to "catch you doing the right thing." Let's talk about how to do that, without you feeling like I'm always checking up on you.

❑ When you're on long or multi-day shifts, I feel like a single parent. It's a lot of work! I need you to (a) express thankfulness for all I do in your absence and (b) not expect me to easily and automatically turn the steering wheel back over to you the moment you walk in the door. But I don't want you to go incognito either. Let's be sensitive to each other during "reentry phase."

❑ Sure, you can save somebody's life or put out a burning building, but can you take out the trash? Mow the lawn? I know they don't seem as important – but we all need to do our part.

❑ When you don't come home when expected, it causes me to worry, but it especially increases the children's anxiety level. Let me know if you're going to come home late.

❑ I love it when you call or text me (or the kids) during the day just to say hi or I love you.

❑ With your unpredictable work schedule, mandatory overtime and call outs, it's hard to schedule things. But let's not allow our dates and romantic times to be pre-empted too often.

❑ The problems I deal with aren't life-and-death, as yours often are. But they are still my problems, and sometimes they seem very difficult. Please don't minimize them. Instead, encourage me to share them with you – otherwise I may be reluctant to.

❑ I worry about your future beyond your first responder career. So much of your identity is wrapped up in it. We need to talk about and prepare for retirement – socially and financially.

❑ You know how much you love to help people? How good it makes you feel? It makes me feel good to help *you!* So let me!

If you feel brave enough, and would like to get some really honest feedback from your spouse, share a clean copy of this list and let him or her check off the statements that apply. Then discuss them.

Eight Things You Can and Should Do for Your Family Despite Your Stress and Trauma

1. Men, remember that you are the "Head" of the family.

But I want you to understand that Christ is the head of every man, and the man is the head of a woman, and God is the head of Christ."

—1 Corinthians 11:3

When many people look at the above verse, they think the word translated "head" here means "authority" or "boss." The Greek word for "head" in this verse is *kephale*. Like its English equivalent, it is used to refer to the part of your body that includes your eyes, nose, mouth, ears and brains. But it also has several metaphorical meanings. In some contexts it means "authority" and could be used as we say, "the *head* of the department." In other places it clearly conveys the idea of "source" or "origin" as it does in English when we speak of the *head*waters of a river.

In the Septuagint – an ancient Greek translation of the Hebrew Old Testament written prior to the birth of Christ – the translators used *kephale* for "ruler" or "leader" only five percent of the time. They used a different word all the other times. On the other hand, there are many, many places in ancient Greek literature where *kephale* is used to describe "source" or "origin." Aristotle believed that semen was produced in the male brain (head), and this thought influenced many generations of philosophers and writers after him – probably including the Septuagint translators and therefore, the Apostle Paul (the human scribe of the above verse). For them, the *head* represented the source of life.[2]

This idea of the husband being the "source of life" for his wife and family could be developed much further – in a book about the Greek language, not this one! But as for a first responder husband's self-concept, it's a good mindset to cultivate.

 Obviously, the true and ultimate source of life for every person is God (Genesis 2:7; Acts 17:28). But in some profound way, husbands are meant to be a source of life for their wives and children. Take a moment and think of how you could bring life into your family – even while fighting the symptoms of stress and trauma – and write your thoughts below. **If you are a female first responder, nothing says you too aren't meant to bring life into your family!** How can you do it?

_____

_____

_____

2. Ask your spouse to take the *Traumatic Stress Self-Test.*

Your spouse may never have considered the possibility that some of the distressing thoughts and feelings he or she has are due to Secondary Traumatic Stress. They might be quite alarmed, thinking that they are the only first responder spouse who feels as they do. It would be to their advantage to be aware of this condition so that healing steps can be taken. Just be sure that you are prepared for some of the answers he/she may share with you. They may not always be pleasant – but hopefully they'll be honest.

The self-test found in **Appendix E** (page 191). Feel free to photocopy it and give it to your spouse. Then discuss it with him or her after it's complete. This test was originally devised by Dr. Charles Figley[3] as a self-test for counselors and therapists to determine how deeply they were being influenced by the trauma of their clients. It was shortened and altered a little later by Figley and two colleagues from Canada's Traumatology Institute, Dr. Anna Baranowsky and Dr. Eric Gentry. We have further adapted it here for use by first responder spouses. It is not a scientific or statistically verified test (Figley's original test was, but this adaptation has yet to be reviewed). However, it should at least give you some idea of how light or heavy your spouse's current stress load is.

3. Examine yourself.

None of us is beyond the need for forgiveness. God's Word says, *"All of us like sheep have gone astray, each of us has turned to his own way..."* (Isaiah 53:6). Jesus made it clear that we need always to be aware of our own sins and humbly seek God's forgiveness for them. After sharing the story about the self-righteous Pharisee who gave God a bullet-pointed list of how awesome he was, and the humble tax collector who understood his sinfulness and asked God to be merciful (Luke 10:9-14), Jesus declared that the latter was forgiven and justified. He went on to say, *"For everyone who exalts himself will be humbled, but he who humbles himself will be exalted."*

It is vital that each of us be intentional about spiritual self-examination and keep short accounts with God. As King David asked God,

> *Search me, O God, and know my heart; try me and know my anxious thoughts;*
> *And see if there be any hurtful way in me, and lead me in the everlasting way.*

— Psalm 139:23, 24

Subsequent to this self-examination, repentance and confession to God, figure out if you also need to ask your spouse for forgiveness. It has been said that the ten most powerful words in the English language are the following:

I am sorry. I was wrong. Will you forgive me?

? If you can be sensitive to your own sins and hurtful actions and be humble enough to admit them to your spouse, you bring life and light into your family. Spend a little time with God right now and ask Him to search your heart and reveal anything in you that is displeasing to Him. Write down anything that God brings to mind that you need to deal with. Do you need to bring this up with your spouse?

_____

_____

_____

4. Are you abusing your spouse?

What? Did you read that correctly? "Abusing? Don't be ridiculous. Things may be a little tense between us sometimes, but in no way do I abuse my spouse."

We honor and respect the men and women who invest so much of their lives as the "Kevlar of our society," but domestic abuse by first responders *does* happen – way too frequently. This abuse can be triggered by a variety of stressors and can take many forms. You may have everything under control. Or you may only think you have. Or you may rationalize that your stress and trauma gives you an excuse to act abusively, or that *it* is to blame and not *you*. This section provides a very practical and profound way to educate yourself and apply point #3 above. It could be very eye-opening for you.

Abuse can take many forms. As first responders, you are most familiar with **physical and sexual abuse** – you probably see their effects frequently as you perform your duties. We won't go into those two most-obvious varieties of abuse in this short section. If either of those are a problem for you, you are already aware of it. If you're not getting help, we strongly urge you to do so.

In any case of abuse, the main objective of the abuser is to establish his superiority and to secure or maintain his power and control over the victim. We'll take a quick look at four forms of abuse which are sometimes present in a marriage relationship, but may not be recognized as abuse to the person engaged in them. Actual physical violence is often the end result of months or even years of these other types of abuse. As you read the following descriptions, ask God to open your eyes to any "hurtful ways" that you may be practicing. Put a tick-mark next to any that might describe how you sometimes treat your spouse.

A. Spiritual Abuse

The misuse of real or perceived spiritual authority to secure superiority, power and control over another or to get their way regardless of the other person's wishes. Appealing to Biblical precepts (usually out of context) to achieve one's personal agenda with either no thought or a misconception regarding God's actual approval of their action.

B. Emotional Abuse[4]

An intentional or unintentional attack on another person's character, worth, or abilities to gain a position of superiority, power, and control through shame, insult, ridicule, intimidation, embarrassment or demeaning. It can also involve:

- Withholding money, limiting access to money or bank accounts, requiring an accounting for every penny, creating debt, not paying child support (also called "Financial Abuse").

- Denying permission to work, see friends or family, make decisions, socialize or keep property ("Social Abuse").

- Threatening abandonment or taking the children away ("Family Threat Abuse").

- Having to prove things to another, mind games, demanding perfection, being made to feel stupid, attacking ideas and opinions, telling the victim he/she is crazy ("Intellectual Abuse")

- Ridiculing another's valued beliefs, religion, race, or heritage; forcing another to adopt one's cultural practices; forbidding another to practice his or her cultural beliefs ("Cultural Abuse")

C. Psychological Abuse[4]

Intentionally or unintentionally attacking another person's reality or perspective in order to gain a position of superiority, power and control in a way that is psychologically harmful.

For a chilling look at a classic example of psychological abuse, watch the 1944 movie *Gaslight,* starring Ingrid Bergman and Charles Boyer. Since that movie, the term "Gaslighting" has been used in clinical and research literature, and describes a form of abuse in which false information is presented with the intent of making victims doubt their own memory, perception and sanity.

D. Verbal Abuse[5]

Intentionally or unintentionally using words to gain a position of superiority, power and control over another through:

- **Withholding** – "I'm in control because I have what you need and you can't have it."

- **Countering** – "I'm right, you're wrong." She doubts herself, so he's in control.

- **Discounting** – "Your opinion is worthless. You don't know what you're talking about."

- **Malicious Joking** – "You can't get mad, I was only joking!"

- **Blocking/Diverting** – Ignoring the subject she brings up and switching to your preferred one.

- **Accusing** – Finding a way to blame all problems on the other person.

- **Judging/Criticizing** – "You are broken, substandard, defective; I know this because I am superior."

- **Trivializing** – "The things that seem so important to you are actually quite insignificant and should be disregarded."

- **Undermining** – Weakening, marginalizing, or denying the other person's authority.

- **Threatening** – Promising harm if the other person doesn't perform as directed.

- **Name-calling** – Capsulizing the other person's identity in a derogatory term.

- **Forgetting** – Not remembering various facts that pertain to the other person in a way that lets them know that they don't count.

- **Ordering/Demanding** – "What you want isn't important. Only what I want is. It's my way or the highway."

? As you look over the descriptions above, were there any that God's Spirit "red flagged" for you as you went through? Were there any that you didn't feel were problems before, but now you are wondering if they might be? Write them down here:

_____

_____

_____

NEXT STEPS: If you listed any practices that concern you –

- Take your observations to your spouse, and ask his/her opinion about them.

- Take your observations to God, and ask Him to free you from engaging in those practices.

- Take your observations to a Bridge friend, your support group, a chaplain, counselor, or pastor, and ask him/her to offer support as you and God seek to eliminate them from your life.

⊕　⊕　⊕　⊕　⊕

5. Learn how to have a good fight.

All relationships encounter conflict from time to time. If one or both of the "combatants" are struggling with traumatic stress, it will probably happen more often than normal. For this reason, you and your spouse need to agree to certain "rules of engagement." Usually, when a couple is in the heat of an argument, there is no interest in rules, it's every man (or woman) for himself! And when a couple is *not* arguing, they aren't interested in discussing rules – why think about negative things when things are going so positively? But if both of you have a clear understanding and agreement about how to *resolve* conflict ahead of time – instead of simply how to win it – your fights will be shorter, less hostile, and less damaging. And over time, there will be fewer.

First, think about what's going on during an argument, and how the basic mechanics of conflict communication can be improved. If you and your spouse can agree to the following eight parameters, your confrontations will be much more productive:[6]

FOCUS ON:	RATHER THAN:
One issue at a time	Many issues
The problem	The person
Behavior	Character
Specifics	Generalities
Expression of feelings	Judgment of character
"I" statements	"You" statements
Observation of facts	Judgment of motives
Mutual understanding	Who's winning or losing

Next, reconsider who you are arguing with, and how he or she should be treated. John Gottman, in his book *The Seven Principles for Making Marriage Work* writes:

> To a certain degree, [solving problems] comes down to having good manners. It means treating your spouse with the same respect you offer to company. If a guest leaves an umbrella, we say, "Here. You forgot your umbrella." We would never think of saying, "What's wrong with you? You are constantly forgetting things. Be a little more thoughtful! What am I, your slave to go

picking up after you?" We are sensitive to the guest's feelings, even if things don't go well... What's really being asked of you is no more than would be asked if you were dealing with an acquaintance, much less the person who has vowed to share his or her life with you.[7]

Why is it easy to be pleasant to a guest who forgets his umbrella, yet so hard to cut our mate some slack? Two reasons: (1) we have low expectations for a stranger, and (2) we have little history with them. On the other hand, we have built high expectations for our spouse, which have been dashed time and time again, establishing a history of disappointments. Each one triggers our memories of all the ones which preceded it.

Instead, ask God to help you become less of a historian and more of an ambassador of goodwill. Ask Him to remind your reactive pathways that you *love* your spouse. He/she is not the enemy. There may be shortcomings (on *both* sides), but you can put up with them as easily as you put up with the umbrella-forgetter. As God says in Ephesians 4:2 (AMP):

> *...bearing with one another and making allowances because you love one another.*

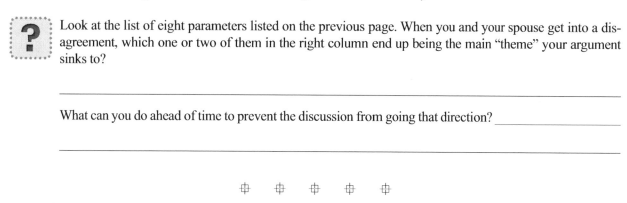 Look at the list of eight parameters listed on the previous page. When you and your spouse get into a disagreement, which one or two of them in the right column end up being the main "theme" your argument sinks to?

_____

What can you do ahead of time to prevent the discussion from going that direction? _____

_____

⊕ ⊕ ⊕ ⊕ ⊕

6. Consider outside support – for both of you.

YOU FIRST. We already examined the importance of "Bridge" People in Step 9. There are two important Bridge people that you should consider admitting to your solar system:

1. **A counselor** – A Christian professional, a chaplain, a pastor, someone who has been trained in how to deal with stress and trauma, especially one with a Biblical mindset. You may want to suggest you both go to a marriage counselor together.

2. **A support group** – Several peers who have experiences similar to yours and who have committed to help each other to a "New Normal" with regard to your stress and trauma.

This is how you can gain supportive feedback, correction, encouragement, and accountability, and it's a crucial element of your healing environment. Trying to go it alone when you're dealing with stress and trauma is always a mistake. The vast majority of both secular and faith-based experts on dealing with traumatized people agree that involving them in a small group is the absolute best environment. Take it from one of the smartest guys in history (King Solomon) inspired by the infinitely intelligent God of the universe:

> *Where there is no counsel, the people fall; but in the multitude of counselors there is safety.*

—Proverbs 11:14 (NKJV)

NOW YOUR SPOUSE. If your mate is struggling with the effects of Derivative Stress (Step 10), he or she may be reluctant to seek outside support. It may be a matter of energy, time, childcare, lack of initiative, shyness, a feeling that he/she should subordinate his/her needs to yours, denial about what she actually needs, etc. Your job – if you truly want to be the hero and not the jerk – is to do whatever you can to encourage her to engage with a counselor or a small group. It will make a *huge* difference in his/her life, and therefore in yours as well.

7. Give your spouse this manual.

Hopefully, you are receiving some helpful input from this manual regarding your line of duty stress and trauma. How much input is your spouse receiving so that he/she can better understand and support you? As of this writing, we haven't put together a "spouse's manual" yet, but it's in the pipeline. In the meantime, you could share with your spouse some of the things you've found helpful in here. If nothing else, give her a photocopy of Step 2 – "What Happened To Me?"

Though it was written for wives of combat veterans, our manual *When War Comes Home* could be a big help to your wife as well. Trauma is trauma, regardless of what door it came through. The principles that are in that manual would apply to a first responder wife too. *Some* of it would be helpful to the husband of a first responder wife, but it's mainly written for the female of the species.

8. Have some fun.

As you sail the ocean of your pain and difficulty, provide some "islands of refreshment" along the way. Think through ways that you and your spouse can engage in satisfying hobbies together, vacations, leisure time with family and friends, recreational activities, romance, relaxing. Give each other things to look forward to. Make some *big* plans for some *big* fun, like a trip to an exotic location, saving up for a ski boat, setting some fitness goals (aim for a marathon together?), etc. Those big plans have a tendency to pull you out of your present doldrums into a pleasurable and highly anticipated event in the future.

Prayer Seed

Heavenly Father, I'm thankful for my mate, and for my kids [if applicable]. I have been blind-sided by the stress and trauma of my years as a first responder, but I'm sure that my spouse has been too. It grieves me that a profession that is meant to help others could end up hurting me and my spouse so deeply. I know this can't be Your perfect will. Please help me to gain insight and motivation so that I may be a "source of life" to my family. Amen.

1. Adapted from Marshele Carter Waddell's journal entry in *When War Comes Home* (by Adsit, Adsit and Waddell, Military Ministry Press, 2008, 2012) "Erin's Journal," p. 23. Marshele is an author, speaker, and Founder and President of "Hope for the Homefront" and "When War Comes Home DON'T RETREAT" weekend retreats for wives of veterans.

2. This concept is developed in detail by Loren Cunningham and David Joel Hamilton in *Why Not Women?* (Seattle: YWAM Publishing, 2000). pp. 159-175.

3. Adapted from C. R. Figley, A. B. Baranowsky & J. E. Gentry, "Compassion Fatigue Scale – Revised" in C. R. Figley (Ed.), Compassion Fatigue: Volume II (NY: Brunner/Mazel, 1999) and also in Figley's *Treating Compassion Fatigue* (NY: Brunner/Mazel, 2002), pp. 134, 135.

4. Definitions for Spiritual, Emotional, and Psychological Abuse from Dawn Bradley Berry, J.D. *The Domestic Violence Sourcebook* (Los Angeles: Lowell House, 2000), p. 3, and from conversations with Jackie Hudson, MS, MFT, LPC, co-founder of Peace and Safety in the Christian Home (PASCH), Eugene, OR. Input also from the "Power and Control Wheel" in Jill Cory and Karen McAndless-Davis, *When Love Hurts* (New Westminster, B.C.: WomanKind Press, 2003), p. 31.

5. Verbal Abuse definition and categories from Patricia Evans, *The Verbally Abusive Relationship* (Avon, MA, Adams Media Corp, 1992, 1996).

6. "Secrets of Loving Confrontation" from Campus Crusade for Christ's FamilyLife *Weekend to Remember* Conference manual (2007). p. 92.

7. John Gottman and Nan Silver, *The Seven Principles for Making Marriage Work* (New York: Three Rivers Press, 1999), pp.158, 159.

Step 12: How Do I Get Back To "Normal?"
...Defining Your Mission

May the God of all grace, who called us to His eternal glory by Christ Jesus, after you have suffered a while, perfect, establish, strengthen, and settle you.

—1 Peter 5:10 (NKJV)

"The test of success is not what you do when you're on top. Success is how high you bounce when you hit bottom."

—General George S. Patton, Jr.

If you have experienced line of duty stress or trauma and you are on the road to recovery, General Patton's words shed light on three very important truths you must hang on to:

1. You have hit bottom.

2. Your impact is now propelling you upward to "success."

3. The incredible force of *your* impact predicts a lofty zenith.

More than most people who currently occupy the "top" positions of peace and comfort in our land, you are intimately acquainted with what the bottom looks like. And you've gained this familiarity not because you sought it or expected it, but because you were taken there forcibly by the stress and trauma resulting from your unselfish commitment to serve and protect the people of the community in which you live.

But as Ralph Waldo Emerson wrote, "He has seen but half the universe who has never been shown the house of Pain."[1] It's an education that you probably would rather have done without, but you have gained much knowledge and wisdom having seen that dark half of the universe.

The payoff.

And it won't be for nothing. As God promised in the Scripture above, *"after you have suffered a while"* you will experience a perfecting, an establishing, a strengthening and a settling which the rest of the world knows nothing about. You have been placed in an environment that has the potential of bouncing you to heights of satisfaction, strength, influence and leadership that were out of reach prior to your wounding. You have gained precious credentials that uniquely qualify you to hold positions that few can occupy. And whether it feels like it or not right now, God is *well-pleased* with you.

I will bring that group through the fire and make them pure.
I will refine them like silver and purify them like gold.
They will call on My name, and I will answer them.
I will say, 'These are My people,' and they will say, 'The Lord is our God.'

—Zechariah 13:9 (NLT)

But it won't be *normal,* as the title to this Step implies. At least, not the normal you remember. When you hear the word "normal" your mind probably snaps back to how things were prior to your period of stress or trauma. How desperately you would love to return to *that* normal! But, if we were to sell you the illusion that you *could* go back there, it would be a cruel deception. You have been changed, and your world has been changed. The pre-trauma "normal" no longer exists.

What God now has in mind for you is a **"new normal."** And it's going to be *better* than the old normal in many, many ways. We're not saying necessarily that your *current* condition is better, nor are we saying that "new normal" will be all puppies and butterflies. But we *are* saying that you are on your way to a level of existence that will be better than ever. Just as Jesus' "normal" was burned away by the trauma of his crucifixion so that He could inherit the "new normal" of the resurrection, so your old normal is being transformed through fire into a glorious *new* normal. As Elisabeth Elliot wrote, "There is a necessary link between suffering and glory."[2] Jesus said,

> *I tell you the truth, unless a kernel of wheat is planted in the soil and dies, it remains alone. But its death will produce many new kernels—a plentiful harvest of new lives.*

—John 12:24 (NLT)

 Would it be too shocking to say you died out there in that fire, or during that shootout, or on that traumatizing call? In some respects you did. Spend a few moments thinking about that concept. In what ways did you die while on the job? Feel free to use extra paper if you need more room…

_____

_____

_____

Jesus' promise in the above Scripture (John 12:24) is that, because of that death (or those deaths), abundant new life is going to be produced – in you and because of you. You have suffered losses, as did Jesus. And just as Jesus' biggest loss became the doorway to His greatest gain, so your sacrifices will crack open the door of your PTSD and give you entrance to a world of light and life that you never could have experienced otherwise.

 Name one outrageous, over-the-top thing that you hope you will find in that "new normal" world:

_____

_____

After you have suffered awhile…

This metamorphosis we've been speaking of doesn't happen quickly or all at once. We don't get to experience "microwave maturity." God likes crockpots – He likes what the *process* produces. He likes quality, and quality can't be rushed. He takes a thousand years to make a decent redwood tree; a squash He can do in a month.

And it doesn't happen if we sit passively and wait for Him to "zap" us. God has required that we partner with Him in the process. He's expecting us to be intentional about creating that environment that gives Him maximum access to our hearts and souls. Our transformation will occur as we respond positively to His overtures and obey His instructions. There is no easy way. The only way to resurrection is through the cross and the tomb. As you look around at your current difficulties, it's easy to see you're on the right road, isn't it?

Becoming Intentional About the New Normal

In this Step, we want to help you define your mission. Just as every mission in a law enforcement action, firefighting, or medical emergency is made up of many interrelated and coordinated movements, so your mission to "new normal" will also have several components that need to be thought through:

- **What Needs To Change?** – Vocation? Location? Companions?

- **Facing Your Fears** – Dealing with triggers.

- **Setting Personal Goals** – Regarding your family, exercise, finances, etc.

- **Serving Others** – How giving becomes receiving.

If you don't set about actually making objective plans in these four areas, you will continue to "float" at your current level of confusion and stagnation. As Benjamin Franklin once said, "The Constitution only gives people the right to *pursue* happiness. You have to catch it yourself." So, let's go catch some!

What Needs To Change?

Vocation?

If you're still employed as a first responder, you may conclude that you are already in the right vocation for the long term. God may have endowed you with all the necessary physical, psychological, and experiential assets to be an outstanding cop, firefighter, emergency room nurse – whatever! Or it may be that after a few years or decades, you visualize yourself contributing to society in other ways, such as through education, business, ministry, a different brand of first responder, etc.

Whatever the case, ask yourself a simple question: *How much do I like my job?* What would you give it on a scale of 1 to 10, with 10 being perfect? Put your answer here:

If you answered anything less than a 7, then you should probably begin thinking and praying about God *eventually* leading you in a different direction.

However, we want to emphasize "eventually" very strongly. If you are still dealing with symptoms of severe stress, trauma or PTSD, you do *not* need the extra stress of trying to learn a new job right now. You shouldn't make *any* major changes to your present routines until you feel good-and-ready – even eager – to do so, with confirmation from your spouse and/or bridge people. If your traumatic experience(s) are relatively recent, give your decision-making skills a chance to calm down and become a bit more objective and less emotional.

On the other hand, *do* make as many smaller, daily decisions as possible (like what or where you want to eat, what movie you want to go to, etc.). This helps you re-establish feelings of control over your life.

Our dreams – God's plans.

This may not be the time for major change – but it is a *great* time for dreams. It's a period where you should be asking God what *He* would suggest for your future. He has something in mind for which you would be perfectly suited. He created you and equipped you in a certain way. He wants to communicate to you what would fulfill you – if you'll be willing to listen and take action.

> *"For I know the plans that I have for you," declares the Lord, "plans for welfare and not for calamity to give you a future and a hope."*

> **—Jeremiah 29:11**

There's a big difference between a "job" and a "career." When you got your first job, it's likely that your only criteria was: "Will they actually pay me *money*?" You landed the burger-flipping job, and quickly realized it wasn't something you wanted to do for the rest of your life. But you didn't quit, because you needed the income. Based on that experience, though, you began to ponder what kinds of jobs you would *prefer*. Once you started to gravitate toward one general vocation, you took steps to break into it – which is why you are where you are today.

The "happily-ever-after" story ends with you finding your ideal vocation which becomes a life-long *career,* and is more like a "calling" because of how satisfying it is. Unfortunately, expectations are sometimes torpedoed along the way to perfection. When that happens, people are often so far down the road they can't figure out how to do a U-turn, so they choose to continue on, abandoning their dreams and considering their disenchantment to be acceptable.

This is a time for new beginnings for you – time to define your "new normal." And if your current job doesn't fit your dream, it's time to imagine what would.

Prayer Assignment:

Start making it a part of your daily prayer time to ask God to give you a vision for what you should do with the rest of your life. And while you're at it, ask Him to show you how to bring that vision into the realm of reality. As scientist and writer Douglas H. Everett wrote: "There are some people who live in a dream world, and there are some who face reality; and then there are those who turn one into the other." God can help you turn your dreams into reality, if you'll look to Him for direction. He wants you in the right spot just as intensely as you do!

 DREAM CAREER. Do you already have a dream? If you could do *anything* career-wise, what would it be? What would you like to see yourself doing ten years from now?

_____

_____

Frederick Buechner a WWII combat veteran, minister, and writer counsels us:

> "The voice we should listen to most as we choose a vocation is the voice that we might think we should listen to least, and that is the voice of our own *gladness.* What can we do that makes us gladdest, what can we do that leaves us with the strongest sense of sailing true north and of peace, which is much of what gladness is? I believe that if it is a thing that makes us truly glad, then it is a *good* thing and it is *our* thing and it is the calling voice that we were made to answer with our lives."[3]

Check the footnotes for this chapter for a few good books that will help you think through what could be a more fulfilling career choice.[4]

Location?

If you are employed full time, getting decent pay, have kids in school and financial obligations that can't handle a few months of unemployment, you probably don't have a lot of control over your location. If you'd like to move, you know the selection process of most municipalities frustratingly slow. You definitely don't need that stress at present. Circumstances would dictate that you sit tight for a while.

But if you are currently in control of where you live, and are thinking about making a geographical and career move, there are some important things to consider.

Live near a bridge.

First of all – whether you go or stay – "bridge people" are one of the most vital elements of your healing environment. If you are married and your spouse is struggling with secondary trauma issues because of your difficulties, he or she also needs a good backup of bridge people. If you've lived in the same area for a long time, and you've made an effort to cultivate good, healthy friendships, those bridge people for both of you are probably right there in your area. The relationships are already established and strong, and no additional energy is needed to find and build new ones. Moving to a new location would mean trying to get established in a place where you don't know anybody, and would therefore be without that key "bridge" element. You might think, "Well, I'll just make new friends," but don't forget that you are probably in a strong self-isolating mode right now. With additional stresses wearing you down, it's likely you'll be hiding in the back room when the Welcome Wagon® shows up.

If it looks like it's a favorable time to move to a new location, it is imperative that you begin looking for new bridge people as soon as you get there. Asking God to help you (and your family, if applicable) assemble a new support network needs to become a part of your daily prayer time.

You may be perfectly content to stay right where you are the rest of your life. Great! If you can match your dream vocation with your current location, that's a good recipe for contentment. But if you're not happy with your location, or if your dream vocation might mean that you need to live elsewhere, there will come a time when you'll feel strong and stable enough to make the move.

Where is Paradise?

But long-term, let your vocation dictate your location. You may find this very difficult to believe, but there are people living in *Hawaii* who have grown tired of it and are thinking about a move to *Arizona!* No lie! Your location can provide a wonderful context for life, but it's *only a context*. What you exchange your time for day-in and day-out forms a much larger portion of your life, and if that isn't satisfying, even the delights of Hawaii seem like a prison. But if your career and calling make you wake up every morning saying, "I can't wait to get to work!" it doesn't really matter where you live. Writer Tad Williams gives us a good perspective:

> "Never make your home in a *place*. Make a home for yourself inside your own head. You'll find what you need to furnish it – memory, friends you can trust, love of learning, and other such things. That way it will go with you wherever you journey."

And as the Apostle Paul put it:

> *I have learned in whatever state I am, to be content.*

> **—Philippians 4:11 (NKJV)**

The ideal, of course, would be to combine your dream vocation with your dream location. Do you feel called to be a dolphin trainer? Then you'd better have an affinity for warm, sunny locales too. Professional snowboarder? You'd better love places that get snowbound from time to time. Launching rockets? Is Houston or Cape Kennedy okay with you?

Then again, your dream *vocation* may involve frequent shifts of *location*. Some people start to feel stagnant after they've been in the same spot for more than a few months. Some people specifically join the military to "see the world," and that mobile lifestyle suits them just fine. There are first responder careers that will keep you flitting around the world to your heart's content. Take your home with you, as Tad Williams recommended above.

 You may not be able to name a particular city, state or country, but you can probably identify certain characteristics of your ideal location. If it could match up with your vocation, what would be five characteristics of your ideal location?

1._____

2._____

3._____

4._____

5._____

Prayer Assignment:

In your prayer times, begin asking God if He would combine your dream vocation with your ideal location. It may seem like too much to ask, but our God *loves* to delight His children – especially those who have had to endure the hardships you have. Jesus said so Himself:

> *Until now you have asked nothing in My name. Ask, and you will receive, that your joy may be full.*

> **—John 16:24 (NKJV)**

As amazing and extravagant as it might seem, sometimes the main criteria God has for answering your prayer with a *Yes!* is simply, "Will it bring My child joy?"

Companions?

Duty-strained or not, *everyone* needs good friends. But *especially* the duty-strained. So many people don't appreciate the wealth represented by a loyal, compassionate friend until they are in desperate need of one. Have you got at least a couple of friends like this:

> "A friend is someone who sees through you and still enjoys the view."

> —Wilma Askinas

> "A real friend is one who walks in when the rest of the world walks out."

> —Walter Winchell

> "A friend knows the song of my heart and sings it to me when my memory fails."

> —Unknown

> "A friend is a person with whom you dare to be yourself."

> —C. Raymond Beran

> "A friend is a single soul living in two bodies."

> —Aristotle

So if you *do* have some friends like this, it is *not* time for a change concerning them! If, in addition, you have shared tough line of duty experiences with them, you are wealthy indeed. They can understand and relate to you at levels that no one else can. Cultivate those friendships like you were growing money trees!

 But not all of your companions are necessarily *good* friends – even among your close first responder buddies. It's natural that you would feel a strong bond with someone you work with and has endured various catastrophes with you. Your shared experiences have connected you at deep levels, and friendships forged on the anvil of crisis are strong indeed. But you may need to do some hard thinking about whether or not some of these companions are a liability to your healing. Think about each "marginal" companion of yours and assess their effect on you:

❑ When you're with them, do they make you feel "up" or do they drag you down emotionally?

❑ Will they let you talk about your traumatic experiences, or do they avoid or change the subject?

❑ Do you tend to drink too much alcohol when you're with them?

❑ Are they encouraging you – either directly or indirectly – to use illegal drugs?

- ❑ Do they influence you to re-take the throne of your life and engage in behavior that you know grieves the Holy Spirit?

- ❑ Are they frequently finding reasons for you to skip church and other Christian functions?

- ❑ Are they antagonistic or critical about your relationship with God?

- ❑ Are they trying to pull you away from other friends that are a positive influence on you?

- ❑ Do they engage in a lot of negative, critical talk, seldom having anything good to say about anyone or anything?

- ❑ Do they stifle your creativity, enthusiasm, hope and faith, or show disdain for your dreams in the name of "Be realistic!"?

If more than two or three of the negative statements above apply to your friend, this person may not be the best companion for you. This doesn't mean you can't be available to support him or her as needed, but for the sake of your own recovery, you should limit your "hang time" with them. You may be thinking unselfishly, "But I can be a good influence on *them*." And you might be. But if you are still struggling with strong PTSD symptoms, the reverse is more likely. As the Apostle Paul warns us:

> *Do not be misled: "Bad company corrupts good character."*

> **—1 Corinthians 15:33 (NIV)**

So choose your company carefully – but do choose! We all need those bridge people from time to time. To try to make it through your current battle without them will prove very difficult. As anthropologist and writer Zora Neale Hurston observed:

> "It seems to me that trying to live without friends is like milking a bear to get cream for your morning coffee. It is a whole lot of trouble, and then not worth much after you get it."

 Taking stock: In Step 9 you made a short list of people that you would begin praying about beginning a formal "bridge relationship" with (page 128). Continue praying about that and cultivating those good friendships! But are there some other people that might fall into the category of "bad company" who – at least for the present – you need to spend less time with? Ask God who they might be. If anyone comes to your mind, write their names down here (if you worry about confidentiality, you could skip writing them down, if you'd prefer):

_____

_____

⊕　⊕　⊕　⊕　⊕

Facing Your Fears

"Fear doesn't just remain level. If not confronted, it grows."

—Dr. Rex "Rocket" Turner[5]

In Step 2, we discussed the physiological and psychological basis of PTSD. What you experienced while on duty was so traumatic that your brain took special note of it, and anytime you approach a person, place, thing or experience that is similar to your original trauma, your right brain whips out its "photo album" and puts on an intense presentation (sights, sounds, smells, tastes) attempting to alert you of the mortal danger that could be waiting there. Your logical left brain gets muted, and the calming influence of your hippocampus gets pinched off. You're off on a "re-experiencing" jaunt which, if your right brain would only *listen,* your left brain could explain why you didn't need to take that detour today.

In Step 4, we introduced the concept of inviting Jesus Christ into the episodic memories of your trauma, visualizing Him experiencing it with you (page 61). Hopefully, you've been able to continue engaging in this spiritual exercise, giving Him more and more access to your places of pain and darkness and thereby bringing about some direct healing.

 In this Step we want to encourage you – with Jesus' help – to take action concerning the things that trigger your re-experiencing episodes. By now, you are probably well-aware of what your triggers are. In the space following, write down any people, places, things or experiences that trigger your re-experiencing episodes, and what the typical effect is (use additional paper if needed):

Trigger   **Effect**

_____

_____

_____

_____

You may have heard the old joke about the guy who said, "Doc, every time I do *this,* it hurts." And the doctor says, "Well, then, don't *do* that. That'll be fifty bucks." That advice keeps the pain away, but it doesn't fix the problem. In the same way, your brain – with every good intention – is giving you advice about how to avoid the pain associated with your trauma: "Don't *go* there!" But it's unrealistic advice. The guy who assaulted you behind that warehouse had a brown, bushy beard, so now every time you see a man with a brown, bushy beard, your brain advises you, "RUN!"

This can't go on for the rest of your life. For one thing, it's rather annoying to the men with brown, bushy beards you encounter. But mainly because it's very disruptive to your "new normal." It's a reaction based on non-reality. It's no longer needed, and it hampers your day-to-day life. The original event was fearfully and explosively real, but all the re-experiencing isn't.

You have a lot in your arsenal to counter this with. With the introduction of God's Word, prayer, the Christian community and the positive mindset for your healing, you've created an environment where the Holy Spirit can transform and heal your wounded soul directly (review Steps 3A and 3B if needed). You have bridge people in your life who will walk with you through the dark forests (Step 9). You have the Spirit of Jesus sharing your traumatic experiences in the past and accompanying you in the present. You have the assurances from God that you have nothing to fear. And you have the testimony of reality that He's telling you the truth – there will probably not be a sniper on the interstate overpass today.

How can you directly face down these fears? First of all, meditate on God's Word where He tells you the facts regarding your anxieties. Allow His healing words to sink deep into your soul and renew you. Memorize them.

> *The Lord is my light and my salvation; whom shall I fear?*
> *The Lord is the defense of my life; whom shall I dread?*

—Psalm 27:1

> *God met me more than halfway, He freed me from my anxious fears.*

—Psalm 34:4 (MSG)

When I am afraid, I will put my trust in You. In God, whose word I praise,
In God I have put my trust; I shall not be afraid.
What can mere man do to me?

—Psalm 56:3,4

"When I am *afraid*"? Who wrote this wimpy, limp-wristed drivel? Who's this fraidy-cat who cowers behind the skirts of religion? Well, it's the guy who killed the 9'8" giant, forcibly circumcised 200 grown men, killed a lion and a bear and was respected and feared by some of the baddest dudes that ever walked the planet, that's who. And he wasn't hiding behind anything, by the way. Even King David struggled with various anxieties and fears. May you never get over the fact that this valiant, conquering general and king was *afraid* sometimes. But he dealt with his fears pro-actively. He faced them head-on, fully aware that God Almighty had his back and both flanks. And that gave him confidence to step forward.

For more insight into King David's struggles with PTSD, the focus of his hope, the foundation of his healing and his attitude toward his God Who rescued him from every enemy, see Appendix D: *Prayer Life of a PTSD Victor: King David* (pages 185-190). It could be an excellent pattern for your own prayer life.

Mission Strategy

 Look over the list of triggers you just wrote. Spend some time in prayer, and ask the Lord to suggest just one of them that you and He could work on. Make it the easiest one. Write it down here:

_____

Like any difficult project, start slow and easy, and build on your successes. Every time you encounter that particular trigger, your trauma-rattled brain switches on its alarm, and you begin to re-experience and probably react with fear. What action could you take that would defy that alarm and help you face that fear ***just a little bit*** in a safe environment?

We realize it's not easy to anticipate or control a trigger. And the variety of triggers is extensive. For you, it could be the sound of a baby crying, the smell of a decaying animal or of gasoline, a sudden loud noise, a person of a certain ethnic origin, etc. You never know when these triggers are going to pop up. But in the same way that an athlete will create artificial scenarios and repeatedly hone his or her reactions in order to be ready for the "real thing," you can proactively devise situations that will help you confront your triggers – with Christ at your side – in a safe, controllable environment.

Example:

Professionals call this approach "Graduated Exposure Therapy" or "Systematic Desensitization." Let's say your trigger has to do with the smell of gasoline. Because of this, you are unable to go to a gas station to fill up the tank and your spouse must always do it. Perhaps you could get your spouse to prepare a small jug of gasoline for you and bring it home. Once a day, you take a few minutes to put on your spiritual armor, seek the filling of the Holy Spirit, ask God and your spouse to stand with you by your side, and then walk to where the jug is and open it up. Your goal: five seconds before you put the lid back on and leave the room. You will find that you can do it! And the next time, perhaps your goal will be seven seconds. Then ten.

After a period of time that only you and God can determine, you and your spouse will take a trip to the gas station. Maybe the first time you won't even get gas – perhaps you'll just drive through it once and go home. The next time you still won't get gas – you'll just park there and sit for thirty seconds. Then for a minute. Eventually, you could sit in the car while your spouse pumps the gas. Then you stand next to him or her. Eventually, you do it yourself. These victorious steps – accompanied by your spouse (or some other bridge person) and Jesus while filled with His Spirit – provide those more-powerful episodes that can eclipse the episodic memories of your original trauma and retrain your mind.

Now it's your turn to be creative and come up with a plan. Based on the trigger you chose and following the pattern above, what steps can you take – just a little bit at a time – to defy your anxieties with Jesus at your side? Ask God to help you think it through and give you some creative ideas. Write them down here:

_____

_____

_____

_____

_____

_____

Eventually, you will find that this trigger is no longer debilitating. You might still feel a little anxious when you encounter it, but it won't control your life any more. Though a trigger isn't the same thing as sin, God's advice to Cain in Genesis 4 could be applied here: "It wants to master you, but you must master it." By confronting it intentionally like this, little by little, you and the Lord *will* show it who's boss!

⊕ ⊕ ⊕ ⊕ ⊕

Setting Personal Goals

"Planning is bringing the future into the present so that you can do something about it now."

—Alan Lakein

This section could have begun with the old and absolutely true adage: "If you fail to plan, plan to fail." But Lakein's observation should help us to recognize the positive side of planning: it is *future oriented.* Your present is *stuck*, and continuing to focus on it isn't going to get you unstuck. Like with a Jeep sunk past its axles in a mud bog, a cable needs to be stretched out and secured to something solid and stable and the winch turned on. In Christ, your future is secure. Spirit-directed planning is your cable-and-winch that will pull you out of your current quagmire.

Besides, as baseball legend and Yankee philosopher Yogi Berra warns us: "You got to be careful if you don't know where you're going, because you might not get there." Your future awaits – and you *do* want to get there!

Setting Goals: How To

Setting goals involves getting a clear idea of what you want to ultimately accomplish (like "graduate from college") and then writing out the steps that will help you attain it. How to actually *write* those goals in a way that will make them achievable takes a little work, but it will be worth it.

A good criterion for writing any goal uses the acronym SMART. Here's what each letter means:

Specific – There must be some detail and precision to it, and some sense of time. To say, "I would like to learn martial arts" is not very specific. But to say, "I want to become a black belt in *tae kwon do* within three years of today" is very specific.

Measurable – It must contain some objective element that will let you know when you've achieved it or are achieving it. To say, "I would like to be a better father" is a worthy goal, but how would you know when you *became* a better father? Instead, link your desire to measurable action. "I will read my son a bedtime story every night I'm home for the next month," or "I will read three books about parenting within the next year and discuss them with my wife," would both be measurable. Can you put it on a checklist? Then it's probably measurable.

Attainable – It must be a goal for which you can devise a plan to attain it. If you can't work out the steps that would be involved in getting you to your destination, it's not attainable. Enthusiasm, faith and courage are advantages when setting out on any journey, but if you leave with no roadmap, they won't help much.

Realistic – Given your present resources, is it reasonable to believe the goal could be achieved? If you're only 5'6" and your name isn't Spud Webb, it probably isn't realistic to think you have a career ahead of you in professional basketball.

Tangible – It must have substance and objectivity rather than be merely a vague desire. "I would like to be happy" is a nice sentiment, but not tangible. What specifically would *make* you happy? That would more likely be a *goal.* Can you put it on your calendar? That's a good test of tangibility.

Setting Goals: Layering Them According to Priorities

As you begin to write out goals, realize that there are only so many hours in a day, and that you probably won't have unlimited time to pursue *all* your goals at all times. So it will be necessary for you to layer and prioritize them.

A very simple way of doing this – relative to each major desire that God brings into your mind – is to set them according to three time frames:

- **Long-range** – Major pursuits that may take five to twenty years to achieve.

- **Medium-range** – Specific goals that can be achieved in one to five years.

- **Short-range** – Specific goals that can be achieved within a day to a year.

A collection of Short-range goals will add up to one Medium-range goal. The achieving of a series of Medium-range goals will bring about the accomplishment of a Long-range goal.

Next, prioritize them according to how passionately you desire each Long-range goal. Decide which goals belong on your "A" list, which on your "B" list, and which go on your "C" list. Based on this prioritizing, it will be much easier for you to decide which specific activities relative to each goal need to be transferred to your "To do list" and your calendar. If you're like most of us, if it doesn't get on the calendar, *it does not exist!* So calendarize your goals whenever possible!

Setting Goals: Dreaming In the Important Areas

"I have had dreams and I have had nightmares, but I have conquered my nightmares because of my dreams."

—Dr. Jonas Salk (developer of the Polio vaccine)

How thoroughly have your nightmares eradicated your dreams? Nightmares happen when you're asleep and passive, but the dreams we're talking about here spring into being when we are awake and intentional. *Those* dreams, fed by God's Spirit, are what have the power to conquer our nightmares.

"Major on the majors" is a popular credo. If we aren't succeeding in the major areas of our lives, no amount of success in the minor areas will gratify us. And minor dreams won't displace major nightmares.

For this reason, we'd like you to spend a little time thinking about those major areas. We're supplying you with a list of eight areas here, but it is not necessarily complete. There may be other issues unique to your life that need to be addressed. Please write them out on additional sheets of paper.

 In each of the following areas, ask God to give you some vision regarding where you need to be headed. What do you think would be *good* for you? What would be good for your family? What are some of your long-range desires in each area? At this point, you don't need to work out layering or prioritizing them. Just write down whatever the Lord brings to your mind.

1. Goals regarding my relationship with my spouse (or parents, if single):

_____

_____

2. Goals regarding my relationship with my kids (or siblings, if single):

_____

_____

3. Goals regarding my vocation:

_____

_____

4. Goals regarding my location:

_____

_____

5. Goals regarding my finances:

_____

_____

6. Goals regarding diet and exercise:

_____

_____

7. Goals regarding my medical issues:

_____

_____

8. Goals regarding my excesses (alcohol, drugs, food, sex, etc.):

_____

_____

Now, if you're serious about this, here's what we want you to do. In a separate notebook, or on separate sheets of paper, write out each of the goals you wrote at the top of a page – one goal per page. Those constitute your "Long-range Goals." Break each down into two to five "Medium-range Goals" that would combine to help you reach the long-range goal at the top of the page. Then, beneath each medium-range goal, write out two to five "Short-range Goals" that would help you accomplish each medium-range goal. If those goals are "SMART" enough, transfer them to your calendar.

By doing this, you are indeed "bringing the future into the present" so that you can truly bring about your "new normal" and the rest of your life. Nothing can be done about what happened to you in the past, but *everything* can be done about what happens to you in the future.

> *Delight yourself in the Lord; and He will give you the desires of your heart.*
> *Commit your way to the Lord, trust also in Him, and He will do it.*

—Psalm 37:4,5

Serving Others

Whoever wants to be great must become a servant. Whoever wants to be first among you must be your slave. That is what the Son of Man has done: He came to serve, not to be served—and then to give away His life in exchange for many who are held hostage.

— Mark 10:44,45 (MSG)

Having been a first responder, you know a little something about "service." You serve every day. It was while you were serving that you – like Jesus – "gave away your life in exchange" for security and peace for your loved ones and fellow-citizens in your community. Some of your brother and sister first responders gave the ultimate sacrifice and they no longer walk among us. But you – and many others – sacrificed profoundly and died in that "kernel of wheat" sense we studied earlier (John 12:24). Yes, you know a lot about service.

And though it was service that got you into your present traumatized condition, it is service that will help pull you out as well.

One of the facts that virtually every expert on PTSD affirms has to do with the healing power of helping others who are hurting. There's something about giving of ourselves to those who are having difficulties that empowers us, takes our focus off ourselves and invigorates us. As Ralph Waldo Emerson wrote: "It is one of the most beautiful compensations of life that no man can sincerely try to help another without helping himself." Or as J.M. Barrie wrote, "Those who bring sunshine into the lives of others cannot keep it from themselves."

 What talents, gifts or abilities do you have that you think might be of use to others who are hurting? There are talents that are common to us all, such as the ability to listen, to sit with someone, to offer some simple manual labor, to buy a cup of coffee, to provide a ride, to tell your story to others who need to hear it. Or even to simply be available to others. Some have called "availability" the most important of all the abilities when it comes to serving others. But what *unique* talents do you own that you could press into the service of others?

_____

_____

Spend some time in prayer, and then spend some time with one of your bridge friends, and talk with him or her about how you might employ your availability and talents to help others who are hurting. Perhaps you might also talk with your pastor, or people at various charities around town about how you might be of service to them. After you've done this, make a plan. Write down three ways that you would like to serve others – either right away, or sometime in the future.

1._____

2._____

3._____

Why Serve: Your Unique Qualifications and Benefits

You probably remember the story in John 11, when Jesus raised Lazarus from the dead. Jesus delayed coming to Bethany on purpose until Lazarus had been dead for four days. He wanted to make sure that everyone was keenly aware of the fact that this man was *really* dead, and that what was about to take place was not a resuscitation, but a genuine resurrection. When Jesus gave the command, "Lazarus, come out!" the dead man got up and walked. Lazarus had been bound in the traditional grave clothes of that day – like fifty Ace Bandages from head to toe. He walked, but not very well.

The next command Jesus gave was interesting and relates to you. He said, "Take off his grave clothes and let him go." Don't you think that a person who just raised somebody from the dead would have the wherewithal to unwrap those grave clothes Himself? Why did he instruct others to do it? Because by partnering with Jesus in this miracle, their faith would be made stronger. By walking up to this astonishing, dreadful figure and touching him, unwrapping the bandages and setting him loose, actually saving his life a second time (because the grave clothes tightly covered his nose and mouth), they were being honored by Jesus, included, and experienced something that would motivate them for the rest of their lives.

You are among the resurrected ones. You died and now new life is being generated in you and through you. You've struggled with your own grave clothes, and this has made you profoundly qualified to unwrap those smelly bandages that bind others. Jesus honors *you* by asking you to now help Him to help others with their grave clothes.

Think, also, of the wisdom of Solomon found in Ecclesiastes 4:1,3:

> *To everything there is a season, a time for every purpose under heaven:*
> *A time to kill, and a time to heal;*
> *A time to break down, and a time to build up.*

You may have experienced an incident – a season – when you were called upon to kill, to break down, to do something that went against your very core convictions. It happened while you were pursuing honorable purposes, unselfishly and courageously. You may have brushed up against death, carnage and malice in the line of duty, and though you didn't cause it, you had to take care of it – perhaps multiple times. And you've paid for it every time, and continue to pay.

But now a new season has come – a new normal. It's a season for healing and for building up. A time for you to heal, and a time for you to help in the healing of others. This, too, is for honorable purposes, and will also require unselfishness and courage. It will also cost you something, for anytime we give, by definition, it costs us. But the benefits you receive will far exceed any disability pay or pension you might ever receive from the sacrifices you made in your previous season. God lists a few of them for you in Isaiah 58:10-12 (NKJV):

If you extend your soul to the hungry
And satisfy the afflicted soul,
    Then your light shall dawn in the darkness,
    And your darkness shall be as the noonday.
    The Lord will guide you continually,
    And satisfy your soul in drought,
    And strengthen your bones;
    You shall be like a watered garden,
    And like a spring of water, whose waters do not fail.
    Those from among you shall build the old waste places;
    You shall raise up the foundations of many generations;
    And you shall be called the Repairer of the Breach,
    The Restorer of Streets to Dwell In.

⊕   ⊕   ⊕   ⊕   ⊕

Prayer Seed

Father, it saddens me that I cannot return to "normal." But, with Your help, I know that I can make the journey to "new normal." Help me see the steps I need to take. Help me recognize the bridge people You have sent to help me walk through the difficult times. Keep my eyes on You, not on the storm that surrounds me. Give me frequent visions of where You are taking me, and how I can get there. Help me face my fears with You alongside me. Give me the same courage that You gave King David as he faced his fears. I need You to let me know for sure that You are right there with me. Bring me to the place where I can minister to the needs of others. Use me in ways that are either common or unique – as long as it will serve those who are hurting, build up Your Kingdom and add to the process of my own healing as well.

You have shown me the house of Pain, O Lord. Now lead me to Your house of Strength. May I be one of the ones called "Repairer of the Breach, Restorer of the Streets to Dwell In." By the authority of the Holy Spirit, with the companionship of Your Son Jesus Christ, and in the sovereignty of Your will, I know it can be accomplished. I ask all these things in the name of my Lord and Savior Jesus Christ, Amen.

⊕   ⊕   ⊕   ⊕   ⊕

1. Quote by Ralph Waldo Emerson in his essay "The Tragic," found in Unspeakable by Os Guinness (NY: HarperCollins, 2005). p. 44.

2. Elisabeth Elliot, *A Path Through Suffering* (Ventura, CA: Regal Books, 1990). p. 14.

3. Spoken by Frederick Buechner in a graduation address, quoted in *Windows of the Soul* by Ken Gire (Grand Rapids: Zondervan, 1996) p. 71.

4. Alan Lakein, *How To Get Control of Your Time and Your Life* (Signet, 1974, 1989). Lakein is one of the most sought-after experts on time management. This classic 3-million seller contains practical suggestions for setting goals, achieving them and organizing your life.
    Julie Jansen, *I Don't Know What I Want, But I Know It's Not This: A Step-by-Step Guide to Finding Gratifying Work* (Penguin, 2003). Jansen is a strong proponent of "one size does NOT fit all." Contains many creative exercises to help you get in touch with what you really love to do, and why you find certain jobs unsatisfying.
    Richard Nelson Boles, *What Color Is Your Parachute?: A Practical Manual for Job-Hunters and Career-Changers* (Ten Speed Press, 2014). This has been the best-selling job hunting book in the world for the past 30+ years (revised almost yearly).

5. Dr. Turner is a Navy Veteran; for 35 years he has been a VA counselor, and has led Branches of Valor small groups for several years. They call him "Rocket" for how he used to drive his motorcycle in his younger days. No fear.

Epilogue

In a certain region of northern Italy, many of the villages produce beautiful vases, each piece fetching a very good price due to the skill that has been passed down from generation to generation.

But there is one particular village that produces vases that command ten times the price of any of their neighbor's goods. They are so valuable because of the crafting technique the artisans of this village use. They make the vases just as all the other villages in the region do, but then they smash them on the ground, shattering them into dozens of pieces.

Then, with the greatest of care and skill, the artisan laboriously reassembles the vase, using glue that has been mixed with gold. When finished, every golden vein contributes a magnificent element to the vase, adding immensely to its beauty and value.

This process is very similar to what you are experiencing currently. The stress and trauma of your experiences as a first responder have shattered your life in many ways, but the eternal Artisan is in the process of rebuilding you, and every re-glued crack, every scarred-over wound will contribute to your beauty and value in ways you can barely imagine.

This is probably why even the resurrected Christ retained His scars, even in His glorified body. For all of eternity, what they symbolize will be *beautiful* to each of us who were saved by them, to all the angels who witnessed His ultimate sacrifice of love, and to the Father Who observed the deadly obedience of His only Son.

So will your scars – seen and unseen – be gloriously beautiful.

You have been in some dark places since line of duty stress and trauma began to alter your life. You are probably still fighting your way out of that darkness into your new normal. God's desire is to *help* you. The sentiment of what God said to His servant Cyrus can be a promise to you as well:

> *I will go before you and will level the mountains;*
> *I will break down gates of bronze and cut through bars of iron.*
> *I will give you the treasures of darkness,*
> > *riches stored in secret places,*
> > > *so that you may know that I am the Lord,*
> > > > *the God of Israel, who summons you by name.*

—Isaiah 45:2,3(NIV)

He knows your name. He has called you. He'll see to it that neither mountains, gates of bronze, bars of iron or the blackest darkness will keep you from where He wants you to go. And there are treasures hidden in that darkness that He wants to give you. As you receive them, you'll know for sure that the God of Israel is the One who has been with you in that dark cave of trauma. Those who have never entered the darkness will never touch them. But He's holding them out to you.

May God give you the sight to see them, accept them and use them for your healing and for the glory of the Kingdom of God.

And may the golden veins of your restored soul be evident to all, for all eternity.

— Chris & Rahnella

Appendix Ⓐ Would You Like to Know God Personally?

Yes, you can know God personally, as presumptuous as that may sound. God is so eager to establish a personal, loving relationship with you that He has already made all the arrangements. He is patiently waiting for you to respond to His invitation. You can receive forgiveness of your sin and assurance of eternal life through faith in His only Son, Jesus Christ.

The major barrier that prevents us from knowing God personally is ignorance of who God is and what He has done for us. Read on and discover for yourself how you can begin a life-changing relationship with God.

The following four principles will help you discover how to know God and experience the abundant life He promised.

1 God LOVES you and created you to know Him personally.

God's Love

God so loved the world, that He gave His only begotten Son, that whoever believes in Him should not perish, but have eternal life.

– John 3:16

God's Plan

Now this is eternal life: that they may know You, the only true God, and Jesus Christ, whom You have sent.

– John 17:3 (NIV)

What prevents us from knowing God personally?

2 Man is SINFUL and SEPARATED from God, so we cannot know Him personally or experience His Love.

Man is Sinful

All have sinned and fall short of the glory of God.
– Romans 3:23

Man was created to have fellowship with God; but, because of his own stubborn self-will, he chose to go his own independent way and fellowship with God was broken. This self-will, characterized by an attitude of active rebellion or passive indifference, is an evidence of what the Bible calls sin.

Man is Separated

> *But your iniquities have made a separation between you and your God, and your sins have hidden His face from you so that He does not hear.* — **Isaiah 59:2**

> *The wages of sin is death.* [spiritual separation from God]
> — **Romans 6:23a**

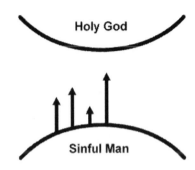

This diagram illustrates that God is holy and man is sinful. A great gulf separates the two. The arrows illustrate that man is continually trying to reach God and establish a personal relationship with Him through his own efforts, such as living a good life, philosophy, or religion – but he inevitably fails.

The third principle explains the only way to bridge this gulf...

3

JESUS CHRIST IS GOD'S <u>ONLY</u> PROVISION FOR MAN'S SIN. THROUGH HIM ALONE WE CAN KNOW GOD PERSONALLY AND EXPERIENCE GOD'S LOVE.

He Died in Our Place

> *God demonstrates His own love toward us, in that while we were yet sinners, Christ died for us.*
> — **Romans 5:8**

He Rose From the Dead

> *Christ died for our sins...He was buried...He was raised on the third day according to the Scriptures... He appeared to Peter, then to the twelve. After that He appeared to more than five hundred...* — **1 Corinthians 15:3-6**

He is the Only Way to God

> *Jesus said to him, "I am the way, and the truth, and the life; no one comes to the Father, but through Me."*
> — **John 14:6**

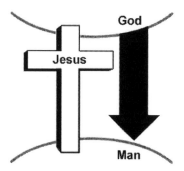

This diagram illustrates that God has bridged the gulf that separates us from Him by sending His Son, Jesus Christ, to die on the cross in our place to pay the penalty for our sins.

It is not enough just to know these three truths...

4 We must individually RECEIVE Jesus Christ as Savior and Lord; then we can know God personally and experience His love.

We Must Receive Christ

> *As many as received Him, to them He gave the right to become children of God, even to those who believe in His name.*
> — **John 1:12**

We Receive Christ Through Faith

> *By grace you have been saved through faith; and that not of yourselves, it is the gift of God; not as a result of works, that no one should boast.*
> — **Ephesians 2:8-9**

When We Receive Christ, We Experience A New Birth

> Read
> **John 3:1-8**
> in your Bible.

We Receive Christ by Personal Invitation

> [Christ speaking] *Behold, I stand at the door and knock; if anyone hears My voice and opens the door, I will come in to him.*
> — **Revelation 3:20**

Receiving Christ involves turning to God from self (repentance) and trusting Christ to come into our lives to forgive us of our sins and to make us what He wants us to be. Just to agree intellectually that Jesus Christ is the Son of God and that He died on the cross for our sins is not enough. Nor is it enough to have an emotional experience. We receive Jesus Christ by faith, as an act of our will.

These two circles represent two kinds of lives:

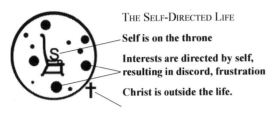

THE SELF-DIRECTED LIFE

Self is on the throne

Interests are directed by self, resulting in discord, frustration

Christ is outside the life.

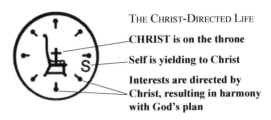

THE CHRIST-DIRECTED LIFE

CHRIST is on the throne

Self is yielding to Christ

Interests are directed by Christ, resulting in harmony with God's plan

Which circle best represents your life?

Which circle would you like to have represent your life?

The following Explains how you can receive Christ:

You Can Receive Christ Right Now by Faith Through Prayer
(Prayer is simply talking with God)

God knows your heart and is not so concerned with your words as He is with the attitude of your heart. The following is a suggested prayer:

> *"Lord Jesus, I want to know You personally. Thank you for dying on the cross for my sins. I open the door of my life and receive You as my Savior and Lord. Thank You for forgiving me of my sins and giving me eternal life. Take control of the throne of my life. Make me the kind of person You want me to be."*

Does this prayer express the desire of your heart?

If it does, pray this prayer right now, and Christ will come into your life, as He promised.

How to Know That Christ Is in Your Life

Did you receive Christ into your life? According to His promise in Revelation 3:20, where is Christ right now in relation to you? Christ said that He would come into your life and be your friend so that you can know Him personally. Would He mislead you? On what authority do you know that God has answered your prayer? (The trustworthiness of God Himself and His Word.)

> *The witness is this, that God has given us eternal life, and this life is in His Son. He who has the Son has the life; he who does not have the Son of God does not have the life. These things I have written to you who believe in the name of the Son of God, in order that you may know that you have eternal life.*
> **— 1 John 5:11-13**

The Bible Promises Eternal Life to All Who Receive Christ

Thank God often that Christ is in your life and that He will never leave you (Hebrews 13:5). You can know on the basis of His promise that Christ lives in you and that you have eternal life from the very moment you invite Him into your life. He will not deceive you.

An important reminder...

Do Not Depend on Feelings

The promise of God's Word, the Bible – not our feelings – is our authority. The Christian lives by faith (trust) in the trustworthiness of God Himself and His Word. This train diagram illustrates the relationship among **fact** (God and His Word), **faith** (our trust in God and His Word), and **feeling** (the result of our faith and obedience) (John 14:21).

The train will run with or without the caboose. However, it would be useless to attempt to pull the train by the caboose. In the same way, we as Christians do not depend on feelings or emotions, but we place our faith (trust) in the trustworthiness of God and the promises of His Word.

Now That You Have Entered Into a Personal Relationship With Christ...

The moment you received Christ by faith, as an act of your will, many things happened, including the following:

1. Christ came into your life (Revelation 3:20 and Colossians 1:27).
2. Your sins were forgiven (Colossians 1:14).
3. You became a child of God (John 1:12).
4. You received eternal life (John 5:24).
5. You began the great adventure for which God created you (John 10:10; 2 Corinthians 5:17 and 1 Thessalonians 5:18).

Suggestions for Christian Growth

Spiritual growth results from trusting Jesus Christ. A life of faith will enable you to trust God increasingly with every detail of your life, and to practice the following:

G – Go to God in prayer daily (John 15:7).
R – Read God's Word daily (Acts 17:11). Begin with the Gospel of John.
O – Obey God moment by moment (John 14:21).
W – Witness for Christ by your life and words (Matthew 4:19; John 15:8).
T – Trust God for every detail of your life (1 Peter 5:7).
H – Holy Spirit – Allow Him to control and empower your daily life and witness (Galatians 5:16,17; Acts 1:8).

> *The righteous man shall live by faith.*
> **– Galatians 3:11**

Fellowship In a Good Church

God's Word admonishes us not to forsake "the assembling of ourselves together..." (Hebrews 10:25). Several logs burn brightly together; but put one aside on the cold hearth and the fire goes out. So it is with your relationship with other Christians. If you do not belong to church, do not wait to be invited. Take the initiative; call the pastor of a nearby church where Christ is honored and His Word is preached. Start this week, and make plans to attend regularly.[1]

[1] This is a version of the Four Spiritual Laws, written by Bill Bright. Copyright 1965, 1988, Campus Crusade for Christ, Inc. Used by permission.

Appendix **B** Doorways and Footholds

From Step 8, pages 116 - 118.

Please keep in mind that this list only represents *possible* doorways. Just because you have experienced one of the occurrences listed below, it doesn't mean that you have necessarily opened a doorway or provided a foothold for the enemy. But you *may* have. That's something you and God will have to discern together.

> *But if any of you lacks wisdom, let him ask of God, who gives to all generously and without reproach, and it will be given to him.*
>
> **—James 1:5**

1. Indulgence in occultic music, literature, art, dancing, etc.

2. Possession of (known or unknown) and/or use of occultic records, tapes, books, pictures, charms, books, souvenirs, tools, games (Ouija Boardtm, Dungeons & Dragons®, etc.).

3. Holding on to grudges or bitterness against God and others.

4. Destructively negative self-image.

5. Anorexia; bulimia.

6. Attempted suicide; thoughts of suicide.

7. Rebellion against authority.

8. Dating relationships or close friendships with demonized people.

9. Sexual immorality with demonized people.

10. Habitually participating in sexual immorality with anyone.

11. Sexual involvement with a prostitute – even once.

12. Parents, relatives or other close authority figures who have accepted satanic influence, i.e. witch, warlock or Satanist.

13. Ancestors or dead relatives who accepted satanic influence.

14. Seeking or giving consent to occult power or revelation (spirit guides, going to a psychic, medium or fortune teller, having an astrological chart made, etc).

15. Fascination with occultic power, occultic revelation, or psychic phenomena in general (taking e.s.p. tests or psychic aptitude tests).

16. Involvement in psychic phenomenon, such as astral projection, levitation, spells, magic, fortunetelling, séances, channeling, or being present when these phenomena occurred.

17. Involvement in or attending occultic rituals, festivals, masses, sacrifices, etc.

18. Involvement in martial arts rituals (no problem with martial arts, it's a matter of how deeply you may have participated in their rituals).

19. Involvement with "New Age" medicine, such as biofeedback, hypnosis, self-hypnosis, subliminal tapes, acupuncture, etc. (some of these procedures are harmless and have even been medically demonstrated to be beneficial, but there is the potential for satanic involvement – so ask God for discernment).

20. Deliberate rejection of what is known and understood to be true.

21. Participation in false religions or cults.

22. Abuse of drugs and/or alcohol.

23. Abuse of herbs.

24. Escapism through thrill-seeking, science fiction, soap operas, or some other addicting hobby or activity (again, these activities can be harmless, but if they have led to an addiction, it's a vulnerability).

25. Hedonism; an absorbing pursuit of entertainment and/or body pleasure.

26. Fascination with violence, especially violence devoid of justice, such as sadism or masochism.

27. Torture - either as a victim or a perpetrator.

28. Prolonged or persistent jealousy or resentment.

29. Habitual use of pornography.

30. Fascination with UFO phenomena; attempts to contract extraterrestrial beings.

31. Prolonged sleeplessness (this could simply be a symptom of PTSD, but you should still ask the Lord if there is a possible doorway here).

32. Chanting or other cultic/occultic forms of worship.

33. Blaspheming the Holy Spirit; i.e. repeatedly and consistently rejecting the work of the Holy Spirit as He reveals truth and convicts of sin.

34. Vivid, recurrent dreams as a child.

35. Victim or perpetrator of rape or incest.

36. Victim or perpetrator of violent sexual, physical or emotional assault.

37. Victim or perpetrator of child abuse.

38. Institutionalization (jail, psych ward, etc.).

39. Shock or trauma. (Yes, your first responder experiences could have created open doors, but not necessarily. Ask God about it.)

40. General anesthesia. (In this totally passive state, open doors are possible, but not probable. Ask God.)

41. Very prolonged, unshakable grief.

42. Involvement at high levels with some fraternal organizations, such as Masons, Eastern Star, Rainbow, etc.

43. Obsession with occultic novels (such as Harry Potter and Goose Bumps).

For direction regarding how to close open doorways, see Step 8, page 118.

Appendix C Spiritual Warfare Ammo Bunker

From Step 8, pages 123, 124.

Use these Scriptures when involved in spiritual warfare. They are your "sword of the Spirit, which is the Word of God" (Ephesians 6:17). Remember how Jesus used these weapons against Satan when He was tempted in the wilderness (Matthew 4:1-11): "It is written…"

ANGER

Proverbs 16:32 – He who is slow to anger is better than the mighty, and he who rules his spirit, than he who captures a city.

James 1:20 – For man's anger does not bring about the righteous life that God desires.

DECEIT/LYING

Leviticus 19:11,12 - Do not steal. Do not lie. Do not deceive one another. Do not swear falsely by my name and so profane the name of your God. I am the Lord.

Proverbs 12:22 - The Lord detests lying lips, but he delights in men who are truthful.

DISOBEDIENCE TO GOD

John 14:21 - Whoever has My commands and obeys them, he is the one who loves Me; and he who loves Me will be loved by My Father, and I too will love him and show Myself to him.

1 Samuel 15:22b - To obey is better than sacrifice, and to heed is better than the fat of rams.

DISRESPECT FOR AUTHORITY

Ephesians 5:21 - Submit to one another out of reverence for Christ.

1 Peter 2:13 - Submit yourselves for the Lord's sake to every authority instituted among men; whether to the king, as the supreme authority, or to governors, who are sent by him to punish those who do wrong and to commend those who do right.

DRUGS AND ALCOHOL

Proverbs 20:21 - Wine is a mocker and beer a brawler; whoever is led astray by them is not wise.

Ephesians 5:18 - Do not get drunk on wine, which leads to debauchery. Instead, be filled with the Spirit.

ENVY

Galatians 5:26 - Let us not become conceited, provoking and envying each other.

Proverbs 14:30 - A heart at peace gives life to the body, but envy rots the bones.

FEARFULNESS

Isaiah 41:10 - Do not fear, for I am with you; do not be dismayed, for I am your God. I will strengthen you and help you; I will uphold you with my righteous right hand.

2 Timothy 1:7 - For God did not give us a spirit of timidity, but a spirit of power, of love and of self-discipline.

GREED/COVETING

Exodus 20:17 - You shall not covet...

Matthew 16:26 - What good will it be for a man if he gains the whole world, yet forfeits his soul?

HATRED

Leviticus 19:17 - Do not hate your brother in your heart...

1 John 4:20 - If anyone says, "I love God," yet hates his brother, he is a liar. For anyone who does not love his brother, whom he has seen, cannot love God, whom he has not seen.

IDOLATRY

Exodus 20:4 - You shall not make for yourself an idol in the form of anything in heaven above or on the earth beneath or in the waters below.

1 John 5:21 - Dear children, keep yourselves from idols.

JEALOUSY

Proverbs 27:4 - Anger is cruel and fury overwhelming, but who can stand before jealousy?

Romans 13:13 - Let us behave decently, as in the daytime...not in dissension and jealousy.

LACK OF FAITH

Romans 1:17 - ...the righteous will live by faith.

Hebrews 11:6 - And without faith it is impossible to please God, because anyone who comes to Him must believe that He exists and that He rewards those who earnestly seek Him.

LAZINESS

Proverbs 6:9-11 - How long will you lie there, you sluggard? When will you get up from your sleep? A little sleep, a little slumber, a little folding of the hands to rest - and poverty will come on you like a bandit and scarcity like an armed man.

Colossians 3:23 - Whatever you do, work at it with all your heart, as working for the Lord, not for men.

LUST

2 Timothy 2:22 - Flee the evil desires of youth, and pursue righteousness, faith, love and peace, along with those who call on the Lord out of a pure heart.

1 Peter 2:11 - Dear friends, I urge you, as aliens and strangers in the world, to abstain from sinful desires, which war against your soul.

MALICE

1 Peter 2:1 - Therefore, rid yourselves of all malice and all deceit...

1 Peter 2:16 - ...not using your liberty for a cloak of maliciousness, but as the servants of God.

Materialism

Hebrews 13:5 - Keep your lives free from the love of money and be content with what you have, because God has said, "Never will I leave you; never will I forsake you."

Luke 12:15 - Then He said to them, "Watch out! Be on your guard against all kinds of greed; a man's life does not consist in the abundance of his possessions."

PRIDE

1 Peter 5:5,6 - ...Clothe yourselves with humility toward one another, because, "God opposes the proud but gives grace to the humble." Humble yourselves, therefore, under God's mighty hand, that He may lift you up in due time.

Proverbs 29:23 - A man's pride brings him low, but a man of lowly spirit gains honor.

PROFANITY

Ephesians 4:29 - Do not let any unwholesome talk come out of your mouths, but only what is helpful for building others up according to their needs, that it may benefit those who listen.

Ephesians 5:3,4 - But among you there must not be even a hint of ... obscenity, foolish talk or coarse joking, which are out of place, but rather thanksgiving.

REBELLION

Proverbs 17:11 – An evil man is bent only on rebellion…

Romans 13:2 – He who rebels against the authority is rebelling against what God has instituted, and those who do so will bring judgment on themselves.

REVENGE

Leviticus 19:18 - Do not seek revenge or bear a grudge against one of your people, but love your neighbor as yourself. I am the Lord.

Proverbs 25:21,22 - If your enemy is hungry, give him food to eat; if he is thirsty, give him water to drink. In doing this, you will heap burning coals on his head, and the Lord will reward you.

Matthew 6:14,15 - For if you forgive men when they sin against you, your heavenly Father will also forgive you. But if you do not forgive men their sins, your Father will not forgive your sins.

SELF-CENTERED

Proverbs 12:15 - The way of a fool seems right to him, but a wise man listens to advice.

Philippians 2:3,4 - Do nothing out of selfish ambition or vain conceit, but in humility consider others better than yourselves. Each of you should look not only to your own interests, but also to the interests of others.

SLANDER/GOSSIPING

Proverbs 10:18 - He who conceals his hatred has lying lips, and whoever spreads slander is a fool.

Ephesians 4:29 - Do not let any unwholesome talk come out of your mouths, but only what is helpful for building others up according to their needs, that it may benefit those who listen.

SULLENNESS

Psalm 118:24 – This is the day the Lord has made; let us rejoice and be glad in it!

Philippians 4:4 – Rejoice in the Lord always. I will say it again: Rejoice!

THEFT

Exodus 20:15 - You shall not steal.

1 Peter 4:15 - If you suffer, it should not be as a murderer or thief or any other kind of criminal...

UNFORGIVING SPIRIT

Matthew 18:21,22 - "...Lord, how many times shall I forgive my brother?" ...Jesus answered, "I tell you, not seven times, but seventy times seven."

Matthew 6:14,15 - For if you forgive men when they sin against you, your heavenly Father will also forgive you. But if you do not forgive men their sins, your Father will not forgive your sins.

WRATH/RAGE

Psalm 37:8 – Refrain from anger and turn from wrath; do not fret – it leads only to evil.

Proverbs 12:16 - A fool's wrath is quickly and openly known, but a prudent man ignores an insult.

Appendix **D** Prayer Life of a PTSD Victor: King David

From Step 12, page 163.

We've made reference in several places in this manual to King David. Not only was he a man of great courage, a brilliant military leader, and the most powerful king the nation of Israel ever had, he was also "a man after God's own heart" (Acts 13:22). But David was one other thing that surprises a lot of people – though it shouldn't. David also was a PTSD sufferer. How could one think otherwise when you read passages like this which David wrote:

> **Psalm 31:9-13** Be gracious to me, O Lord, for I am in distress; my eye is wasted away from grief, my soul and my body also. For my life is spent with sorrow, and my years with sighing; my strength has failed because of my iniquity, and my body has wasted away. Because of all my adversaries, I have become a reproach, especially to my neighbors, and an object of dread to my acquaintances; those who see me in the street flee from me. I am forgotten as a dead man, out of mind, I am like a broken vessel. For I have heard the slander of many, terror is on every side; While they took counsel together against me, they schemed to take away my life.

David wrote over seventy-five desolate, anguish-filled passages like this in the Psalms. So why would we want to offer King David to you as an example of a PTSD victor when he writes such despairing words? Because David recognized that God was his Healer, his only hope of escape from his distress. When you read many of David's Psalms, you are reading the writings of a man in process. He fought with depression, guilt, fear, anger, despair – probably many of the same emotions you fight with. But in practically every one of his Psalms, you will see him lifting his eyes and his hopes to God. Here's what he wrote in the very next section in the Psalm we just shared:

> **Psalm 31:14-22** But as for me, I trust in You, O Lord, I say, "You are my God." My times are in Your hand; deliver me from the hand of my enemies and from those who persecute me. Make Your face to shine upon Your servant; save me in Your lovingkindness . . . How great is Your goodness, which You have stored up for those who fear You, which You have wrought for those who take refuge in You, before the sons of men! You hid them in the secret place of Your presence from the conspiracies of man; You keep them secretly in a shelter from the strife of tongues. Blessed be the Lord, for He has made marvelous His lovingkindness to me in a besieged city. As for me, I said in my alarm, "I am cut off from before Your eyes"; Nevertheless You heard the voice of my supplications when I cried to You.

David's "normal" was the youngest son of a rural shepherd, peacefully tending his father's sheep in the hills around Bethlehem. You couldn't ask for a more idyllic life. But God had other plans for the boy. Looking at death in the face of a giant, having his country's king attempt to murder him twice, running for his life, being pursued by thousands of soldiers because the king had put a bounty on his head, seeking refuge in a hostile country with an enemy king, fighting battles without number, being betrayed by his own son, punished by God Himself for an adulterous affair and murder – these things shattered David's life over and over, and he had to find his "new normal."

And he did. God sustained him throughout his many years of trauma, crisis and despair, and finally brought him to a place of peace. His life was not without turmoil and disappointment, even in his latter years. He was reaping what he sowed in many ways. But he had come to a place where he could live triumphantly above the storms that had so completely engulfed his life in his earlier days.

Following are a number of David's prayers. We hope that you will identify with this man who, despite his courage, skills and accomplishments, was only a man. He was a man who recognized his need for a Savior, and his need for God's help. He's a good man for us to imitate as we grow through our dark days.

PRAYERS FROM A HEART OF STRESS AND TRAUMA

Note David's honesty as he pours out his heart to God. He doesn't hold back – and you don't need to either. You won't hurt God's feelings; He already knows what's in your heart, and He wants you to communicate it to Him, no holds barred. Try making David's words your words. Pray David's prayers as if they're coming from your heart. They probably are in many ways. David – and the Spirit of God – are just helping you to find the words to say. When David talks about his "adversaries," he could be talking about his literal adversaries, or he could be talking about his spiritual ones. There are forces of darkness that are "rising up against you." As David did, ask God for His help in defeating them.

Psalm 3:1-6 O Lord, how my adversaries have increased! Many are rising up against me. Many are saying of my soul, "There is no deliverance for him in God." But You, O Lord, are a shield about me, my glory, and the One who lifts my head. I was crying to the Lord with my voice, and He answered me from His holy mountain. I lay down and slept; I awoke, for the Lord sustains me. I will not be afraid of ten thousands of people who have set themselves against me round about.

Psalm 5:1-3 Give ear to my words, O Lord, consider my groaning. Heed the sound of my cry for help, my King and my God, for to You I pray. In the morning, O Lord, You will hear my voice; in the morning I will order my prayer to You and eagerly watch.

Psalm 16:1 Preserve me, O God, for I take refuge in You. I said to the Lord, "You are my Lord; I have no good besides You."

Psalm 22:1-5 My God, my God, why have You forsaken me? Far from my deliverance are the words of my groaning. O my God, I cry by day, but You do not answer; and by night, but I have no rest. Yet You are holy, O You who are enthroned upon the praises of Israel. In You our fathers trusted; they trusted and You delivered them. To You they cried out and were delivered; in You they trusted and were not disappointed.

Psalm 25:15-20 My eyes are continually toward the Lord, for He will pluck my feet out of the net. Turn to me and be gracious to me, for I am lonely and afflicted. The troubles of my heart are enlarged; bring me out of my distresses. Look upon my affliction and my trouble, and forgive all my sins. Look upon my enemies, for they are many, and they hate me with a violent hatred. Guard my soul and deliver me; do not let me be ashamed, for I take refuge in You.

Psalm 32:7 You are my hiding place; You preserve me from trouble; You surround me with songs of deliverance.

Psalm 38:21,22 Do not forsake me, O Lord; O my God, do not be far from me! Make haste to help me, O Lord, my salvation!

Psalm 40:17 Since I am afflicted and needy, let the Lord be mindful of me. You are my help and deliverer; do not delay, O my God.

Psalm 42:1-3,5,8 As the deer pants for the water brooks, so my soul pants for You. My tears have been my food day and night, while they say to me, "Where is your God?" Why are you in despair, O my soul? And why have you become disturbed within me? Hope in God, for I shall again praise Him for the help of His presence. The Lord will command His lovingkindness in the daytime; and His song will be with me in the night, a prayer to the God of my life.

Psalm 51:15-17 O Lord, open my lips, that my mouth may declare Your praise. For You do not delight in sacrifice, otherwise I would give it; You are not pleased with burnt offering. The sacrifices of God are a broken spirit; a broken and a contrite heart, O God, You will not despise.

Psalm 56:8-13 You have taken account of my wanderings; put my tears in Your bottle. Are they not in Your book? Then my enemies will turn back in the day when I call; this I know, that God is for me. In God, whose word I praise, in the Lord, whose word I praise, in God I have put my trust, I shall not be afraid. What can man do to me? Your vows are binding upon me, O God; I will render thank offerings to You. For You have delivered my soul from death, indeed, my feet from stumbling, so that I may walk before God in the light of the living.

Psalm 69:1-3,13-17 Save me, O God, for the waters have threatened my life. I have sunk in deep mire and there is no foothold, I have come into deep waters, and a flood overflows me. I'm weary with my crying; my throat is parched; my eyes fail while I wait for my God. But as for me, my prayer is to You, O Lord, at an acceptable time. O God, in the greatness of Your lovingkindness, answer me with Your saving truth. Deliver me from the mire and don't let me sink; may I be delivered from my foes and from the deep waters. May the flood of water not overflow me, nor the deep swallow me up, nor the pit shut its mouth on me. Answer me, O Lord, for Your lovingkindness is good; according to the greatness of Your compassion, turn to me, and do not hide Your face from Your servant, for I am in distress; answer my quickly.

Psalm 71:1-3 In You O Lord, I have taken refuge; let me never be ashamed. In Your righteousness, deliver me and rescue me; incline Your ear to me and save me. Be to me a rock of habitation to which I may continually come; You have given commandment to save me, for You are my rock and my fortress.

Psalm 86:1-7 Incline Your ear and answer me, for I am afflicted and needy. Preserve my soul, for I am a godly man; You are my God, save Your servant who trusts in You. Be gracious to me, for to You I cry all day long. Make glad the soul of Your servant, for to You I life up my soul. For You, O Lord, are good and ready to forgive, and abundant in lovingkindness to all who call on You. Give ear, O Lord, to my prayer; and give heed to the voice of my supplications! In the day of trouble I shall call upon You, for You will answer me.

There are many additional passages that you can find on your own in the Psalms that reflect David's mix of honest expression of his despair balanced by his faith in God as his Healer and Deliverer. Find them, and underline them or highlight them in your Bible.

PROMISES TO A WOUNDED WARRIOR

The next set of passages expresses David's confidence in God's ability to deliver, strengthen, heal him, and to cause him to triumph. Read these verses over when your faith is flagging. Meditate on them. Pray them back to God, proclaiming your confidence in them just as David did.

Psalm 4:3 Know that the Lord has set apart the godly man for Himself; the Lord hears when I call to Him.

Psalm 4:8 In peace I will both lie down and sleep, for You alone, O Lord, make me to dwell in safety.

Psalm 9:9,10 The Lord will be a stronghold for the oppressed, a stronghold in times of trouble; and those who know Your name will put their trust in You, for You, O Lord, have not forsaken those who seek You.

Psalm 10:17,18 O Lord, You have heard the desire of the humble; You will strengthen their heart, You will incline Your ear to vindicate the orphan and the oppressed, so that man who is of the earth will no longer cause terror.

Psalm 12:5 "Because of the devastation of the afflicted, because of the groaning of the needy, now I will arise," says the Lord; "I will set him in the safety for which he longs."

Psalm 16:11 You will make known to me the path of life; in Your presence is fullness of joy; in Your right hand there are pleasures forever.

Psalm 23:1-6 The Lord is my shepherd, I shall not want. He makes me lie down in green pastures; He leads me beside quiet waters. He restores my soul; He guides me in the paths of righteousness for His name's sake. Even though I walk through the valley of the shadow of death, I fear no evil, for You are with me; Your rod and Your staff, they comfort me. You prepare a table before me in the presence of my enemies; You have anointed my head with oil; my cup overflows. Surely goodness and lovingkindness will follow me all the days of my life, and I will dwell in the house of the Lord forever.

Psalm 30:4,5 Sing praise to the Lord, you His godly ones, and give thanks to His holy name. For His anger is but for a moment, His favor is for a lifetime; weeping may last for the night, but a shout of joy comes in the morning.

Psalm 34:7 The angel of the Lord encamps around those who fear Him, and rescues them.

Psalm 34:15-19 The eyes of the Lord are toward the righteous and His ears are open to their cry. The face of the Lord is against evildoers, to cut off the memory of them from the earth. The righteous cry, and the Lord hears and delivers them out of all their troubles. The Lord is near to the brokenhearted and saves those who are crushed in spirit. Many are the afflictions of the righteous, but the Lord delivers him out of them all.

Psalm 37:23,24 The steps of a man are established by the Lord, and He delights in his way. When he falls, he will not be hurled headlong, because the Lord is the One who holds his hand.

Psalm 46:10-11 "Cease striving and know that I am God, I will be exalted among the nations, I will be exalted in the earth." The Lord of hosts is with us; the God of Jacob is our stronghold.

Psalm 50:15 Call upon Me in the day of trouble; I shall rescue you, and you will honor Me.

Psalm 55:22 Cast your burden upon the Lord and He will sustain you; He will never allow the righteous to be shaken.

Psalm 91:1-16 He who dwells in the shelter of the Most High will abide in the shadow of the Almighty. I will say to the Lord, "My refuge and my fortress, my God, in whom I trust!" For it is He who delivers you from the snare of the trapper and from the deadly pestilence. He will cover you with His pinions, and under His wings you may seek refuge; His faithfulness is a shield and bulwark. You will not be afraid of the terror by night, or of the arrow that flies by day; of the pestilence that stalks in darkness, or of the destruction that lays waste at noon. A thousand may fall at your side and ten thousand at your right hand, but it shall not approach you. You will only look on with your eyes and see the recompense of the wicked. For you have made the Lord, my refuge, even the Most High, your dwelling place. No evil will befall you, nor will any plague come near your tent. For He will give His angels charge concerning you, to guard you in all your ways. They will bear you up in their hands, that you do not strike your foot against a stone. You will tread upon the lion and cobra, the young lion and the serpent you will trample down. "Because he has loved Me, therefore I will deliver Him; I will set him securely on high, because he has known My name. He will call upon Me, and I will answer him; I will be with him in trouble; I will rescue him and honor him. With a long life I will satisfy him and let him see My salvation."

Psalm 92:12-15 The righteous man will flourish like the palm tree, he will grow like a cedar in Lebanon. Planted in the house of the Lord, they will flourish in the courts of our God. They will still yield fruit in old age; they shall be full of sap and very green, to declare that the Lord is upright; He is my rock, and there is no unrighteousness in Him.

Psalm 121:1-8 I will lift up my eyes to the mountains; from where shall my help come? My help comes from the Lord, who made heaven and earth. He will not allow your foot to slip; He who keeps you will not slumber. Behold, He who keeps Israel will neither slumber nor sleep. The Lord is your keeper; the Lord is your shade on your right hand. The sun will not smite you by day, nor the moon by night. The Lord will protect you from all evil; He will keep your soul. The Lord will guard your going out and your coming in from this time forth and forever.

Psalm 139:7-10 Where can I go from Your Spirit? Or where can I flee from Your presence? If I ascend to heaven, You are there; if I make my bed in Sheol, behold, You are there. If I take the wings of the dawn, if I dwell in the remotest part of the sea, even there Your hand will lead me, and Your right hand will lay hold of me.

Psalm 146:7b-9 The Lord sets the prisoners free. The Lord opens the eyes of the blind; the Lord raises up those who are bowed down; the Lord loves the righteous; the Lord protects the strangers; He supports the fatherless and the widow, but He thwarts the way of the wicked.

PRAISES FROM A WOUNDED WARRIOR

We know that God came through for David because of how saturated the Psalms are with his praise and thanksgiving to God. Read through David's expressions of praise and make them yours. You may not feel too much like praising God at the moment, but try praising Him "by faith." The Bible says that God is enthroned upon the praises of his people (Psalm 22:3). As you intentionally make the attempt, you will sense His presence.

Psalm 13:5,6 I have trusted in Your lovingkindness; my heart shall rejoice in Your salvation. I will sing to the Lord, because He has dealt bountifully with me.

Psalm 16:5,6 The Lord is the portion of my inheritance and my cup; You support my lot. The lines have fallen to me in pleasant places; indeed, my heritage is beautiful to me.

Psalm 18:1-3 I love You, O Lord my strength. The Lord is my rock and my fortress and my deliverer, my God, my rock, in whom I take refuge; my shield and the horn of my salvation, my stronghold. I call upon the Lord, who is worthy to be praised, and I am saved from my enemies.

Psalm 18:16-19 He sent from on high, He took me; He drew me out of many waters. He delivered me from my strong enemy, and from those who hated me, for they were too mighty for me. They confronted me in the day of my calamity, but the Lord was my stay. He brought me forth also into a broad place; He rescued me, because He delighted in me.

Psalm 18:46-49 The Lord lives, and blessed by my Rock; and exalted be the God of my salvation, the God who executes vengeance for me, and subdues peoples under me. He delivers me from my enemies; surely You lift me above those who rise up against me; You rescue me from the violent man. Therefore I will give thanks to You among the nations, O Lord, and I will sing praises to Your name.

Psalm 28:6-8 Blessed be the Lord, because He has heard the voice of my supplication. The Lord is my strength and my shield; my heart trusts in Him, and I am helped; Therefore my heart exults, and with my song I shall thank Him. The Lord is their strength, and He is a saving defense to His anointed.

Psalm 29:1,2 Ascribe to the Lord, O sons of the mighty, ascribe to the Lord glory and strength. Ascribe to the Lord the glory due to His name; worship the Lord in holy array.

Psalm 30:1-3 I will extol You, O Lord, for You have lifted me up, and have not let my enemies rejoice over me. O Lord my God, I cried to You for help, and You healed me. O Lord, You have brought up my soul from Sheol; You have kept me alive, that I would not go down to the pit.

Psalm 30:11-13 You have turned for me my mourning into dancing; You have loosed my sackcloth and girded me with gladness, that my soul may sing praise to You and not be silent. O Lord my God, I will give thanks to You forever.

Psalm 31:7,8 I will rejoice and be glad in Your lovingkindness, because You have seen my affliction; You have known the troubles of my soul, and You have not given me over into the hand of the enemy; You have set my feet in a large place.

Psalm 34:4-6 I sought the Lord, and He answered me, and delivered me from all my fears. They looked to Him and were radiant, and their faces will never be ashamed. This poor man cried, and the Lord heard him and saved him out of all his troubles.

Psalm 36:5-9 Your lovingkindness, O Lord, extends to the heavens, Your faithfulness reaches to the skies. Your righteousness is like the mountains of God; Your judgments are like a great deep. O Lord, You preserve man and beast. How precious is Your lovingkindness, O God! And the children of men take refuge in the shadow of Your wings. They drink their fill of the abundance of Your house; and You give them drink of the river of Your delights. For with You is the fountain of life; in Your light we see light.

Psalm 40:1-3 I waited patiently for the Lord; and He inclined to me and heard my cry. He brought me up out of the pit of destruction, out of the miry clay, and He set my feet upon a rock making my footsteps firm. He put a new song in my mouth, a song of praise to our God; many will see and fear and will trust in the Lord.

Psalm 57:7-11 My heart is steadfast, O God, my heart is steadfast; I will sing, yes, I will sing praises! Awake, my glory! Awake, harp and lyre! I will awaken the dawn. I will give thanks to You, O Lord, among the peoples; I will sing praises to You among the nations. For Your lovingkindness is great to the heavens and Your truth to the clouds. Be exalted above the heavens, O God; let Your glory be above all the earth.

Psalm 59:16,17 But as for me, I shall sing of Your strength; yes, I shall joyfully sing of Your lovingkindness in the morning, for You have been my stronghold, and a refuge in the day of my distress. O my strength, I will sing praises to You; for God is my stronghold, the God who shows me lovingkindness.

Psalm 63:6-8 When I remember You on my bed, I meditate on You in the night watches, for You have been my help, and in the shadow of Your wings I sing for joy. My soul clings to You; Your right hand upholds me.

Psalm 68:19,20 Blessed be the Lord, who daily bears our burden, the God who is our salvation. God is to us a God of deliverances, and to God the Lord belong escapes from death.

Psalm 71:14-16 But as for me, I will hope continually, and will praise You yet more and more. My mouth shall tell of Your righteousness and of Your salvation all day long; for I do not know the sum of them. I will come with the mighty deeds of the Lord God; I will make mention of Your righteousness, Yours alone.

Psalm 84:5a How blessed is the man whose strength is in You.

Psalm 86:10,12,13 You are great and do wondrous deeds; You alone are God. I will give thanks to You, O Lord my God, with all my heart, and will glorify Your name forever. For Your lovingkindness toward me is great, and You have delivered my soul from the depths of Sheol.

Psalm 94:17-19 If the Lord had not been my help, my soul would soon have dwelt in the abode of silence. If I should say, "My foot has slipped," Your lovingkindness will hold me up. When my anxious thoughts multiply within me, Your consolations delight my soul.

Psalm 94:22 The Lord has been my stronghold, and my God the rock of my refuge.

Psalm 100:1-5 Shout joyfully to the Lord, all the earth. Serve the Lord with gladness; come before Him with joyful singing. Know that the Lord Himself is God; it is He who made us, and not we ourselves; we are His people and the sheep of His pasture. Enter His gates with thanksgiving and His courts with praise. Give thanks to Him, and bless His name. For the Lord is good; His lovingkindness is everlasting and His faithfulness to all generations.

Appendix ⓔ Traumatic Stress Self-Test for Spouses of First Responders

From Step 11, page 149.

Consider each of the following statements about you and your current situation. Write in the number that best reflects your experience using the rating system where "1" signifies rarely or never and "10" means very often. Answer all items, even if they do not seem applicable. Then read the instructions at the end to get your score.

Rarely/Never = 1----2----3----4----5----6----7----8----9----10 = Very Often

1. _____ I force myself to avoid certain thoughts or feelings that remind me of frightening experiences from my past (any experiences, not necessarily associated with your spouse's job).

2. _____ I find myself avoiding certain activities or situations because they remind me of frightening experiences from my past.

3. _____ I have gaps in my memory about frightening events in my past.

4. _____ I feel isolated and estranged from others.

5. _____ I have difficulty falling or staying asleep.

6. _____ I have outbursts of anger or irritability with little provocation.

7. _____ I startle easily.

8. _____ I have thought about violence against the people who caused my spouse's stress or trauma.

9. _____ I have had "flashbacks" about some of the traumatic incidents my spouse has shared with me.

10. _____ I have had first-hand experience with traumatic events in my adult life.

11. _____ I have had first-hand experience with traumatic events in my childhood.

12. _____ I have thought that I need to "work through" a traumatic experience in my life.

13. _____ I am frightened by things my spouse has said or done to me.

14. _____ I experience troubling dreams similar to those of my spouse.

15. _____ I have experienced thoughts that intrude unbidden into my mind about my spouse's traumatic incidents (or other traumatic events from my past)

16. _____ I have suddenly and involuntarily recalled a frightening experience from my past while with my spouse.

17. _____ I am losing sleep over the traumatic experiences my spouse has shared with me.

18. _____ I have thought that I might have been "infected" by the traumatic stress of my spouse.

19. _____ I remind myself to be less preoccupied about my spouse's well-being.

20. _____ I have felt trapped by my marriage.

21. _____ I have felt a sense of hopelessness about my marriage.

22. _____ I have been in danger from my spouse.

23. _____ I have thought that there is no one to talk with about my highly stressful life.

[Continued next page.]

24. _____ I have felt "on edge" about various things, and I attribute this to being married to a first responder who is experiencing or has experienced line of duty stress and trauma.

25. _____ My relationship with my spouse has made me feel weak, tired, and rundown.

26. _____ My relationship with my spouse makes me feel depressed.

27. _____ I am not successful at separating my ministry to my spouse from my personal life. I feel absorbed by his/her difficulties.

28. _____ I have a sense of worthlessness/disillusionment/resentment associated with my marriage.

29. _____ I have thoughts that I am a "failure" as a spouse.

30. _____ I have thoughts that I am not succeeding at achieving my life goals.

_____ TOTAL

Scoring Instructions:

- Be certain you responded to all questions.
- Add up the values (1 to 10) you wrote next to each of the statements.
- This is your risk of developing Compassion Fatigue (equivalent to Posttraumatic Stress Disorder):
  - ➢ 94 or less = Low risk
  - ➢ 95 to 128 = Some risk
  - ➢ 129 to 172 = Moderate risk
  - ➢ 173 or more = High risk

Admittedly, this is not a scientifically or statistically verified test (Dr. Charles Figley's original test was, but this spouse-specific adaptation has yet to be reviewed). However, it should at least give you some idea of how light or how heavy the stress load you're currently carrying is.

 Based on your test score, what do you think your next steps should be?

_____

_____

_____

---

1. Adapted from C. R. Figley, A. B. Baranowsky & J. E. Gentry, "Compassion Fatigue Scale – Revised" in C. R. Figley (Ed.), *Compassion Fatigue: Volume II* (NY: Brunner/Mazel, 1999) and also found in Figley's *Treating Compassion Fatigue* (NY: Brunner/Mazel, 2002), pp. 134, 135.

Branches of Valor International

PO Box 2212 – Eugene, OR 97402 – 541-345-3458 – www.branchesofvalor.org
Founder & CEO: Rev. Rahnella Adsit – National Director: Rev. Chris Adsit

Our Mission:

To bring hope and healing to the Warrior Community and their families impacted by service-related stress and trauma.

Our Mission Target:

- ★ Active Servicemembers and Veterans
- ★ First Responders
- ★ Their Families

Our Strategy:

To accomplish this mission, we link the Warrior Community with practical resources, supportive connections and Biblical solutions through retreats, conferences, weekly Resiliency Group meetings and peer mentoring.

Our Ministry Philosophy:

"Bridges to Healing." God is the Healer (Exodus 15:26) and *we* are *not.* But God desires to partner with His people – "bridges" – to create an environment in which He has optimal access to a trauma-sufferer's body, soul and spirit for the purpose of healing.

Our Branches:

- ★ **Men of Valor** – For men who struggle with military-related stress and trauma.
- ★ **Women of Valor** – For women who struggle with military-related stress and trauma.
- ★ **Sisters of Valor** – For women in the lives of combat troops (wives, mothers, daughters, girlfriends, ex-wives, etc.) struggling with secondary trauma and compassion fatigue.
- ★ **Shields of Valor** – For those serving as First Responders.
- ★ **Shields of Valor/Families** – For the Families of those who are serving as First Responders.

Our Canopy – Communities of Valor:

- ★ **Resiliency Groups** – weekly meetings that provide a healing environment and support for growth.
- ★ **Peer Mentors** – single point-of-contact for resources, connection and discipling.
- ★ Trained and equipped **staff and volunteers**.
- ★ **Momentum events** – conferences and retreats.
- ★ **Supporting military and First Responder chaplains** and linking them to the Faith Community and their resources.

Our Fruit:

Sustainable, reproducible, God-generated, eternal results among veterans, First Responders and their families, and equipping them to pass these results on to others.

 http://facebook.com/BranchesOfValor

BRIDGES TO HEALING SERIES

This is the manual from which *The First Responder Healing Manual* was adapted. It was originally written for combat veterans who were impacted by war-related trauma and were struggling with the symptoms of Posttraumatic Stress Disorder. Regardless of its source, stress and trauma affect people in similar ways and with the same crippling intensity. Physical and psychological solutions can only go so far. But what God can do for someone who has experienced the horrors of war can make a life-or-death difference. Thousands of combat veterans have benefitted greatly from the principles in this manual – including many who went into first responder careers after their military service. Principle #1: secure a vital relationship with your Creator and Healer.

In the course of writing *The Combat Trauma Healing Manual,* the authors realized that there is a vast population of Americans who were profoundly affected by the stress and trauma of war, but were receiving almost no help at all: the wives of combat veterans. So the Adsits teamed up to write this manual with Marshéle Carter Waddell, a writer and speaker whose Navy SEAL husband had been deployed 11 times and struggled with severe PTSD. The manual deals with issues that wives of traumatized troops must uniquely confront: secondary trauma, compassion fatigue, their physical and emotional safety and that of their children, building a support network, helping their husband and children, forgiveness issues, self-care and more. Many of the principles in this manual would be applicable to wives of first responders who have been impacted by their husband's stress and trauma.

A self-paced instructional course co-produced by Cru Military and the American Association of Christian Counselors (AACC). Suitable for home study and includes 30 one-hour video presentations by experts in counseling, psychology, medicine, and military life. The program also comes with a 200+-page workbook, and a post-test. Upon successful submittal of the post-test, the participant will receive a Certificate of Completion from the AACC. The course is suitable for anyone with an interest in combat trauma and Post-Traumatic Stress Disorder and is particularly relevant for: military, first responder and hospital chaplains, mental health professionals, EMS personnel, support group facilitators, and anyone affected by combat trauma.

To purchase: crumilitary.org/grow/resource-store

Printed in Poland
by Amazon Fulfillment
Poland Sp. z o.o., Wrocław